VENERATION

"...Lest they rise and possess the earth..."
ISAIAH 14:21

Sharon K. Gilbert & Derek P. Gilbert

VENERATION

*Unveiling the Ancient Realms of Demonic Kings
and Satan's Battle Plan for Armageddon*

DEFENDER

CRANE, MO

Veneration: Unveiling the Ancient Realms of Demonic Kings and Satan's Battle Plan for Armageddon
by Sharon K. Gilbert and Derek P. Gilbert

All Scripture is taken from the ESV of the Bible unless otherwise noted.

Cover design by Jeffrey Mardis.

ISBN: 9781948014298

CONTENTS

INTRODUCTION

In the Beginning:
Order from Chaos

I am Alpha and Omega, the beginning and the ending, saith
the Lord, which is, and which was, and which is to come, the
Almighty.

—REVELATION 1:8

In the beginning God created the heaven and the earth. And the
earth was without form, and void; and darkness was upon the
face of the deep. And the Spirit of God moved upon the face of
the waters.

—GENESIS 1:1–2

Prepare slaughter for his children for the iniquity of their fathers;
that they do not rise, nor possess the land, nor fill the face of the
world with Watchers.[1]

—ISAIAH 14:21

And death and hell were cast into the lake of fire.
This is the second death.
—REVELATION 20:4

The universe has always been planned. From beginning to ending, the Creator of all has known precisely what He would do, and when He would do it. And that even goes for the existence of sin, death, and resurrection. He's foreseen rebellion, warfare, paganism, child abuse, thefts, and every dark thing done in every darkened place since the beginning of time itself. He is all-knowing, yet all-loving. He is the Father who stands at the end of the lane, watching for the return of His prodigal son. And you, dear reader—you are part of His wonderful plan. Each of us has a place in His design, and as of this moment, you're reading this from a battlefield. Why, you ask? Because the Lord of Hosts (Armies) has been marching to war since Genesis. That's when the war started, and Revelation is when it ends. And it's all about life and death.

The first action recorded in this ongoing war commenced just prior to Genesis 1:2. We cannot know for certain what happened, but a rebellion of some kind can be presumed. It is called the *chaoskampf* by scholars, and it's a theme repeated throughout all civilizations and all cosmogonies.

The term is composed of two words: *chaos* and *kampf*. The first is Greek and refers to a state of disorder but also to a primordial god known as Chaos. *Kampf* is German for "war" or "struggle."

Nearly every civilization has a mythology within its cosmogony that describes the subduing of a primordial "dragon." The hero in these tales is the storm-god, and the villain is the monstrous god (sometimes goddess) of the sea:

- Zeus subduing Typhon
- Marduk taking out Tiamat

- Baal clubbing Yam
- Yahweh versus Leviathan
- Thor taking out Jömungandr
- Tarhunz defeating Illuyanka
- Indra against Vritra
- Yamata versus No Orochi (Japanese)

In all of these tales, the conquering hero uses a mace, a club, an ax, or another weapon to subdue the beast, but in the TRUE version of events, YHWH only spoke. He then sealed the primordial dragon beneath the waves of the sea and placed His Holy Spirit upon it.

But if that was phase one of this long war, what comes next? In the Old Testament, we see YHWH again and again using the wiles of the enemy against them, turning their rituals on their heads as a means to foil their plots, and in the New Testament, Christ takes a claim made by the mighty men of old, the spirits of the Nephilim, those called the *Rephaim*, shades of the dead. These long-dead princes plan to rise again, when their leader calls them to life. It will take them three days to arrive, according to the ritual texts. Three days? It's no coincidence that our Savior rose three days after the infernal realm killed Him.

We who watch for His return expect our Lord to set the world to rights, but the Fallen believe once again (foolishly) that they can circumvent that arrival by raising up their own army.

An army of the dead. It will be the ultimate zombie apocalypse, and these infernal demonic spirits will try to use humans as shields against the Almighty.

In this book, we hope to give you new insights into the traditions of the fallen realm; into their gods and goddesses, their rituals and rites, and the expectations of the humans who served them (and still serve them today). And we'll reveal how these rituals describe the infernal realm's battle plans.

So, let's begin.

Gardens

Human history began in a garden. Many of the myths and legends told by bards, storytellers, shamans, and priests through the ages originated with a dim, shared memory of a lost paradise. Much of the blood, sweat, and tears shed by mankind over the millennia has been in the service of gods who promised our ancestors a path back to that paradise.

The concept of "garden" has changed over time. Today, we think of a pleasant patch of earth for flowers, vegetables, fruit, or maybe herbs we can pick to spice up our cooking. It wasn't that way in the beginning.

To really understand what God communicated through His prophets and apostles, we need to get inside the heads of the men who wrote the books of the Bible. Sadly, most of us don't make much of an effort; it's easier to read ourselves into the Bible than to put ourselves into the minds of people who lived two or three thousand years ago on the other side of the world. While it's uplifting to read the story of, say, David and Goliath as a symbol for how God empowers us to slay the "giants" in our lives, it's also a historic account of how David defeated the champion of an elite cult of pagan warriors who worshiped the dead.

Reading the Bible with the worldview of the ancient Hebrews takes a little work, but it's worth it. The payoff is seeing the stories we've known since Sunday school through new eyes, almost as children reading them for the first time. It will bring a level of excitement to your study of God's Word you haven't felt in years, if ever, and it will instill a deep appreciation for what's at stake in this long, supernatural war, and for God's sacrifice to get you off the battlefield in one piece—and bring you back to where it all began—Eden.

The original garden wasn't what we think of when we hear the word, and neither were the gardens in the days of the Hebrew prophets and apostles. There is a spiritual sense to the word that's been lost over the years. Archaeologists who specialize in the ancient Near East—the lands we now call Israel, Jordan, Lebanon, Syria, and Iraq—have known this for some time. They know many things that haven't been passed along to us in the pews, either because they don't see the information through a biblical lens or because there just isn't much interaction between professional scholars and us lay people.

We will dig deeper into this concept as we unpack the importance of the dead in the ancient world. Gardens held a special place in the culture of the ancient Near East, and it was part of a very different way of looking at the world. This wasn't just because they lacked modern conveniences, our understanding of the sciences, and access to the Internet, but because they understood that the spirit realm was part of daily life—something we've lost in the modern world, especially in the West. Part and parcel of their reality was interacting with the dead.

The dead were gone only in the physical sense. It was understood that those who'd gone before had moved on to a different type of existence. It wasn't necessarily enjoyable, and one's happiness in the afterlife depended on his or her descendants performing the correct rituals every month.

The exception was the dead kings of old. They held a place of esteem in the afterlife, and the pagan kings of the ancient Near East aspired to join the ranks of their venerated fathers who could still affect the world of the living. To that end, special rituals were performed at special locations—and that brings us back to gardens.

This will make more sense as we dig into the beliefs and practices of the neighbors of ancient Israel. The significance of the cults of the dead will become clear, and you'll see that the venerated dead are prophesied to play a role at Armageddon. The mother of all battles will be fought at the end of human history outside the walls around the Garden of God.

And the enemy host at the gates will literally be an army of the evil dead.

Part One

NAMING THE DEAD

1

Mighty Men Who Were of Old

Once upon a time, giants roamed the earth.

That sounds like the beginning of a fairy tale. Most Christians have never been taught that a similar story is told in the Book of Genesis, and in very similar language: "The Nephilim (or *giants*) were on the earth in those days, and also afterward, when the sons of God came in to the daughters of men and they bore children to them. These were the mighty men who were of old, the men of renown."[2]

Pastors, priests, and Sunday school teachers tend to skip the first four verses of Genesis 6 and go right to the story of Noah because—well, the verses are weird. They contradict the scientific consensus. They're hard to understand.

Please remember this: God didn't inspire the prophets and apostles to write filler. Moses was not assigned a minimum word count. If it's in the Bible, it's relevant—and if it's weird, it's important.

The reason we're writing this book is that it's become clear to us that the episode described in Genesis 6:1–4, and expanded upon in the noncanonical Book of 1 Enoch, is far more important to human history and biblical theology than we realized.

We are Bible-believing, blood-bought Christians, so let's put to bed right now any concerns you might have that this book is going off the theological rails to add something to the salvation story. If you don't accept the evidence we'll present here, that's fine; as long as we agree that salvation comes only through grace by faith in Jesus Christ, we're good. The purpose of this study is to show you how viciously and for how long the Fallen have been waging war against our Creator. Their ultimate objectives are control of God's mount of assembly, Zion, and authority over your eternal soul.

So, what role did the giants play in the biblical narrative?

First, we need to establish that the children of human women to the "sons of God" were literally angel-human hybrids. This is consistent with similar stories from the ancient world of gods commingling with humans to produce demigods such as Gilgamesh, who claimed to be two-thirds god and one-third human, and Hercules, the son of Zeus by the mortal woman Alcmene.

Obviously, researchers can't produce DNA from pre-Flood human remains that will support this theory. However, it's worth noting that for all of the faith placed by science in Darwinian evolution, only two hundred specimens of "pre-human" fossils have ever been found.[3] If humanity has been around for ten thousand years, where are all the skeletons? But we digress.

It's important to note that the phrase translated "sons of God" in the Old Testament, Hebrew *bənê hā'ělōhîm*, always means supernatural beings—angels, if you like. It does not refer to human men.

Yes, there are references in the New Testament to "sons of God" that *do* mean humans, but those passages are translated from Greek into English, and the context is different. The arc of history is all about restoring humanity to the garden, like the prodigal son returning home and being restored to the family as a co-heir. Someday, we will once again be "sons (and daughters)" of God in the Old Testament sense. That's why Jesus went to the cross.

At the risk of beating a horse that's already on life support, we repeat:

"Sons of God" in Genesis 6:4 refers to spirit beings, supernatural entities who rebelled against the Father—fallen angels who spawned an evil race of giants mingling the bloodlines of angels with humans. The "sons of God" were not evil human rulers or men from the line of Seth, or any other naturalistic explanation that's been put forward since Augustine decided he couldn't believe it in the early fifth century AD. Casting the "sons of God" as human men simply ignores the linguistic and cultural foundation of the Book of Genesis. To interpret the Nephilim as fully human means mistranslating the Hebrew and ignoring the way the very same phrase was used by the cultures around ancient Israel that spoke and wrote similar languages.

Besides, the apostles believed it. And we dare say their theology teacher was better than ours.

> For if God did not spare angels when they sinned, but cast them into hell and committed them to chains of gloomy darkness to be kept until the judgment; if he did not spare the ancient world, but preserved Noah, a herald of righteousness, with seven others, when he brought a flood upon the world of the ungodly; if by turning the cities of Sodom and Gomorrah to ashes he condemned them to extinction, making them an example of what is going to happen to the ungodly; and if he rescued righteous Lot, greatly distressed by the sensual conduct of the wicked (for as that righteous man lived among them day after day, he was tormenting his righteous soul over their lawless deeds that he saw and heard); then the Lord knows how to rescue the godly from trials, and to keep the unrighteous under punishment until the day of judgment, and especially those who indulge in the lust of defiling passion and despise authority. (2 Peter 2:4–10)

The only place in Scripture where we know of angels who sinned (Satan excluded) is Genesis 6. By connecting the rebellious angels to

Sodom and Gomorrah, Peter made it clear that the sin of the angels was sexual—a point he reinforced in verse 10. Like the "angels who sinned," the wicked would be kept under punishment until the Judgment— "especially those who indulge in the lust of defiling passion and despise authority," exactly the sin of the sons of God in Genesis 6.

The apostle Jude was even more explicit:

> And the angels who did not stay within their own position of authority, but left their proper dwelling, he has kept in eternal chains under gloomy darkness until the judgment of the great day—just as Sodom and Gomorrah and the surrounding cities, **which likewise indulged in sexual immorality and pursued unnatural desire**, serve as an example by undergoing a punishment of eternal fire. (Jude 6–7, emphasis added)

It could not be clearer: By connecting Genesis 6 to the sin of Sodom and Gomorrah, Jude emphasized that the sin of the angels was sexual. (It also indicates that the sin of Sodom wasn't just homosexuality; it was the desire to cross the boundary between species. Physical relations between angel and human was just as "unnatural" as between human and animal.)

Interestingly, just a few verses later, Jude quotes the *Book of 1 Enoch*, which suggests that we might learn something from Enoch even though it's not in the Bible.

> When the sons of men had multiplied, in those days, beautiful and comely daughters were born to them. And the watchers, the sons of heaven, saw them and desired them. And they said to one another, "Come, let us choose for ourselves wives from the daughters of men, and let us beget children for ourselves."...
>
> These and all the others with them took for themselves wives from among them such as they chose. And they began to go in

to them, and to defile themselves through them, and to teach them sorcery and charms, and to reveal to them the cutting of roots and plants. And they conceived from them and bore to them great giants. And the giants begot Nephilim, and to the Nephilim were born Elioud ["gods of glory"]. And they were growing in accordance with their greatness. They were devouring the labor of all the sons of men, and men were not able to supply them. And the giants began to kill men and to devour them. And they began to sin against the birds and beasts and creeping things and the fish, and to devour one another's flesh. And they drank the blood.[4]

Dr. Michael Heiser makes a convincing case in his book *Reversing Hermon* that a key aspect of the mission of Jesus was to reverse the evil of the Watchers. It's obvious in *1 Enoch* that the impact of the Watchers went well beyond producing monstrous hybrid offspring. Besides sorcery and potions, the fallen angels of the Hermon rebellion taught humanity the arts of divination, cosmetic enhancement, metalworking, fashioning weapons, making "hate-inducing charms," and "the eternal mysteries that are in heaven,"[5] which clearly were things man was not meant to know. In short, because of the forbidden knowledge passed from the Watchers to humans, the earth became filled with sex and violence.

For this, as Peter noted, God imprisoned the rebels in the abyss. While most English Bibles translate 2 Peter 2:4 as "cast them into hell," the Greek word, *tartaroō*, literally means "thrust down to Tartarus." That's different from Hades, the word most commonly used to designate the underworld home of the evil dead. In Greek cosmology, Tartarus was as far below Hades as the earth is below heaven. It was a special prison reserved for supernatural threats to the divine order—hell for angels, basically. Since this is the only place in the New Testament where *tartaroo* is used, it's important. It referred to a unique event, but one with

13

which Peter's readers were obviously familiar—the famous story of the Watchers who attempted to corrupt humanity physically and spiritually.

Now, if all of this invective against an ancient race of giants was unsupported elsewhere in the ancient world, you would be right to be skeptical. But that happens not to be the case. Similar stories, told from slightly different perspectives, are attested in many of the cultures in the ancient Near East. Mesopotamians knew the Watchers as antediluvian sages called *apkallu*. They were supernatural agents of the god Enki, lord of the *abzu* ("abyss"), who sent them into the world to deliver the gifts of civilization to humanity.

Despite this, the *apkallu* were considered potentially dangerous, capable of malicious witchcraft. An Assyrian exorcism text names two *apkallus* who angered gods and thus brought punishment on themselves and the land, and in a popular Mesopotamian text called the *Epic of Erra* (the god of pestilence and mayhem), the chief deity Marduk tells of how he banished the *apkallus* to the *abzu* (after he caused the Flood!) and told them not to return to the earth.[6] That's exactly the punishment that God decreed for the Watchers, and likewise connected to the great deluge remembered for centuries across Mesopotamia.

Interestingly, the last four *apkallus* were described as partly human, and thus able to mate with human women, just like the Watchers and their offspring, the Nephilim.

The giants created by the lecherous Watchers were destroyed in the Flood of Noah. While the Bible doesn't make this explicit, it's implied in 1 Peter 3:18–20, where the apostle links the Flood to the angels who "formerly did not obey…in the days of Noah.[7] The text in *1 Enoch*, however, does specifically connect the Flood to the punishment of the Watchers and the evil acts of their children, the Nephilim.[8]

Here's the key to understanding why this is in the Bible at all: The neighbors of the ancient Hebrews, especially the Amorites who lived in and near Canaan, apparently believed that these mighty men of old were the ancestors of their kings. The spirits of the Nephilim were called *rapha*—Rephaim. What's more, texts discovered at the ancient Amorite kingdom of Ugarit and translated within the last fifty years indicate that the Amorites venerated these entities, summoned them through necromancy rituals, and believed that their kings joined their assembly after death.

While the Bible names tribes called Rephaim in the Transjordan, lands that later became the kingdoms of Ammon, Moab, and Edom, in the time of Abraham (around 1850 BC),[9] it appears that, by the Exodus, the Rephaim were the spirits of the venerated dead (except, of course, Og, king of Bashan, the last "of the remnant of the Rephaim").[10] The Rephaim and Anakim encountered by the Israelites were not literal blood descendants of the Nephilim, but tribes who worshiped their spirits in the deluded belief that those demons were their heroic royal ancestors. So, when 1 Chronicles 20:4–8 and 2 Samuel 21:15–20 refer to the Goliath and the other Philistine "descendants of the giants" (*yelîdê hārāpâ*), it's in the spiritual sense—an elite warrior cult, perhaps the "sons of Rapha," dedicated to the mighty men who were of old.[11]

Likewise, the Anakim, who are identified with the Rephaim in the books of Deuteronomy and Joshua, appear to have been a class of pagan warrior kings rather than supernaturally big. Contrary to the popular explanation that *anak* means "long-necked," the term most likely derives from a Greek word, *anax* ("god," "hero," or "master of the house").[12] Anakim, then, wasn't a proper name but a title, and the "sons of the Anakim" were not genetic descendants of giants but a warrior elite who ruled the hill country of Judah and Israel before the Conquest.

Veneration of the dead among the ancient Amorites was an integral part of their culture. A monthly ritual called *kispum* summoned dead ancestors to a ritual meal, which we'll describe in detail in another chapter. The *kispum* took on greater importance when it came to their dead kings; while the dead could be dangerous if they were unhappy, dead royalty were especially menacing. They posed a threat to the ruler himself, and that was a problem that could affect the entire kingdom. Bedeviled kings weren't just a threat to their families; everyone in the kingdom suffered when a ruler was tormented by angry spirits.

The standard practice in the ancient Near East was to perform the *kispum* rite twice a month for kings, usually on the 15th and 30th. As with the family *kispum*, long-dead rulers had to be called to the meal by name. Forgetting the dead meant their spirits were unsettled and thus unpredictable. Proper performance of the ritual was key to maintaining the health and stability of the realm.

Several fascinating texts from Ugarit are especially relevant to our discussion. Around 1200 BC, just before its destruction by the so-called Sea Peoples, Ugarit crowned its last king. A ritual text designated KTU 1.161 by scholars suggests that the ill-fated Ammurapi III, who was probably killed when his city was overrun, was crowned with a necromancy rite that summoned the spirits of his royal ancestors, the Rephaim.

> You are summoned, O Rephaim of the earth,
> You are invoked, O council of the Didanu!
> Ulkn, the Raphi', is summoned,
> Trmn, the Raphi', is summoned,
> Sdn-w-rdn is summoned, Ṯr 'llmn is summoned,
> the Rephaim of old are summoned!
> You are summoned, O Rephaim of the earth,
> You are invoked, O council of the Didanu![13]

There is no question that these Rephaim are the same group called by that name in the Bible.

> Sheol beneath is stirred up to meet you when you come; it rouses the shades [*rephaim*] to greet you, all who were leaders of the earth; it raises from their thrones all who were kings of the nations. (Isaiah 14:9)

The "shades"—Rephaim—were "leaders of the earth" and "kings of the nations," the same way they are described in the Ugaritic texts.

This appears to be a belief that extends back at least to the time of Abraham. A bone talisman dated to about 1750 BC found in the tomb of a king at Ebla, an ancient kingdom in northern Syria, depicts a scene that suggests three ranks in the hierarchy of the afterlife: A lower level for the human dead, a top level inhabited by the gods, and a middle level occupied by entities that probably represent Rephaim or the Eblaite equivalent.[14] It's been suggested by scholars who have tried to interpret the symbols on the artifact that the item was a guide to the spirit of the dead king on how to attain status among the venerated dead—the "men of renown," as it were. Even the name "Rephaim" may originate with an Akkadian word that means something like "great ones."[15]

What ties this together into a cohesive package is the reference in the Ugaritic "Sacrifice of the Shades Liturgy" to the "council of the Didanu." That shadowy group shares the name of an Amorite tribe from antiquity (variously spelled Didanu, Ditanu, and Tidanu) that was known and feared throughout the Near East. The last Sumerian kings of Mesopotamia, the Third Dynasty of Ur, actually built a wall 175 miles long north of modern Baghdad that they dubbed the "Amorite Wall That Keeps Tidanu Away."

Too bad for the Third Dynasty of Ur that it didn't keep the Tidanu away. Within a century of the wall's construction, Ur was overwhelmed by waves of invaders that included the Tidanu, savage Gutian tribesmen from the mountains to the northeast, and Elamites, from what is today northwestern Iran.

The key point is this: Amorite kings from Babylon to Canaan traced their ancestry to this Tidanu/Ditanu tribe. And modern scholars have concluded that the name of this tribe is the origin of the name given by the ancient Greeks to their old gods, the Titans.[16]

So, consider the evidence: We know that in the days of the judges in Israel, Amorite kings in what is now northern Syria aspired to become *rapha* and join the council of the Didanu after death, a religious belief that may have existed for more than a thousand years already by that time. The Rephaim were a sort of middle-tier deity, higher in rank in the cosmological order than humans, but not at the level of the great gods like El, Baal, Asherah, and Astarte.

Like the Didanu, the Titans of the Greeks were supernatural inhabitants of the underworld who'd roamed the earth long ago, just like the *apkallu* of Babylon and the Watchers of the Hebrews. This is not coincidence.

And it's relevant today. You see, the *Rephaim Texts* from ancient Ugarit call the Rephaim "warriors of Baal." The mountain sacred to Baal is the rally point for the end-times army of Gog, the Antichrist. Jesus identified Baal as Satan.

As this book unfolds, we'll put those pieces together to show you that veneration of the dead was not a quaint religious belief by primitive pagans who didn't know any better. What we are unraveling here is an ancient plot by the infernal council to create a demonic army to assault the throne of God.

2

The Abominable Branch

Chapter 14 of the Book of Isaiah is absolutely fascinating. It's long been interpreted as a condemnation of the rebel in the Garden of Eden. It certainly is that; Jerome's Hebrew-to-Latin translation of the rebel's name, *Helel ben Shachar*[17] (literally, "Day Star, son of Dawn"), is the origin of the name "Lucifer." But this chapter goes much deeper; it probably reveals in one short chapter more about the rebellion of the Fallen, and God's response to it, than any other single chapter in the Bible.

On the surface, it's a biting criticism of the king of Babylon. From our perspective, it seems natural that a Hebrew prophet would write such a thing, but we're looking at these matters with 2,700 years of hindsight. When Isaiah lived and wrote, Babylon was a vassal state of Assyria. It was more than eight centuries after the Amorite founding dynasty of Babylon had been ended by the Kassites, a tribal people from the mountains of what is now western Iran. The Kassites continued many of the religious traditions of the Amorites, but they changed the name of the city to Karduniash. They ruled for more than four hundred years, which means the Kassites controlled Babylonia longer than any other people in history.

By the time of the Judges in Israel, about four hundred years before Isaiah, the Kassite kingdom had fallen to the Chaldeans, a Semitic people probably descended from the Amorites. But the Chaldeans never extended their control as far west as the Holy Land in the years leading up to Isaiah. Israel and Judah had more trouble with the Aramaeans, Ammonites, Moabites, Edomites, Midianites, and Philistines.

The Assyrians, based in what is now northern Iraq, emerged after the time of David and Solomon in the tenth century BC as the scourge of the Near East. Assyria destroyed the kingdom of Israel around 722 BC, flattening its capital city, Samaria, and scattering the northern tribes throughout Assyrian territory.

The Assyrians ravaged the southern kingdom, too. In the days of Isaiah and Hezekiah, Sennacherib sent his army to conquer Judah. The invaders overran most of the country, and it was only divine intervention that stopped the Assyrian army outside the walls of Jerusalem.[18] Sennacherib withdrew to his home country, where he was assassinated by his sons. Sometimes it's *not* so good to be the king.

At the time of Sennacherib's invasion of Judah, the rise of Babylon was still more than a century in the future, in the days of Josiah, grandson of Hezekiah. So, Isaiah's polemic against the king of Babylon, which begins in the thirteenth chapter of Isaiah, appears to be an anachronism, out of sync with the political events of the time.

When the LORD has given you rest from your pain and turmoil and the hard service with which you were made to serve, you will take up this taunt against the king of Babylon: "How the oppressor has ceased, the insolent fury ceased! The LORD has broken the staff of the wicked, the scepter of rulers, that struck the peoples in wrath with unceasing blows, that ruled the nations in anger with unrelenting persecution." (Isaiah 14:3–6)

This text was unquestionably a prophecy of the future Babylon, an oracle of the destruction of the oppressor before Babylon became Judah's oppressor. But clues in the chapter, mainly overlooked by Bible teachers, point to other targets of the prophet's oracle—not just the divine rebel from Eden, but also his colleagues and their minions.

> Sheol beneath is stirred up
> to meet you when you come;
> it rouses the shades to greet you,
> all who were leaders of the earth;
> it raises from their thrones
> all who were kings of the nations. (Isaiah 14:9)

As noted earlier in the book, the Hebrew word translated "shades" is *rephaim*. That's the mysterious group named in Genesis, Deuteronomy, and Joshua as the tribes who lived east of the Jordan River in the lands of Bashan, Ammon, Moab, and Edom. By the time of the judges in Israel, the Rephaim were considered the spirits of the "mighty men who were of old"—in other words, "leaders of the earth" and "kings of the nations." Isaiah's description is consistent with the depiction of the Rephaim in the texts found at the Amorite kingdom of Ugarit. Whether the Amorite neighbors of ancient Israel knew it or not, they venerated the spirits of the half-breed giants created by the supernatural sons of God, the Watchers. This means that the role of the rebel from Eden takes on new significance.

First, we need to identify this character. Who is Helel ben Shachar? It would be easy to say "Lucifer," and leave it at that. But, as we noted above, Lucifer is just an Anglicized version of the Latin words *lux* ("light") and *ferre* ("to carry"). In other words, "Lucifer" is English for the Latin translation of the original Hebrew name. But who is he, really? Isaiah gives us the information we need.

21

How you are fallen from heaven,
O Day Star, son of Dawn!
How you are cut down to the ground,
you who laid the nations low!
You said in your heart,
"I will ascend to heaven;
above the stars of God
I will set my throne on high;
I will sit on the mount of assembly
in the far reaches of the north;
I will ascend above the heights of the clouds;
I will make myself like the Most High." (Isaiah 14:12–14)

"Day Star" is a reference to Venus, from a Hebrew word based on a root that means "to shine."[19] Scholars who've tried to find a similar story in the religions of the ancient Near East have come up empty so far. The closest parallel is the Ugaritic myth of the war-god Attar, the male aspect of Astarte (Ishtar), who found that he was too small for the throne of the king of the gods, the storm-god Baal, who was temporarily dead. (It's a pagan myth. It doesn't have to make sense.) The point is that Attar was represented by Venus in the morning; Venus in the evening was believed to represent the goddess of "love," Astarte.

Well, that doesn't quite work. The key bit of evidence is in verse 13. The Hebrew phrase "far reaches of the north," variously rendered in other English translations as "sides of the north," "recesses of the north," "remotest parts of the north," and simply "the far north," is *yarkete tsaphon*. This appears only three times in the Bible, which makes it weird. And if it's weird, it's important.

The other verses where we find *yarkete tsaphon* are in Psalm 48, where the psalmist compares God's holy mountain, Zion, with another mountain (Zaphon—although it's rendered "far north," which means you have to read between the lines to grasp the wordplay of the verse: *har-tziyon, yarkete tsaphon*), and Ezekiel 38 and 39, the prophecy of Gog of Magog.

Why is this significant? Because Zaphon (or Saphon, or *tsaphon*) was the name of the mountain sacred to the storm-god Baal.

> Then Valiant Baal said,
> "Depart, Kothar-and-Hasis!
> Hasten! Build a house indeed;
> hasten! Construct a palace!
> Hasten! Let them build a house;
> Hasten! Let them construct a palace,
> in the midst of the uttermost parts of Saphon."[20]

So, if the mount of assembly of the rebel in Eden is the mountain sacred to Baal, the text of Isaiah 14 can't have been borrowed from a myth about Baal's would-be replacement.

Why does this matter? Because Jesus specifically identified Baal the storm-god as Satan. When He was confronted by Pharisees who accused Him of casting out demons by the power of Beelzebul ("Baal the Prince"), Jesus replied, "If Satan casts out Satan, he is divided against himself. How then will his kingdom stand?"[21] And in the Book of Revelation, Jesus told the church at Pergamum, "I know where you dwell, where Satan's throne is."[22] That was a reference to the altar of Zeus, who was the Greek incarnation of the storm-god.

That gives us a simple equation: Lucifer = Baal = Satan. And since Gog (the Antichrist) is Satan's commander-in-chief, it makes sense that he comes from *yarkete tsaphon*—Mount Zaphon. (That's in Turkey, by the way. Contrary to what you've probably been taught, Gog and Magog have nothing to do with Russia.)[23]

But there is more here than just a polemic against the Accuser, Satan.

Isaiah gives us enough information to confirm what the Israelites' pagan neighbors knew about Baal—that the king of their pantheon was also lord of the dead.

This was probably some kind of honor in the minds of Canaanites. The Rephaim spirits were called "warriors of Baal" and "warriors of Anat" (their incredibly violent war-goddess), and some scholars believe that one of Baal's functions may have been to resurrect them at the ritual meals to which the Rephaim were summoned.

However, the prophets Isaiah and Ezekiel make it very clear that this was a demotion.

> You were in Eden, the garden of God;
> every precious stone was your covering,
> sardius, topaz, and diamond,
> beryl, onyx, and jasper,
> sapphire, emerald, and carbuncle;
> and crafted in gold were your settings
> and your engravings.
> On the day that you were created
> they were prepared.
> You were an anointed guardian cherub.
> I placed you; you were on the holy mountain of God;
> in the midst of the stones of fire you walked.
> You were blameless in your ways
> from the day you were created,
> till unrighteousness was found in you.
> In the abundance of your trade
> you were filled with violence in your midst, and you sinned;
> so I cast you as a profane thing from the mountain of God,
> and I destroyed you, O guardian cherub,
> from the midst of the stones of fire. (Ezekiel 28:13–16)

All of [the Rephaim] will answer
and say to you:
"You too have become as weak as we!
You have become like us!"
Your pomp is brought down to Sheol,
the sound of your harps;
maggots are laid as a bed beneath you,
and worms are your covers." (Isaiah 14:10–11, 15)

From the pinnacle of creation to a bed of maggots. A real comedown. Even the Rephaim, who are supposed to be Satan's warriors, recognize his diminished status.

Lest you think we're reading our preconceptions of Satan into Isaiah 14, let's take this a bit further. Scholars have known for a long time that the prophet was a brilliant writer, and he was a master of wordplay. The influence of Egypt on the kingdom of Judah during Isaiah's lifetime provided him with another opportunity to make his point.

All the kings of the nations lie in glory, each in his own tomb;
but you are cast out, away from your grave, like a loathed branch,
clothed with the slain, those pierced by the sword, who go down
to the stones of the pit, like a dead body trampled underfoot.
(Isaiah 14:18–19)

At the risk of pointing out the obvious, the phrase "a loathed branch" in verse 18 is weird. And remember: weird = important. What in the world did Isaiah mean by that?

The Hebrew word *netser* is easy. It means "branch." The adjectives translators chose to describe the branch includes "loathed," "repulsive," "rejected," "worthless," and "abominable," but they convey the same sense—something utterly detestable. The Hebrew word rendered "abhorred" or "abominable," *ta'ab*, is significant. It modifies the noun *netser*, which would normally have a positive connotation. In this context, *ta'ab* means something like "unclean" or "ritually impure."[24]

Still, even trying to allow for differences in cultures over the last twenty-seven hundred years, calling someone an "unclean or impure branch" is puzzling. But there is a likely explanation: Isaiah meant something other than "branch" because the Hebrew *netser* wasn't the word he used at all.

[The] term is best explained as a loanword from the common Egyptian noun *ntr*. **Ntr is generally translated "god," but is commonly used of the divinized dead and their physical remains.** It originally came into Hebrew as a noun referring to the putatively divinized corpse of a dead king, which is closely related to the Egyptian usage.[25] (Emphasis added.)

The Egyptian word *ntr* is especially relevant here. Isaiah connects the divinized dead god, Baal/Satan, with the dead kings venerated by the pagan Amorites and Canaanites, the Rephaim—the spirits of the Nephilim destroyed in the Flood.

This is not a weird, out-of-left-field stretch to force the Scriptures to fit a pet theory involving antediluvian giants. The prophet devoted several chapters, especially Isaiah 30 and 31, to condemning Israel for turning to Egypt instead of Yahweh for protection against Assyria. Sennacherib's official mocked Hezekiah for "trusting in Egypt, that broken reed of a staff, which will pierce the hand of any man who leans on it."[26]

Recently, a seal of Hezekiah was found in Jerusalem at the foot of the southern wall of the Temple Mount. While this one, apparently from later in Hezekiah's reign, featured an Assyrian-style winged solar disk,[27] his older seals were decorated with a scarab beetle, which represented the Egyptian sun-god Ra. This was apparently part of Hezekiah's foreign policy, an attempt to curry favor with his stronger neighbor, Egypt, to further his dream of reunifying Judah and Israel.[28] This required standing up to the Assyrian juggernaut, which had destroyed the northern half of the kingdom of David and Solomon about six years after Hezekiah became king.

By using a loan word from Egypt that meant "dead god"—and not "branch," as translated in our English Bibles—Isaiah was emphasizing the theme of chapter 14: The entity who rebelled in Eden, the storm-god Baal (whom Jesus identified as Satan), was cast down to the land of the dead to become the unclean, profane, abominable lord of the shades—the Rephaim.

This theme is echoed by Ezekiel in chapter 28. A deeper dive into the Hebrew of that text reveals a surprising parallel with Isaiah.

Your heart was proud because of your beauty;
you corrupted your wisdom for the sake of your splendor.
I cast you to the ground;
I exposed you before kings,
to feast their eyes on you. (Ezekiel 28:17)

Reading this as another account of Lucifer's fall to Sheol is a bit of a stretch, but only until we dig into the original Hebrew behind the English text. The word translated "kings," *məlākîm*, uses the same consonant sounds, M-L-K, as *mal'akh*, or "messenger," a word usually translated into English as "angel." But in the Semitic languages spoken in the lands to the north and east of the ancient Israelites, similar words such as *maliku* and *malku* referred to underworld spirits who received *kispum* offerings and were possibly linked to the Rephaim.[29]

Translators, both English and Hebrew, seeing the consonants *mlkm* would understandably assume that the word referred to kings. Translators may not have been aware of the *maliku* spirits of ancient Ebla or Mari or why they were relevant to Ezekiel's verse. But in the context of the cults of the ancestors and divinized dead kings who were an integral part of the pagan religions in and around ancient Israel, it seems more likely that Ezekiel was referring to *malakim*, the malevolent spirits of the dead Nephilim, rather than "kings," just as Isaiah called the demoted rebel from Eden an unclean dead god and not a "loathed branch."

This has interesting implications. It suggests that the fall of Satan, or at least his punishment, took place *after* the Flood, because the "shades," the Rephaim (the spirits of the Nephilim), were already in Sheol when Satan landed there. That assumes, of course, that time in the spirit realm moves in a linear manner, the way it does for us. But that kind of speculation is way outside the scope of this book.

The bottom line is this: Satan's ambition got the better of him. He was thrown out of Eden, cast down from the mountain of God, where he was greeted by the shades, the Rephaim—and not exactly with praise and thanksgiving ("You have become as weak as we!").

However, while Satan was down, he wasn't out. Although he'd been demoted from guardian of the throne of God to overseer of the disembodied spirits of the Nephilim, Satan took the form of the storm-god under names like Hadad (Baal), Zeus, Jupiter, and Thor, and set himself up as king of pagan pantheons from India to Rome to Scandinavia. And the Rephaim, called "warriors of Baal" in ancient Amorite ritual texts that have only been translated within the last fifty years, have been hard at work literally bedeviling humanity until Jesus returns.

Meanwhile, another nefarious group connected to the Rephaim has been confined to the abyss. But they're not out of touch; they've been influencing humanity for millennia, and those Amorite texts show that the myths of Greece and Rome are integrally linked to the history written on the pages of the Bible.

3

Council of the Titans

The Greeks and Romans shared a good deal of their religion. The names were different (with the notable exception of Apollo), but the gods were pretty much the same. Zeus of the Greeks was Jupiter of the Romans. Likewise, Aphrodite was Venus, Ares was Mars, Hera was Juno, Hephaestus was Vulcan, and so on.

Similarly, the old god of the Romans, Saturn, was the equivalent of Kronos, king of the Titans. In both Roman and Greek religion, this was the old god who ruled the earth during a long-ago Golden Age, when humanity lived like gods, free from toil and care. Both were overthrown by their son, the storm-god, and confined to the netherworld. To the Greeks, this was Tartarus, a place as far below Hades as the earth is below heaven; in Roman myth, Saturn was chained by Jupiter to ensure that he didn't overeat. It was believed that Saturn consumed the passing days, months, and years. It obviously would have been a problem if the old god had turned his voracious appetite to consuming the present and future as well.

The most famous of the Roman religious festivals, Saturnalia, was adapted from the Kronia celebrated in the Greek world. The Kronia is first recorded in Ionia, the central part of western Anatolia (modern Turkey) in the eighth century BC, roughly the time of Isaiah.[30] From there, the celebration spread to Athens and the island of Rhodes,[31] and ultimately westward to Rome, although the festival shifted from midsummer to the winter solstice. Both festivals were a time of merriment and abandoning social norms, with gambling, gift-giving, the suspension of normal business, and slaves being served by their masters.[32]

The annual party notwithstanding, the god had a darker side. It's well documented that both Saturn and Kronos were connected to human sacrifice. Classical sources report that condemned prisoners were sacrificed to Kronos at Rhodes,[33] children were offered to the god at Crete,[34] and, as Baal-Hammon, the god was offered sacrifices of Phoenician children well into the Christian era.[35] Perhaps most horrifying of all is the description of the first-century philosopher Plutarch.

> [Carthaginians] offered up their own children, and those who had no children would buy little ones from poor people and cut their throats as if they were so many lambs or young birds; meanwhile the mother stood by without a tear or moan; but should she utter a single moan or let fall a single tear, she had to forfeit the money, and her child was sacrificed nevertheless; and the whole area before the statue was filled with a loud noise of flutes and drums so that the cries of wailing should not reach the ears of the people.[36]

Historians of the classical age made no distinction between Saturn, Kronos, and Baal-Hammon; to them, they were the same god worshiped under different names by Romans, Greeks, and Phoenicians. The parallel between child sacrifice and the myth of Saturn/Kronos devouring his own children to prevent their eventual rebellion is obvious. Diodorus Siculus, writing in the first century AD, drily noted that "the story passed down among the Greeks from ancient myth that Kronos did away with his own children appears to have been kept in mind among the Carthaginians through this observance."[37] Christian apologist Tertullian was less charitable:

> Since Saturn did not spare his own children, of course he stuck to his habit of not sparing those of other people, whom indeed their own parents offered of themselves, being pleased to answer the call, and fondled the infants, lest they should weep when being sacrificed. And yet a parent's murder of his child is far worse than simple homicide.[38]

Indeed. In our modern, civilized world, we've mostly avoided the guilt associated with infanticide by convincing ourselves that an unborn child is simply a clump of cells that's part of a pregnant woman's body—heartbeat and unique DNA sequence notwithstanding.

We cannot lay the blame for the cult of Kronos, and the sacrifices offered later to his alter egos Saturn and Baal-Hammon, entirely on the Greeks. Careful reading of ancient texts reveals that this god is much older than the Greek civilization and originated farther east, in northern Mesopotamia. As at Saturnalia, the Kronia featured a reversal of normal social roles, most notably slaves served by their masters and eating with them at a common meal. It appears that this festival was very old by the time the Greeks established themselves as a world power.

A text discovered in 1983 at the site of the capital city of the Hittite kingdom, Hattuša, dated to about 1400 BC, the time of the Israelite conquest of Canaan, describes a myth in which the king of the gods, the storm-god Teshub (Baal/Zeus/Jupiter by a different name) has a ritual meal with the sun-goddess, Allani, and the "primeval gods" who'd been banished to the netherworld. Not only were the old gods at the table; they sat in the place of honor at Teshub's right hand.

The celebration of the temporary suspension of the cosmic order surely accompanied the temporary suspension of the social order on earth. In other words, the myth with the "primeval gods" will have been associated with a ritual of reversal between masters and slaves. Now the Titans were also called "the old gods," old and/or dumb people were insulted as Kronoi, and Attic comedy used expressions such as "older than Kronos" and "older than Kronos and the Titans." Evidently, the antiquity of this divine generation had become proverbial at a relatively early stage of the tradition. The Titans thus can be legitimately compared to the Hurrian "primeval" gods.[39]

It's no coincidence that, like Kronos and Saturn, the Hurrian-Hittite god Kumarbi became king of the gods for a while by castrating his father, the sky-god, and was in turn deposed by his son, the storm-god, called Teshub by the Hurrians and Tarhunz by the Hittites. In other words, Kumarbi, who was worshiped in what is now Turkey and northern Syria, was an older incarnation of Kronos/Saturn/Baal-Hammon.

West drew attention to the conceptual similarity of the (Hittite) "former gods" (*karuilies siunes*) with the Titans, called Πρότεροι Θεοι in *Theogony* 424, 486. Both groups were confined to the underworld (with the apparent exceptions of Atlas and Prometheus), and as Zeus banished the Titans thither, so Tešup [Teshub] banished the *karuilies siunes*, commonly twelve in number, like the Titans. They were in turn identified with the Mesopotamian Anunnaki. These were confined by Marduk to the underworld, or at least some of them were (half the six hundred, Enuma Elish vi 39–47, see 41–44), where they were ruled over variously by Dagan or Shamash.[40]

The evidence for the earliest traces of this god point to a Mesopotamian origin, not Greek. Specifically, the trail leads to northwest Mesopotamia, in the area of the Mediterranean coast along the border between modern Syria and Turkey.

But this goes farther back than the Hittites and Hurrians of Joshua's day. Scholar Amar Annus, who has done some absolutely brilliant work tracing the Watchers, Peter's "angels that sinned," back from Hebrew texts to older Mesopotamian sources, came to an astonishing conclusion when he dug into the origin of the name of the former gods of the Greeks, the Titans.

Annus notes first the existence of an ancient, and by the time of the judges in Israel, almost mythical Amorite tribe called the Tidanu or Ditanu. They had a bad reputation in Mesopotamia—uncivilized, warlike, and dangerous.[41] In fact, they were so threatening to the last Sumerian kings of Mesopotamia, the Third Dynasty of Ur, that around 2037 BC they began building a wall 175 miles long north of modern Baghdad specifically to keep the Tidanu away. We know this because the Sumerians literally named it *bàd martu muriq tidnim*,[42] the "Amorite Wall Which Keeps the Tidnum at a Distance."[43]

Annus notes that the name "*Ti/Di-ta/da-nu(m)*—most possibly 'large animal; aurochs; strong, wild bovide'—is the name of the eponymic tribe."[44] Then he points out that this tribe was linked to the Rephaim in ritual texts at Ugarit, the Amorite city-state destroyed around 1200 BC.

> Greatly exalted be Keret
> In the midst of the *rpum* (Rephaim) of the earth
> In the gathering of the assembly of the Ditanu[45]

So, the Ditanu/Tidanu were linked to the Rephaim in mind and ritual among the ancient Amorites, who, you remember, considered the

Rephaim to be the divinized ancestors of their kings. What's more, this assembly was summoned in what can only be described as a necromancy ritual for the coronation of Ugarit's last king, Ammurapi III.

> You are summoned, O Rephaim of the earth,
> You are invoked, O council of the Didanu!
> Ulkn, the Raphi', is summoned,
> Trmn, the Raphi', is summoned,
> Sdn-w-rdn is summoned,
> Tr 'llmn is summoned,
> the Rephaim of old are summoned!
> You are summoned, O Rephaim of the earth,
> You are invoked, O council of the Didanu![46]

This council or assembly was more than just a group of honored forefathers, like the framers of the Constitution. One text from Ugarit makes reference to ritual offerings for the temple of Didanu,[47] and temples owed sacrifices are typically devoted to gods. It appears, then, that between the birth of Abraham, around 1950 BC, and the time of the judges, circa 1200 BC, the Tidanu/Ditanu were transformed from a scary tribe of Amorites named for a giant wild bull into divine beings connected to the Rephaim, who likewise disappeared from the earth (in physical form) during that period.[48]

And the Tidanu/Ditanu are probably the origin of the name of the bad old gods of the Greeks.

> Then it may not be overbold to assume that the Greek *Titanes* originates from the name of the semi-mythical warrior-tribe (in Ugarit) *tdn*—mythically related to the *Rpum* in the Ugarit, and once actually tied together with Biblical Rephaim in II Samuel 5:18-22, where we have in some manuscripts Hebrew *rp'm* rendered into LXX as *Titanes*.[49]

So, the veneration of this group of ancient entities extends at least as far back as the time of the judges, and probably much further. But why would the Greeks choose the name of an Amorite tribe for the old gods confined to Tartarus? Was that tribe literally descended from the old gods—the rebellious "sons of God" in Genesis 6? In other words, were the Tidanu/Ditanu literally Nephilim?

While it's possible, we think it's unlikely. The Nephilim were destroyed in the Flood. Their spirits survived to become demons, a belief shared by Jews of the Second Temple period and early Church fathers such as Origen, Philo, and Justin Martyr.[50] This was also the belief of the Greeks, although they tended to think that *daimones* were "pure Spirits dwelling on the earth, and are kindly, delivering from harm, and guardians of mortal men."[51]

What's clear is the link between the religions of the Amorites of the patriarchal age, the Hurrians and Hittites who lived to the north of Mesopotamia, and the Greeks of the classical era who lived west of the Hittites in what we know today as western Turkey and Greece. It's not surprising that scholars are shifting from the consensus view of a hundred years ago, that Greek and Roman religion came from early Indo-Europeans, to what appears obvious in light of modern archaeology: The religion of Greece and Rome originated with the Semitic people of the Near East, specifically the Amorites.

The biggest change regarding the relationship of humanity to the "former gods" was that by the time the Greeks emerged onto the world stage, Kronos/Saturn was the only one of the old gods who received any kind of worship. His brothers and sisters had small roles in the cosmologies of the Greeks and Romans, but Kronos/Saturn was the only one with official rites.

This is a little odd, since the assembly, or council, of the Ditanu had its own temple at Ugarit as late as the time of the judges. Over the centuries, the only one of the spirits in the abyss who still commanded respect was their leader.

We can identify these spirits in the Bible. You have already seen the clues; Peter and Jude both refer to angels who sinned against God by committing an act of sexual perversion, for which they were *tartaroō*, "thrust down to Tartarus." The Greeks and Romans knew of only one group of gods confined to Tartarus, and that was the Titans.

If the Titans were the angels who defied their Creator in the distant past on Mount Hermon, then it appears the Amorites worshiped those angels long after the Flood had destroyed their progeny, the Nephilim. Under the influence of the demon spirits of the Nephilim who were destroyed in the deluge, these descendants of Canaan, son of Ham,[52] terrorized the ancient Near East from before the time of Abraham until the time of David, when the soldiers of Israel finally wiped out the Philistine Sons of Rapha.

Identifying the Titans as the Watchers who swore an oath on Mount Hermon is consistent with the evidence from the myths of later civilizations. Textual evidence from ancient Mesopotamia identifies Kronos/Saturn as the Phoenician Baal-Hammon, and the earlier Mesopotamian deities Kumarbi (Hittites and Hurrians), El (Canaan), Dagan (Amorites and Philistines), and Enlil (Akkad and Sumer). All of them, from Kumarbi to Enlil, have their origins in northwest Syria or southeast Turkey, in an area generally bounded on the south by Jebel Bishri in northeast Syria and the Amanus mountains in southern Turkey. And this is precisely the region that eventually produced the Amorites, and the tribe from which the Amorite kings of Babylon claimed descent, the Tidanu/Ditanu, which apparently took the name of the old gods called Titans by the later Greeks. In fact, one of the mountain peaks in the Bishri range northeast of Palmyra is called Jebel Diddi, which may preserve the name of the ancient Amorite tribe.[53]

In other words, after the Flood, spirits working in the vicinity of modern-day Aleppo led a group of Amorites to believe a twisted version of history—that the ancestors of this tribe had been demigods, "mighty men who were of old," and that the old gods were still available to serve if only the Amorites pledged their worship and made regular sacrifices to them. Over time, as the influence of these old gods spread westward through the lands of the Hurrians and Hittites, they were adopted into the religion of the Greeks as the Titans, a name that reflects the bull-like appearance of these entities, who may be, like the divine rebel from Eden, rebellious cherubim who thought they could overthrow their Creator.

Is it a coincidence that Satan is usually depicted with horns?

The most powerful of these rebels, known to us through the ages as the Watcher called Shemihazah, or the creator-god variously called El, Enlil, Dagan/Dagon, Kumarbi, Kronos, Saturn, and Baal-Hammon, continued to influence the world around the Mediterranean and probably elsewhere under other names. To this day, one can make the case that the child sacrifice that's become an industry unto itself is just a sanitized version of the ancient worship of a dark god who sits in Tartarus, waiting for what he believes will be the time to emerge and finally claim what is rightfully his—the very throne of God.

Part Two

APPEASING THE DEAD

4

The Pourer of Water

Before God revealed the true nature of the afterlife to us through Jesus and, to a lesser degree, the prophets and apostles, the ancient world had a very different idea about what came after death. The people who dominated the world during the time of the patriarchs, the Amorites, believed that the quality of life after death depended on one's children, and their children, and their children, et cetera, until the end of time.

There was more to it than that. The people of the Near East in Abraham's day never really said goodbye to their ancestors. The dead hung around, always near, as part of everyday life. In fact, they required the attention of their descendants, and through the rituals of the living, those who'd passed on remained an active part of family, tribe, and community. Life among the Amorites of the second millennium BC, at least as far as one's relationships with family and tribe, both living and dead, were very similar to the ancestor veneration found today in many parts of the world. It may seem odd to Protestants, for whom praying to saints is anathema, but the practice is widespread and very old. The earliest written accounts that describe and explain the practice come from the Amorites of the ancient Near East.

Mesopotamians four thousand years ago believed the netherworld was a dark, dreary place. The only food and drink available to the dead was what was provided by one's descendants. The living were bound by duty to summon the ancestors to a ritual meal called the *kispum* on the thirtieth day of each month. This was the night of no moon, the darkest night, when the veil between the world of the living and the land of the dead was apparently thinnest. This is likely why one text in Sumerian and Akkadian from the time of Abraham described the last day of the month as "the evil day," "dangerous day," "the day of the *kispum*," "day of the disappearance," and "the day of 'purification'."[54]

This wasn't like children putting out cookies and milk for Santa Claus on Christmas Eve. The *kispum* was a necromancy ritual at which the family called the ancestors by name. Failure to perform the rite condemned the ancestors to a gloomy existence of dull, constant hunger.

Amorite society was based on a moral code that held the family together, a set of values called *ahhutum* ("brotherhood").[55] These principles included a family's obligations to its dead ancestors, which were embodied in the term *kubbutum*, based on a root word meaning "to be heavy."[56] It means something like "gravitas," implying dignity, respect, and honor paid to those who'd gone on before. We find a similar term in the Book of Job as he reflects on the inevitability of suffering and death:

His sons come to honor, and he does not know it;
they are brought low, and he perceives it not. (Job 14:21)

The word translated "honor" is *yikbədû*, which comes from the Hebrew root *kâbad*. It's similar to the Akkadian *kubbutum* and conveys the same sense of responsibility and honor. The bottom line is that, unlike modern Western society, in which friends, coworkers, and Internet contacts have largely replaced family bonds, the dead in the ancient Near East were never really gone. They were inextricably connected to the world of the living, and the responsibility of the living for the departed was weighty, indeed.

The monthly *kispum* rite may have originated with the Amorites. The first written references to it date from the early second millennium BC,[57] which is when control of Mesopotamia shifted from the Akkadians and Sumerians to the Amorites. The ritual was comprised of three elements: a communal meal, *šuma zakāru* ("remembering the name"), and *mē naqû* ("pouring the water").[58] Dead ancestors were represented by statues call *en-en-ku-ku* ("lords who are sleeping").[59] These statues are probably what the Bible calls teraphim, the household gods stolen by Rachel when Jacob fled from his father-in-law Laban (see Genesis 31).[60]

The form of the ritual has been preserved in a text from Assur:

[Name], who died a natural death in his bed, the son of [Name], who laid him in the grave (*ina qabri*). You are Man (*amelūta*)! I called your name. I called your name among the ghosts of the dead (*eṭemmē*). I called your name for kispum. I sat you before Šamaš. I called your name as a ghost before Šamaš. I placed you in your grave ("house"). I placed food for you in the entrance to your grave. For the ghosts of your family I performed kispum (*kispa aksip*).[61]

The food provided to the dead was simple—bread, cold water, hot broth, flour, honey, and maybe some wine or beer flavored with roasted grain. Liquids might be poured into a pipe inserted into the earth, presumably to deliver it directly to the deceased.[62] The provision of water was so important that the family heir who was responsible for the monthly *kispum* was called a "pourer of water."[63]

It's hard for us in the modern world to grasp how crucial these monthly rites were in ancient Mesopotamia. Participation in the afterlife absolutely depended on one's descendants faithfully fulfilling their duties every new moon.[64] This not only nourished the dead through the

long years in the netherworld; it kept them pacified. This was important. The dead were dangerous![65] To guarantee that the heir, usually the
eldest son, did right by the expired ancestors, inheritance was tied to the
performance of the *kispum*. Receiving one's birthright was conditional
on performing the monthly rites.[66] Disobedient children might be punished in a will by being barred from accessing the gods and the dead of
the recently deceased.[67]

The anxiety of children who struggled to meet their obligation to
the ancestors is captured in a number of ancient Mesopotamia texts.
This letter was sent by a woman who berated her brother for failing to
send the needed items for the *kispum*:

> As you, my brother, know, this year you have sent me neither
> garlic, nor onions, nor *sirbittum* fish. If I do not write you, you
> do not call my name (i.e. remember me). I am now sending
> Muballiṭ Marduk (a messenger) before you (with this). Assem-
> ble together and send me one shekel silver worth of garlic, one
> shekel silver worth of onion, and one shekel silver worth of *sir-
> bittum* fish. (Or else) what shall I give (during) the whole year
> for the *kispum* offering for the day of the new moon for the
> house of your family?[68]

Although the responsibility for performing the *kispum* fell to the
oldest male child, the letter above shows that women sometimes took on
the duty. In fact, daughters in Abraham's day could be legally adopted
as sons to identify them as heirs, which gave them the right to approach
the family's dead and family gods—a high honor.[69]

The month of Abu in the Babylonian calendar (the Hebrew month
of Ab, or July/August) seems to have been especially important in the
annual cycle of the *kispum*. A letter from Ammi-ditana, the Amorite
king of Babylon during the seventeenth century BC, a contemporary of
Jacob and Joseph, calls for milk and butter for the offerings that month.[70]

It seems that Abu was believed to be a good time to ask dead relatives to leave the living in peace and to consult them for supernatural advice about how to cope in the world of the living.[71]

Interestingly, the name of the month may derive from a Semitic term *ab*, meaning "entrance to the netherworld."[72] In Hebrew, *ab* means "father," but in a broader sense of honored ancestors or deities. Many of the gods worshiped in Mesopotamia were called "father," such as the creator-god of Canaan, El, the "father of mankind," and the war-god Chemosh, who is described as the father of the Moabites in Numbers 21:29. This has relevance beyond trying to understand the ancient Mesopotamian monthly meal for the dead, because another word based on *ab*, the Hebrew *abarim* ("travelers"), identifies the mountain from which Moses got his only look at the Promised Land and the battleground where the army of the Antichrist will fall.[73] *Ab* is also a component of the name "Moab," where the Israelites camped before crossing the Jordan (and the site of the "mountain of the Abarim," Mount Nebo). The most common explanation of the etymology of Moab ("from father") derives from the Bible's origin story of the nation; the patriarch of the Moabites was a child of incestuous unions between Abraham's nephew Lot and his daughters, who plied their father with wine when they despaired of having children after losing their fiancés in the destruction of Sodom and Gomorrah.[74] Likewise, Moab's northern neighbor, Ammon, was founded by Lot's other son/grandson, Ben-Ammi, whose name means "son of my people."[75] We'll address the significance of those names in the context of honored ancestors in another chapter.

The relationships between the living and the dearly departed were so important that scholars haven't found any communal cemeteries in the ancient Near East from the Old Testament period—in other words, when the Amorites controlled the lands of the Bible. Families buried their dead under the floors of their homes,[76] maybe so the dead only had to travel about six feet, more or less, to attend the *kispum*. This practice is even mentioned in the Bible. Have you ever wondered why the prophet

Samuel was buried "in his house at Ramah"?[77] That wasn't a figure of speech; it was the custom of the time and culture in which Samuel, Saul, David, and Solomon lived.

This dedication of the living to the dead, and the dependence of the dead on the living for their existence after death, is likewise reflected in the story of Abraham. If you're reading this book, you are no doubt familiar with the basic outline of the story of Father Abraham: He faithfully followed God's call and left his home in northern Mesopotamia, near Harran (it's spelled with two *R*s outside the Bible) and traveled to Canaan. God promised that his descendants would return from Egypt to Canaan and become a great nation. As time passed, Abraham and Sarah began to doubt because they reached their senior years without a child and heir. Trying to jump-start God's promise, Sarah gave her servant, Hagar, to Abraham, who promptly fathered Ishmael, considered the father of the Arabian tribes. But even with this display of disbelief, God reappeared to Abraham and Sarah and promised a son, who arrived in the form of Isaac, the son of the promise.

Most of us, reading this with a modern, Western worldview, interpret Abraham's distress at the lack of an heir as the understandable sadness a father might have over not seeing his family line continue, or over leaving his (rather large) estate to an outsider.

> After these things the word of the Lord came to Abram in a vision: "Fear not, Abram, I am your shield; your reward shall be very great." But Abram said, "O Lord God, what will you give me, for I continue childless, and the heir of my house is Eliezer of Damascus?" (Genesis 15:1–2)

Having read this far into the chapter, you already have a better understanding of why Abraham was distressed about not having a son. Since he didn't know what later prophets and the apostles knew about the afterlife, Abraham can be excused for thinking that he needed a son to call his name and feed him on the thirtieth of every month. This is confirmed by a closer examination of Genesis 15:2:

> *mâ titten-lî wĕ'ānōkî hôlēk 'ărîrî ûben mešeq bêtî {hû' dammešeq}*
> *'ĕlî 'ezer*

What can you give me, since I am childless, and the one who will pour libations on my tomb… is Eliezer?

The expression *hû' dammešeq* is a scribal gloss, explaining what was felt to be a damaged text, since the meaning of *mešeq* was lost until the Ugaritic texts were found. It may be translated "that is, Damascus", but is an ill-directed attempt to explain an obscure term, and should be omitted. *Ben mešeq*, "son of the cup", alludes to the eldest son's ritual duties at the obsequies of his father.[78]

In short, Abraham wasn't upset that he might have to leave his wealth to a distant relative in Damascus. In fact, Eliezer may not even have been related; he might have been the servant Abraham sent north to find a bride for Isaac.[79] Abraham was distressed that he'd have to name a servant his *ben mešeq*, "son of the cup," to pour the water every month for the *kispum*.

Oddly enough, this practice of "pouring the water" for the ancestors is one more religious rite that appears to be connected to, if not inspired by, the Watchers and Mount Hermon.

In September of 1869, Sir Charles Warren climbed the mountain as part of a survey of the Levant for the Palestine Exploration Fund. We quote an excerpt from his report for the PEF later in this book, but the relevant point right now is this: In addition to discovering a four-foot-high stela inside the ruins of a temple near the summit inscribed in archaic Greek with a reference to "those who swore an oath" (i.e., the Watchers), Warren found that the summit of the mountain was scooped out to form a giant bowl about nine feet across and at least six feet deep.

If you're familiar with the *Book of 1 Enoch*, you probably know that the two hundred rebellious Watchers descended to the summit of Hermon and bound one another with a mutual oath before proceeding to mate with human women and corrupt most of the living things on the planet. The text of Enoch puts the event "in the days of Jared."[80]

Scholar Edward Lipiński, however, has a different view:

The word *yarīd*... is not the name of a person, as authors generally believe, but a cultic term denoting the rite of hydrophory, which consisted in going down to a well in order to draw water out of it and bring it up in procession to pour it out as a libation.[81]

In other words, the descent of the Watchers didn't take place in the days of Jared, it happened in the days of the *yarīd*, or perhaps in the days when the *yarīd* was introduced. Lipiński documents from classical sources that the ritual was performed in a number of places in the Levant, including Hierapolis (modern Manbij, Syria) to honor Atargatis, another name for the goddess Inanna/Ishtar (about whom more later), and Tyre, for the chief god of that city, Melqart—the Phoenician name for the most famous of the Greek demigods, Herakles.[82]

The practice of venerating one's ancestors probably predates Abraham's day, but we can only definitely date the practice of the monthly care and feeding ritual, the *kispum*, to the rise of the Amorites around 2000 BC. It's difficult to believe that religious rites based on the worship of ancestors would have continued for the last four thousand years without *some* evidence to compel cultures as different as South Korea and rural Madagascar to continue it to this day. The evidence must have been in the form of supernatural intervention in the physical realm, since it was fear of the power of the dead motivated Amorites to feed them in the first place.

As Christians, we understand that the dead only visit the living under special circumstances sanctioned by God. The only example in the Bible was the visit by the prophet Samuel to the medium at En-dor (1 Samuel 28:1–25). So, it's safe to say that demands for food and drink from the dead weren't coming from dead ancestors. Those demands came from another kind of spirit. They were spirits of the dead, all right, but not dead humans—dead hybrids. Nephilim. In other words, what the Amorites of old and the people of Madagascar today believed were the spirits of the ancestors were actually demons.

And that begs a question: What do the demons get out of this deal? Obviously, a spirit without flesh needs no food or drink, so why the demands for sustenance? The *Book of 1 Enoch* suggests that the spirits of the giants, barred from heaven and Sheol, were condemned to wander the earth, neither eating nor drinking, causing misery among humans as they hunger and thirst.[83] Do the demands for food and drink stem from an ancient longing for the pleasures of the flesh again? Since their hunger and thirst can't possibly be fulfilled through ritual offerings of food and poured water, we're left to speculate. What do they gain?

Why have the spirits of the mighty men who were of old pretended to be the dearly departed of grieving humans for thousands of years?

5

Sacrifices to the Dead

During the Exodus, one of the more unusual confrontations between the Hebrews who were faithful to Yahweh and those who preferred a more—shall we say—tolerant view of the pagan religions they encountered occurred in the plains of Moab, the fertile area northeast of the Dead Sea, across the Jordan from Jericho.

> While Israel lived in Shittim, the people began to whore with the daughters of Moab. These invited the people to the sacrifices of their gods, and the people ate and bowed down to their gods. So Israel yoked himself to Baal of Peor. And the anger of the LORD was kindled against Israel. And the LORD said to Moses, "Take all the chiefs of the people and hang them in the sun before the LORD, that the fierce anger of the LORD may turn away from Israel." And Moses said to the judges of Israel, "Each of you kill those of his men who have yoked themselves to Baal of Peor."
>
> And behold, one of the people of Israel came and brought a Midianite woman to his family, in the sight of Moses and in the sight of the whole congregation of the people of Israel, while

they were weeping in the entrance of the tent of meeting. When Phinehas the son of Eleazar, son of Aaron the priest, saw it, he rose and left the congregation and took a spear in his hand and went after the man of Israel into the chamber and pierced both of them, the man of Israel and the woman through her belly. Thus the plague on the people of Israel was stopped. Nevertheless, those who died by the plague were twenty-four thousand. (Numbers 25:1–9)

This requires some unpacking. To our twenty-first-century minds, the reaction of Phinehas seems excessive. Some in America today would call him out for his intolerance and accuse him of xenophobia, racism, or both. To them, this story makes God out to be a monster since He obviously approved of Phinehas' violent act. But that's because most Americans today, especially those most likely to throw around that kind of epithet, view the world through a naturalistic bias. There is a lot here that's only obvious if you understand what was happening in the spirit realm.

The first clue that there's more to this story than is obvious at first read is the description of Phinehas' killing stroke. Did you notice that he killed both the Israelite prince and the Midianite princess with one thrust of his spear? Without getting too graphic, there are only a couple of physical positions in which Phinehas could have speared both of them with one jab.

There is other evidence in the text that suggests the sexual sin of Zimri and Cozbi, the young lovers who dared transgress "in the sight of all Israel." The Hebrew word translated "belly," *qevah*, means the lower abdomen and can refer to the womb or pubic region,[84] emphasizing that Phinehas caught the young couple in the act. The word translated "chamber" in the ESV (other translations use "tent" or "pavilion"), *qubbah*, appears only here in the Old Testament. The passage is a little obscure, but the sense is that the couple were engaged in some rite to the

Baal of Peor, possibly a fertility ritual. So, what do we know about this pagan deity?

The name Baal-Peor is actually a title, the "lord of Peor." The location of Peor isn't known exactly, but it must be near Mount Nebo, where Moses got his only look at the Holy Land. On a clear day, visitors to Nebo today can see the Dead Sea, Jericho, and the Mount of Olives, which is only about twenty-five miles away. Shittim, or Abel-Shittim, was the name given to the place of the Israelites' camp in the plains of Moab, directly below the western slope of Mount Nebo. Shittim means "acacia," the desert tree that provided the wood of the Ark of the Covenant. It's a hardy plant, surviving where most other vegetation can't because of its resistance to drought and tolerance for salt water.

A team led by Dr. Steven Collins of Trinity Southwest University has been digging at a site in Jordan that overlooks the ancient plains of Moab since 2005. Dr. Collins is convinced that this site, called Tall el-Hammam, is the biblical Sodom. Based on its estimated population, it would have been the largest city in the Levant in the time of Abraham next to Hazor, near the Sea of Galilee.

The evidence suggests that it was destroyed around 1700 BC by an air blast similar to the 1908 Tunguska event in Siberia.[85] Soil samples taken from the lower city revealed a high concentration of salts and sulphates in the ash layer from the city's destruction, and the chemical composition of the salts and sulphates was "virtually identical to the chemical composition of Dead Sea water."[86] So, whatever exploded over the north end of the Dead Sea around the time of Abraham had enough force to kick up a small tsunami of superheated brine that swept over the lower part of the city. This was devastating—the lower city was built on a hill 75 to 150 feet above the surrounding plain!

Further investigation of the plain itself, the Kikkar, revealed that the salty water essentially poisoned the ground. It was at least six hundred years—about the time of Saul, David, and Solomon—before agriculture and civilization could resume.[87] So, when the Israelites arrived on the plains of Moab, it was well named Abel-Shittim, "meadow of aca-cias"[88]—because virtually nothing would grow there besides acacia for another 250 years.

Now, why is all of that relevant? Because the area east of the Dead Sea, and especially near the ruined city of ancient Sodom,[89] was a place where it was believed that the dead intervened in the affairs of the living. In fact, two of the stops along the Exodus route refer to places where the veil between worlds was believed to be thin.

> And the people of Israel set out and camped in Oboth. And they set out from Oboth and camped at Iye-abarim, in the wilderness that is opposite Moab, toward the sunrise. (Numbers 21:10–11)

The name of the first, Oboth, derives from *'ôb*, which refers to nec-romancy, the practice of summoning and consulting with spirits of the dead.[90] This is the Hebrew behind the English word "medium," as in the woman consulted by Saul to summon the spirit of Samuel.

This is a controversial topic among Christians. Those of us who take the Bible seriously are inclined to believe that there's no such thing as ghosts. But there is nothing in the biblical account[91] to suggest that the spirit who delivered God's message to Saul was anything but the ghost of Samuel—who, it's important to note, was called an *elohim* as he emerged from the earth.

"Elohim" is not a proper name, and it doesn't refer specifically to "gods." It's a designator of place, like "American" or "New Yorker." Spir-its live in the spirit realm, but not all spirits are equal. Some are archan-gels and others are demons, but all are spirits. In the same way, spirits are all *elohim*, even the spirits of dead humans, but there is only one capital-*E* Elohim.

Interestingly, this casts new light on the name of one of the giants who fell before the swords of David's mighty men.

There was war again between the Philistines and Israel, and David went down together with his servants, and they fought against the Philistines. And David grew weary. And Ishbi-benob, one of the descendants of the giants, whose spear weighed three hundred shekels of bronze, and who was armed with a new sword, thought to kill David. But Abishai the son of Zeruiah came to his aid and attacked the Philistine and killed him. (2 Samuel 21:15–17)

Contrary to the most common definitions of the name, the giant wasn't Ishbi-benob, he was *Ishbi ben Ob*—Ishbi, son of the medium! And remember, the "descendants of the giants" (*yĕlîdê hārāpâ*) were probably a Philistine warrior cult that venerated the "mighty men who were of old,"[92] a practice that had persisted for at least 1,500 years in the Levant by the time of David.

Not a surprise for this one, since his mother was apparently in contact with those same demon spirits. Wouldn't it be interesting, as author Brian Godawa speculated in his novel, *David Ascendant*, if Ishbi was the son of the medium consulted by Saul the night before he died in battle?[93]

But this goes even deeper. *'Ôb*, in turn, is related to the Hebrew word *'ab*, which means "father." In the Old Testament, the word "fathers" most often refers to one's dead ancestors. For example:

And when the time drew near that Israel [Jacob] must die, he called his son Joseph and said to him, "If now I have found favor in your sight, put your hand under my thigh and promise to deal kindly and truly with me. Do not bury me in Egypt, but let me lie with my fathers [*ăbōṯ*]. (Genesis 47:29–30)

Looking at all of this in context, then, we can pretty safely say that Oboth essentially means "Spirits of the Dead."[94]

The other place mentioned in the Scripture from Exodus, Iye-abarim, or "ruins of the Abarim," is based on the same root. Abarim is the anglicized form of *ōbĕrîm*, a plural form of the verb *'br*, which means "to pass from one side to the other."[95] In this context, it refers to a spirit that passes from one plane of existence to another, or crosses over, in the same sense that the ancient Greeks believed the dead traveled across the River Styx to reach or return from the underworld.

The placement of Oboth and Iye-abarim in Numbers 33 suggests that they were east of the Dead Sea, not far from Mount Nebo and the plains of Moab. This is confirmed by the proximity of Shittim to Beth-Peor. That's a name that needs a deeper dive.

Peor is related to the Hebrew root *p'r*, which means "cleft" or "gap," or "open wide."[96] In this context, that's consistent with Isaiah's description of the entrance to the netherworld:

Therefore Sheol has enlarged its appetite and opened [*pa'ar*] its mouth beyond measure. (Isaiah 5:14)

This is similar to the depiction of the Canaanite god of death, Mot, in Ugaritic texts as a ravenous entity with a truly monstrous mouth:

He extends a lip to the earth, a lip to the heavens, he extends a tongue to the stars.[97]

So, it appears that Baal-Peor was "lord of the entrance to the netherworld," Thus Beth-Peor, "house (or temple) of the entrance to the netherworld," was somewhere close to the plains of Moab and Mount Nebo—which, you'll note in Deuteronomy 32:49, God called "this mountain of the Abarim."

All of this leads to the *real* reason God was angry with the Israelites when they camped at Shittim. The worship of Baal-Peor was not about sexual fertility rites, as you might think after reading the story of the zeal of Phinehas.

> Then they yoked themselves to the Baal of Peor,
> and ate sacrifices offered to the dead;
> they provoked the Lord to anger with their deeds,
> and a plague broke out among them.
> Then Phinehas stood up and intervened,
> and the plague was stayed. (Psalm 106:28–30)

Writing about four hundred years after the incident at Shittim, the psalmist didn't even mention the young couple caught in the act by Phinehas. It was *eating sacrifices offered to the dead* that angered Yahweh. And judging by the words of later prophets, the Israelites were slow to learn their lesson.

> But you, draw near,
> sons of the sorceress,
> offspring of the adulterer and the loose woman.
> Whom are you mocking?
> Against whom do you open your mouth wide
> and stick out your tongue?
> Are you not children of transgression,
> the offspring of deceit,
> you who burn with lust among the oaks,
> under every green tree,
> who slaughter your children in the valleys,
> under the clefts of the rocks?
> Among the smooth stones of the valley is your portion;
> they, they, are your lot;
> to them you have poured out a drink offering,

you have brought a grain offering.
Shall I relent for these things? (Isaiah 57:3–6)

Isaiah wrote nearly seven hundred years after the Exodus, but the Israelites were still engaged in the occult practices that compelled God to smite them with a devastating plague. To "burn with lust among the oaks" suggests fertility rites, which seems obvious given the prophet's condemnation of the children of the adulteress and "loose woman," which is also rendered "prostitute" and "whore" in other English translations. Ah, but once again, there is more in the Bible verse than meets the English-reading eye.

First, did you notice how God, through the prophet Isaiah, used the description of the death-god Mot ("open your mouth wide," "stick out your tongue") to characterize those who mocked Him with pagan rituals? This is not a coincidence.

The Hebrew word translated "sorceress," 'anan, is difficult to pin down. "Witch" and "fortune teller" have also been used in translation. More likely, however, is a correlation with the Arabic 'anna, meaning "to appear," which suggests that the sorceress was actually a female necromancer.[98]

This, then, may explain why the word rendered "oaks" or "terebinths," normally spelled 'êlîm, is 'ēlîm in Isaiah 57:5. This slight difference could be a scribal error, but it seems more likely that it's the same word we find in Psalm 29:1:

Ascribe to the LORD, O heavenly beings (banē 'ēlîm),
Ascribe to the LORD glory and strength.

As we saw above in the story of Saul and the medium of En-dor, *elohim* and its shortened form, *elim*, were used in Hebrew to refer to departed ancestors. So, Isaiah wasn't necessarily railing against sex rites among the sacred oaks, but rather something like, "You sons of the necromancer…who burn with lust among the spirits of the dead." It's likely the prophet was engaging in the wordplay for which he's well known, using a pun to emphasize the spirits behind the rituals—the *'êlîm* among the *'ēlîm*.[99]

Isaiah continues his diatribe by connecting the death cult to the rites of Molech. The valley of the son of Hinnom, later called Gehenna, was the location of the tophet, where Israelites sacrificed their children to the dark god of the underworld.[100] The Valley of Hinnom surrounds Jerusalem's Old City on the south and west, connecting on the west with the Valley of Rephaim (interesting coincidence) and merging with the Kidron Valley near the southeastern corner of the city. It's as Isaiah described it, a narrow, rocky ravine that was used as a place for burying the dead. Tombs along the sides of the valley are plainly visible to visitors to Jerusalem today. This helps us better understand the real meaning behind verse 6, which begins, "among the smooth stones of the valley is your portion."

> An alternative understanding of the phrase *challeqe-nachal*, "smooth things of the wadi," is the "dead" of the wadi. This meaning is based on examples of the related Semitic word *chalaq* found in Arabic and Ugaritic with the meaning "die, perish."[101]

The picture comes into focus. This chapter of Isaiah is obscure and hard to understand only if we read it without knowing what the prophet knew about the Amorite cult of the dead that had persisted from the time of the conquest to his own day. This is confirmed by the next few verses of the chapter:

> On a high and lofty mountain
> you have set your bed,
> and there you went up to offer sacrifice.
> Behind the door and the doorpost

Sharon K. Gilbert and Derek P. Gilbert

you have set up your memorial;
for, deserting me, you have uncovered your bed,
you have gone up to it,
you have made it wide;
and you have made a covenant for yourself with them,
you have loved their bed,
you have looked on nakedness.
You journeyed to the king with oil
and multiplied your perfumes;
you sent your envoys far off,
and sent down even to Sheol. (Isaiah 57:3–9)

The high places were almost constantly in use in Israel and Judah, even during the reigns of kings who tried to do right by God, like Hezekiah. The imagery of adultery and sexual license is a common metaphor in the Old Testament for the spiritual infidelity of God's people. But even here, there are some deeper things to bring out.

This section of Scripture confirms that the target of Isaiah's condemnation was a cult of the dead. Because Hebrew is a consonantal language (no vowels), similar words in the original Hebrew text, written before diacritical marks were used to indicate vowels, can be confusing. Verse 9 is a case in point. The consonants *mem*, *lamed*, and *kaph* can be used for *melech* ("king," which is how it's interpreted in Isaiah 57:9), *malik* ("messenger," especially as a type of angel), or the name of the god Molech. Considering what precedes that verse, specifically Isaiah's reference to slaughtering children in the valleys, the latter option is most likely.

So, Isaiah 57:3–9 should be understood as God's condemnation of the worship of the dead. Isaiah calls out the "sons of the necromancer" who "burn with passion" among the spirits of the dead, sacrificing their children among the dead of the wadis, who were offered food and drink consistent with the Amorite *kispum* ritual for the ancestral dead. But it was worse than that—the apostate Jews "journeyed to Molech with

60

oil…and sent down even to Sheol," the realm of the spirits worshiped as the long-dead, mighty kings of old.

To conclude this section of his book, Isaiah relates a warning and a promise from God:

> When you cry out, let your collection of idols deliver you!
> The wind will carry them all off,
> a breath will take them away.
> But he who takes refuge in me shall possess the land
> and shall inherit my holy mountain. (Isaiah 57:13)

The "wind" is the *ruach*, translated elsewhere as "spirit," as in the Spirit of God. It's another bit of wordplay by Isaiah, showing who will be responsible for the ultimate defeat of the pagan entities worshiped by the backslidden Jews and how easily it will be done. And more—it's a picture of the process of winnowing on a threshing floor, where the chaff is blown away to leave behind the grain. (We have more to say about the spiritual significance of threshing floors in chapter 10.)

The prophet concludes by reminding us what this spiritual war is all about—reclaiming our inheritance, the holy mountain of God.

6

Ruins of the Travelers

One of the most interesting and overlooked parallels in Scripture is the location of the Israelite camp just before the conquest of Canaan and what appears to be the route of attack by the end-times army of the Antichrist when it comes against the holy mountain of God at Jerusalem. We know from Exodus and Deuteronomy that the Israelites camped on the plains of Moab before crossing the Jordan to begin the assault on Jericho.

Likewise, Gog of Magog, whom we'll show later in the book to be the Antichrist, will bring his army to the very same place—to die.

> And you, son of man, prophesy against Gog and say, Thus says the Lord GOD: Behold, I am against you, O Gog, chief prince of Meshech and Tubal. And I will turn you about and drive you forward [or, "drag you along"], and bring you up from the uttermost parts of the north [*yerekah tsaphon*, Baal's mount of assembly], and lead you against the mountains of Israel. Then I will strike your bow from your left hand, and will make your arrows drop out of your right hand. You shall fall on the mountains of

Israel, you and all your hordes and the peoples who are with you. I will give you to birds of prey of every sort and to the beasts of the field to be devoured. You shall fall in the open field, for I have spoken, declares the Lord GOD. I will send fire on Magog and on those who dwell securely in the coastlands, and they shall know that I am the LORD. (Ezekiel 39:1–6, 11)

"The Valley of the Travelers, east of the sea." Many of us have read that verse and paid little attention to the name of Gog's burial place, maybe assuming it was symbolic.

If you assume the sea is the Mediterranean, that could be any-place from Dan to Beersheba—in other words, just about anywhere in Israel. This has allowed prophecy scholars to keep the war of Gog and Magog separate from Armageddon, which many still incorrectly place at Megiddo. But "east of the sea" actually means ancient Moab, which was east of the Dead Sea. This opens a fascinating new look at the war of Gog and Magog.

The Hebrew word rendered "traveler" is *ōbĕrîm*, a plural form of the verb *'br*, which means "to pass from one side to the other."[102] In this con-text, then, a Traveler is a spirit that passes from one plane of existence to another, in the same sense that the ancient Greeks believed the dead had to travel across the River Styx to reach or return from the underworld.

It is interesting that this was the very place, just northeast of the Dead Sea, where Israel camped before crossing the Jordan to begin the conquest of Canaan. How do we know this? Because places where Israel stopped after the Exodus refer to the dead, and specifically to the Travelers.

And the people of Israel set out and camped in Oboth. And they set out from Oboth and camped at Iye-abarim, in the wilderness that is opposite Moab, toward the sunrise. (Numbers 21:10–11)

Oboth has the same sense as *ōbĕrîm*, although it's more specific. *Oboth* derives from *ʾôb*, which refers to necromancy, the practice of summoning and consulting with spirits of the dead.[103] *ʾÔb*, in turn, is related to the Hebrew word *ʾab*, which means "father." In the Old Testament, the word "fathers" most often refers to one's dead ancestors. For example:

> And when the time drew near that Israel must die, he called his son Joseph and said to him, "If now I have found favor in your sight, put your hand under my thigh and promise to deal kindly and truly with me. Do not bury me in Egypt, but let me lie with my fathers [*ăbōt*]". (Genesis 47:29–30)

Oboth, then, means "Spirits of the Dead."[104] And, you've probably already noticed that the second half of the compound name *Iye-abarim* is very similar to *ōbĕrîm*. Excellent work! *Iye-abarim* means "heaps (or ruins) of the Travelers."[105]

Not coincidentally, this area east of the Jordan Rift Valley, from ancient Moab to Bashan, southeast of Mount Hermon, is home to thousands of dolmens, megalithic tombs made from slabs of basalt and limestone that weigh as much as fifty tons.[106]

While dolmens are found all over the world, there are more of these tombs in Jordan and the Golan Heights than anywhere else. They are simple structures, mostly in a trilithon formation—two standing stones and a capstone, like a "table" across the top, with no cement holding the slabs together. Sometimes additional stones are placed at the front and back, occasionally with a porthole cut to include a frame around the opening that held a removable flat stone. Skeletal remains have been found at enough of them to conclude that the primary function of these intriguing structures was burial of the dead.[107]

These ancient monuments are fascinating for a couple of reasons. First, although Iye-Abarim was located just northeast of the Dead Sea, the highest concentration of dolmens in the region is on and around the Golan Heights, where the Rapha king Og and the deity called Rapi'u, King of Eternity, once ruled. A recent survey of the Golan found more than five thousand megalithic burial sites, most of which are dolmens.[108] In Jordan, another twenty thousand dolmens have been found,[109] although many are threatened by the expansion of modern cities and quarrying for rock and gravel. (Which makes sense—dolmens were built where great big rocks were close to the surface and easy to find.) Secondly, and this is an interesting admission: Scholars really don't know anything about the people who built them.

The dolmens are generally dated to the third millennium (3000–2000) BC. On the Golan Heights, they are more narrowly dated to between 2250 BC and about 1800 BC.[110] Based on pottery shards found near some of the dolmens in Jordan, the megaliths closer to the Dead Sea may be as old as the beginning of the Early Bronze Age, circa 3300 BC.[111]

If the Bible is accurate, and we believe it is, then the time and location suggest that the builders of the dolmens were the Rephaim tribes, who constructed them in the centuries before Abraham's arrival in the area. By the time the Israelites returned from Egypt around 1406 BC, only Og's small kingdom remained of the Rephaim—possibly the last of the dolmen-builders in the Levant.

It's tempting to go overboard with speculation, but we don't serve our God well by wandering too far afield without evidence. Still, credentialed scholars link the megaliths to the Rephaim, although instead of identifying the dolmen-builders as Rephaim they tend to view things the other way around, believing the dolmens "were the basis for belief in giants, the Rephaim, Anakim, Emim, Zamzummim, and the like."[112] In other words, scholars think the people who moved into the lands alongside the Jordan River invented stories of giants because they imagined really big men must have moved those really big rocks.

Over the centuries, tomb robbers have removed most of the useful evidence from the dolmens. The few bones left behind in burial chambers don't show any evidence of giantism, or at least we haven't found any papers reporting it. Most of the dolmens are oriented north-south, although about 10 percent appear to be oriented east-west, perhaps to face the rising sun.

Is this significant? While it's interesting to note that the Pole Star was Thuban (*Alpha Draconis*) in the constellation Draco, the Dragon, when the dolmens were built, we don't know if that was relevant. In spite of their ability to lift stupendously heavy blocks of stone, the dolmen-builders weren't considerate enough to leave behind any written evidence.

That makes a recent discovery in the Golan all the more intriguing and frustrating at the same time. In 2012, archaeologists examined a massive, multichambered dolmen in the Shamir Dolmen Field on the western foothills of the Golan Heights, a site with over four hundred dolmens. What was truly remarkable about this particular dolmen was the discovery of rock art on the underside of the capstone, a basalt monster weighing about fifty tons.[113] (For comparison, that's about twice as heavy as a fully-loaded, eighteen-wheel, tractor-trailer in the United States.) That's the first time art has been found inside any of the thousands of dolmens in the region, possibly the first written or artistic record that might be connected directly to the biblical Rephaim.

The dolmen itself is surrounded by a tumulus, a burial mound of about four hundred tons of stone. Think about that! Four thousand years ago, maybe a century or so before Abraham arrived in Canaan, a government on the Golan Heights was powerful enough to organize the manpower and logistics (food, water, etc.) to move and assemble some eight hundred thousand pounds of stone into a multichambered tomb for—who? The king and his family? Archaeologists recovered enough bones and teeth to identify "an 8–10 year-old child, a young adult and a 35–45 year-old adult."[114]

Were they—dare we speculate—of the dynasty that produced Og, the enemy of Israel, about six hundred years later? Well, probably not. Most dynasties don't last that long. But it's interesting to wonder.

The engravings were fourteen figures comprised of a vertical line and a downturned arc. What did the symbol mean? No idea. Nothing like it has been found anywhere in the Levant or anywhere else.[115] It might be a representation of the human soul taking flight, but because the artist didn't leave a note, we're guessing. Or—and again, we're speculating—this could be an ancient symbol with occult meaning even today. Three-dimensional scanning of the images show that at least some of them look very much like the Greek character *psi*, which is a trident (and the logo for Indiana University, Sharon's alma mater), the three-pronged spear traditionally carried by the Greco-Roman god of the sea, Poseidon/Neptune. Today it's used, among other things, as a symbol for parapsychology, especially research into extrasensory perception, and in a mathematical formula that claims to guide occultists in how to perform rituals in chaos magick.

What did that symbol mean in the twentieth century BC? We have no way to know. It might have been doodling by a bored Bronze Age stonemason.

The takeaway for this section is this: For at least a thousand years, people living in lands the Bible identifies as the home of Rephaim tribes built burial tombs with massive slabs of limestone and basalt. And those huge burial tombs inspired place names linked to the dolmen-builders (*Iye-Abarim*, "ruins of the Travelers") and to the restless dead (*Oboth*, "Spirits of the Dead").

Get this: Even the place where Moses died was called the Mountain of the Travelers.

Go up this **mountain of the Abarim**, Mount Nebo, which is in the land of Moab, opposite Jericho, and view the land of Canaan, which I am giving to the people of Israel for a possession. And die on the mountain which you go up, and be gath-

ered to your people, as Aaron your brother died in Mount Hor
and was gathered to his people....

So Moses the servant of the LORD died there in the land of
Moab, according to the word of the LORD, and he buried him
in the valley in the land of Moab opposite Beth-peor; but no
one knows the place of his burial to this day. (Deuteronomy
32:49–50, 34:5–6, emphasis added)

Here's a thought: Moses was buried in the valley of the Travelers, a
place where the Rephaim spirits were believed to cross over to the land
of the living. Is that why Satan, lord of the dead, thought he had a claim
to Moses' body after his death?[116]

Another question comes to mind: Were all those dolmens up and
down the Jordan Rift Valley thought to be portals to the underworld?

Here's another connection between this valley and the realm of the
dead: Remember the prophecy of Balaam? After the king of Moab tried
to buy a curse from the pagan prophet, Israel began drifting away from
Yahweh again.

While Israel lived in Shittim, the people began to whore with
the daughters of Moab. These invited the people to the sacrifices
of their gods, and the people ate and bowed down to their gods.
So Israel yoked himself to Baal of Peor. And the anger of the
LORD was kindled against Israel. (Numbers 25:1–3)

Who was Baal of Peor? Remember, *baal* in Hebrew simply means
"lord." So, the Lord of Peor was a local deity linked to a mountain near
Shittim in Moab, northeast of the Dead Sea. The clue to the character
of Baal-Peor is in the name.

Peor is related to the Hebrew root *p'r*, which means "cleft" or "gap,"[117]
or "open wide."[118] In this context, that definition is consistent with Isaiah's description of the entrance to the netherworld:

Therefore Sheol has enlarged its appetite and opened [*pa'ar*] its mouth beyond measure. (Isaiah 5:14)

Since we're looking at a place associated with the dead, it's worth noting that the Canaanite god of death, Mot, was described in the Ugaritic texts as a ravenous entity with a truly monstrous mouth:

He extends a lip to the earth,
a lip to the heavens,
he extends a tongue to the stars.[119]

Yeesh. But that's what's in view here: Baal-Peor was apparently lord of the entrance to the underworld.

Yes, the Canaanites believed the entrance to the underworld was at Bashan. But both Molech (or Milcom) and Chemosh, the national gods of Ammon and Moab, which controlled most of the land east of the Jordan from the Dead Sea to Mount Hermon, demanded child sacrifice. Veneration of the dead and appeasing the gods of the dead through human sacrifice appear to have been the norm in this region east of the Dead Sea.

This was also the general location of Sodom and Gomorrah. Now, we try not to put too much stock in the influence of territorial spirits. After all, God created us with free will. But you have to admit this is an awful lot of evil concentrated in a small area.

Anyway, perhaps because of the association with death and the dead, there was, shall we say, a fertility aspect to the cult of Baal-Peor.

And behold, one of the people of Israel came and brought a Midianite woman to his family, in the sight of Moses and in the sight of the whole congregation of the people of Israel, while they were weeping in the entrance of the tent of meeting. When Phinehas the son of Eleazar, son of Aaron the priest, saw it, he rose and left the congregation and took a spear in his hand and went after the man of Israel into the chamber and pierced both of them, the man of Israel and the woman through her belly. (Numbers 25:6–8)

How to put this delicately? There are only a couple of physical positions in which Phinehas could have speared both the Israelite man and Midianite woman with one thrust. If you're an adult, I don't need to draw you a picture. Emphasizing the point, the Hebrew word translated "belly," *qevah*, can refer to a woman's womb.[120] In other words, the sin here wasn't that an Israelite man brought a foreign woman home for dinner, it's that the couple performed a lewd ritual act in full view of Moses and the assembly of Israel!

Well, it's no wonder the men of Israel were tempted to follow Baal-Peor. Roughly 60 percent of the Christian pastors in America today struggle with addiction to pornography.[121] Just imagine the temptation of being surrounded by people whose god decreed that extramarital sex was a form of worship. We don't mean to be flippant, but it might take the real threat of death to keep men away from the temples! Indeed, twenty-four thousand people died in the plague that God sent as punishment for that apostasy because it wasn't just the one couple involved.

And there was even more to it than that. Not surprisingly, given the Amorite/Rephaim culture in that time and place, one of the pagan rites the Israelites adopted during their time in Moab was veneration of the dead:

Then they yoked themselves to the Baal of Peor,
and ate sacrifices offered to the dead;
they provoked the LORD to anger with their deeds,
and a plague broke out among them. (Psalm 106:28–29)

The psalmist remembered the sacrifices to the dead, which is a basic description of the Amorite *kispum* ritual. The sexual sin of the young

71

couple (and Phinehas' violent reaction) is shocking to us today, but apparently the psalmist didn't find it worth mentioning. The *real* sin that provoked God's anger was venerating the dead, one of the "abominable practices" of the pagan nations He'd promised to drive out of the land before them.

That brings us back to the point: We've identified the area that Ezekiel called the Valley of the Travelers as the east side of the Jordan Rift Valley, specifically ancient Moab east and just northeast of the Dead Sea. And by now you're asking, "Why are we spending all of this time identifying the area and unraveling the meaning behind the word Travelers?"

Here's why: It's the link that connects the Rephaim to Ezekiel's prophecy of Gog and Magog.

How? Stay tuned.

Part Three

ABODES OF THE DEAD

7

Gatekeeper of the Dead

All of the sacrifices and rituals directed toward the realm of the dead had purpose. The communal meals, the pouring of water, the fertility rites, the children burned on detestable altars—they were intended to produce a desired result. They were deals offered to the spirit realm; if we do this, we hope you'll do that in return. Obviously, this assumed that the dead were able to interact with the living; to travel or cross over the boundary between the land of the living and the abode of the dead. This was not an easy journey, even for the gods.

A myth called *The Descent of Inanna* describes a series of indignities that the Queen of Heaven endured as she passed through the seven gates that lead to the netherworld. It seems that Inanna wasn't happy being the queen bee in the world above; she wanted to rule the world below as well.

Her sister Ereshkigal, Queen of the Underworld, saw through Inanna's ploy. Ereshkigal insisted that Inanna remove an item of clothing or give up a symbol of divine authority at each of the seven gates. Inanna finally arrived in the underworld, naked and helpless. Ereshkigal clearly wasn't pleased to see her:

The Annuna, the judges of the underworld, surrounded her
They passed judgment against her.
Then Ereshkigal fastened on Inanna the eye of death.
She spoke against her the word of wrath.
She uttered against her the cry of guilt.
She struck her.
Inanna was turned into a corpse,
A piece of rotting meat,
And was hung from a hook on the wall.[122]

Harsh. Inanna finally escaped the netherworld after three days (!) when her faithful servant went to the clever god, Enki, who gave instructions to two androgynous demons on how to free the goddess from her corpse-prison. Even then, however, underworld demons called *galla* refused to let her go. They demanded a replacement as a condition for Inanna's freedom. The goddess refused to give up her servant or her son. Instead, she threw her husband under the bus—Dumuzi the Shepherd, king of Uruk. Apparently, Dumuzi wasn't showing enough grief over the temporary death of the goddess to please her, so the *galla* dragged him away.

A later myth tells of the sacrifice of Dumuzi's sister, who offered to take his place in the underworld for half the year, resulting in the annual change of seasons. This is similar to the Greek myth of Persephone, who was tricked by the death-god, Hades, into remaining with him for six months out of the year. Thus, Dumuzi became the first of the ancient Near East's "dying and rising" gods, still worshiped as Tammuz in the time of Ezekiel[123] nearly fifteen hundred years after *The Descent of Inanna* was written.

The point of this introduction is to illustrate the pagan belief in the difficulty of getting out of the netherworld, even for their gods. So, for human spirits to make the journey back required at least permission, if not assistance.

That much, at least, is consistent with the Bible. We've noted elsewhere in this book that the *elohim* of Samuel returned to deliver a message to Saul, the only example in Scripture of a human spirit returning to the land of the living. This was done with the approval of God. Note that when the medium saw Samuel, "she cried out with a loud voice."[124] Probably because she was expecting her familiar spirit!

In the pagan mind, however, which god had control over the entrance to the netherworld? There are several possibilities.

We've already mentioned Baal-Peor, the "lord of the entrance to the netherworld" who was worshiped in ancient Moab around the time of the Exodus. But, as we noted, that's a title, not a name. Can we ID this mysterious entity?

Further north, texts from Ugarit specifically identify the land of Bashan as the home of a Canaanite deity called Rapi'u, the "King of Eternity," who reigned, like King Og, at the cities of Ashtaroth and Edrei.[125] This means that at the time of the conquest, Amorites in Canaan believed that the god Rapi'u, which is the singular form of Rephaim, ruled the underworld from exactly the same two cities at the center of Og's kingdom.

Does it make a little more sense now that Og, last of the remnant of the Rephaim, was the first enemy specifically targeted by the Israelites (at God's direction) during the campaign to take the Holy Land?

There's more. One of Rapi'u's home cities, Ashtaroth, links the King of Eternity with another dark god who's mentioned in the Old Testament.

Mother Šapšu, take a message
To Milku in ʿAṭṭartu [Ashtaroth]:
"My incantation for serpent bite,
For the scaly serpent's poison."[126]

Mother Šapšu was the sun-goddess in Ugarit. In this ritual, she was asked to carry a message to a god ruling in Ashtaroth, Milku, which is another form of the name Molech.

This isn't surprising. At the time of the judges in Israel, Bashan, basically the modern Golan Heights, was on the border of the relatively new nation of Ammon. The national god of the Ammonites was Milcom, who was likewise one and the same with Molech.[127]

Here's where things get interesting. Molech was an ancient deity, worshiped at least a thousand years before the Exodus. A god called Malik, an early form of the name, is known from texts found at Ebla dated to around 2400 BC. Of the approximately five hundred deities identified at Ebla, one of most common theophoric elements in personal names—like *el* in Daniel ("God is my judge") or *yahu* in Hezekiah ("YHWH strengthens")—was *ma-lik*.[128]

By the time of Abraham, Isaac, and Jacob, Malik was still worshiped in the Amorite kingdom of Mari, centered on the Euphrates River near the modern border between Syria and Iraq. Further, it appears that the god was served by a group of underworld deities called *maliku*. And five hundred years after the time of the Mari texts, during the time of the judges in Israel, Malik and the *maliku* (called *malikim*) were still venerated at Ugarit.[129]

Here's the interesting bit: Molech was equated with the Babylonian plague-god and gatekeeper of the underworld, Nergal. Not only are both connected to death and the afterlife, Akkadian deity lists record the equation Malik = Nergal. Further, Semitic *mlk* and Sumerian *"ner-gal"* can both be understood as "king," confirming the connection.[130]

Now, this gets a little weird, but hang on. We'll pull all these connections together by the end of the chapter.

While it might seem strange to you and me, chairs played an important role during funerary rituals in the culture of the ancient Amorites. At each funeral, it seems, a chair was designated for use by the *etemmu*, the spirit, of the newly deceased.

The chair is integral to the funerary rites and later, part of the *kispum*, as a concrete form for souls to inhabit. The chair…

was a locus for the soul, and a vehicle for its appropriate transition to the netherworld.... It is not known if a full size chair that belonged to the dead in life was used in the ritual (texts show people owned a bed and chair), or if it could have been a model.[131]

A number of chair models made from clay have been found at the site of ancient Ur. In Sumer, as in modern Iraq, trees are scarce, and so wood for making chairs was a luxury many common folk wouldn't have been able to afford. It seems that the spirits of the dead were not only transferred to the netherworld via the ritual chair, they'd also return to it when their names were called during the *kispum* rite.[132] In some cases, model chariots appear to have served, rather than chairs.[133] File a mental bookmark on that detail because we'll reference it later.

The terra-cotta chairs from Ur, about three and a half to four inches tall (they would have been taller, but the legs had broken off), are finely decorated with various symbols, including the crescent moon representing the moon-god Sîn. The chariot models with crescents also depict a *kusarikku*, a bull-man, which, like the chariot itself, represented Nergal. Since the model chariots were to carry the dearly departed to their eternal rest, it makes sense that they were decorated with symbols of the gatekeeper of the underworld.

At Ugarit, Nergal was equated with the West Semitic deity, Resheph.[134] Like Nergal, Resheph was a warrior and a plague-god who spread disease with his arrows, and he likewise served as gatekeeper to the underworld.[135] (We'll explore the link between Resheph and royal mortuary gardens in an upcoming chapter.) It may surprise you to learn that this entity had a bigger part in the stories of the Old Testament than you've been taught.

Resheph has a long history. He was one of the most prominent gods in ancient Ebla, where one of the four city gates was named for him. Records from Ebla note that one of the cities sacred to Resheph was

Shechem in Canaan, modern Nablus in Israel.[136] That city was the site of key scenes during the age of the patriarchs.

First, it was where God appeared to Abram (before the name change) near the oak of Moreh to confirm His promise that the descendants of Abram would one day inherit the land.[137] Shechem is where Jacob's daughter Dinah was raped by the son of the prince of the city, which enraged Simeon and Levi, who murdered the men in the city and plundered its wealth.[138] Interestingly, at the end of his life, Jacob—who wasn't too happy with his boys for making him "stink to the inhabitants of the land,"[139] blessed Joseph and said, "I have given to you rather than to your brothers one mountain slope that I took from the hand of the Amorites with my sword and my bow."[140]

The Hebrew word translated "mountain slope" is *shĕkem*, which sounds a lot like Shechem. And indeed, when the Israelites returned to the land centuries later, the land around Shechem was allotted to the tribe of Ephraim, and it's where the tomb of Joseph is located to this day.

But it's a lot more interesting than that.

As it happens, the cult of Resheph was brought to Egypt by Amorites who emigrated and settled there during the second millennium BC. He became a popular deity among the native Egyptians, especially as a god of horses and chariots.[141] In the fifteenth century BC, the powerful pharaoh Amenophis II, also known as Amenhotep II, thought so much of the warlike plague-god that he adopted Resheph as his personal protector in battle.[142]

Get this: Scholar Douglas Petrovich has made a convincing case that Amenhotep II was Pharaoh of the Exodus.[143] You know, the guy played by Yul Brynner in the movie. The irony is delicious: The Pharaoh who worshiped the warrior plague-god Resheph, protector of horses and chariots, was compelled to let God's people go by a series of devastating plagues—including one that took the life of Pharaoh's son—and the destruction of his chariot warriors!

The prophet Habakkuk described the humiliating aftermath for the plague-god:

> God came from Teman,
> and the Holy One from Mount Paran. *Selah*
> His splendor covered the heavens,
> and the earth was full of his praise.
> His brightness was like the light;
> rays flashed from his hand;
> and there he veiled his power.
> Before him went pestilence,
> and plague followed at his heels. (Habakkuk 3:3–5)

Mount Paran is another name for Mount Sinai, and Teman was in Edom (which argues against the Mount Sinai in Arabia theory, but we digress). These verses recall the last stage of the Exodus—God leading His people from Sinai toward the Promised Land and the ultimate conquest of Canaan.

Verse 5 is key: "Pestilence" is the Hebrew *Deber*, a Semitic deity that had been worshiped for more than a thousand years by the time of the Exodus (he was the patron god of ancient Ebla), and "plague" is *Resheph*—and Habakkuk describes him following at the heels of Yahweh like a whipped puppy.

Now, to add insult to injury: Where did God tell Moses to proclaim the blessings and curses the Israelites would receive depending on how closely they followed His Law?

At Shechem. The city sacred to Resheph, god of plagues and gate-keeper of the underworld. Mount Ebal, where Joshua built his altar, rises above Shechem to the north. And this declaration of God's sovereignty was made immediately after the Israelites crossed the Jordan and destroyed the Amorite cities of Jericho and Ai.

But there's more.

Not only was Resheph equated with Nergal; he was identified as the divine archer and plague-god of the Greeks, Apollo.[144] The connection between this entity and chariots is captured in the myths of the Greeks, who believed the god hitched a team of horses to the chariot of the sun-god, Helios, for his daily journey across the sky. Interestingly, divine chariots called *merkavah* were a key aspect of a mystical form of Judaism that flourished between about 100 BC and AD 1000. And you'll remember that Apollo was the name chosen for the NASA "chariots" that carried American astronauts to the heavens and on to the moon.

The role of Apollo/Resheph/Nergal as the gatekeeper of the underworld is reflected in the Bible's prophecies of the last days. In Revelation 9, terrifying things emerge to torment those still on the earth when "a star fallen from heaven to earth" is given the key to the abyss.

In appearance the locusts were like horses prepared for battle: on their heads were what looked like crowns of gold; their faces were like human faces, their hair like women's hair, and their teeth like lions' teeth; they had breastplates like breastplates of iron, and the noise of their wings was like the noise of many chariots with horses rushing into battle. They have tails and stings like scorpions, and their power to hurt people for five months is in their tails. They have as king over them the angel of the bottomless pit. His name in Hebrew is Abaddon, and in Greek he is called Apollyon. (Revelation 9:7–11).

The name "Apollyon" is Greek for "destroyer." And yes, it's an allusion to Apollo, the god of plague and destruction. Thus, "Ἀπολλύων can be seen as a demon who brings destruction and whose realm is the underworld."[145] While that's almost the absolute opposite of how Apollo was characterized by the Greeks and Romans, who saw him as the "perfect blend of physical superiority and moral virtue,"[146] it's an accurate description of the way he was viewed by the prophets and apostles—and we suggest that they had a better handle on theology than you, me, our high school mythology teachers, and the classical philosophers of Greece and Rome.

It isn't clear from Revelation whether Apollyon/Apollo is the fallen angel with the key to the abyss or just the king of the locust-things that swarm out of it. Either way, the ancient gatekeeper to the underworld was obviously important in the history of Israel, especially around the time of the Exodus, and he's still part of the Infernal Council's rebellion against the Creator.

8

Garden of the King

The modern word "garden" has a much different connotation today than it did three thousand years ago. To you and me, it evokes images of flowers or vegetables, carefully tended to yield blossoms or produce, according to their kind. Back in the day, however, gardens were often reserved for royalty, and not only because kings and queens naturally get the best stuff.

For example, we read in the Bible that the son and grandson of Judah's king Hezekiah, Manasseh and Amon, were buried in a garden. That seems a little odd, although modern cemeteries here in the US often incorporate "garden" into the name. But in Judah, tombs were usually cut into rock. Tombs of the kings of Judah were usually located in the City of David, the narrow hill that extends south from the Temple Mount. But Manasseh and Amon were buried "in the garden of Uzza,"[147] which was apparently connected to the palace. Uzza may be King Uzziah (also called Azariah), the great-grandfather of Hezekiah, who ruled Judah from about 791 to 740 BC. What was special about his garden? And why wasn't it used for royal burials until Manasseh died about a hundred years after the death of Uzziah?

To find the answer, we have to look at Near Eastern culture long before the time of Hezekiah and Manasseh. It's also important to remember that Manasseh was not one for keeping to the teachings of Moses and the prophets. God Himself said through His prophets that Manasseh "has done things more evil than all that the Amorites did, who were before him,"[148] namely, setting up altars to "all the host of heaven" in the courts of the Temple, burning his son as an offering, presumably to Molech, and consulting with mediums and necromancers.[149]

It's that last bit that concerns us here, because that's the clue that will help us unravel the mystery of the garden of the king.

As we noted elsewhere in this book, the practice of *kispum*, the ritual meal offered to, and in honor of, the ancestral dead probably originated with the Amorites. While there is some disagreement among scholars, it's generally agreed that these Semitic-speaking people moved from northern Mesopotamia to the southeast, the regions of Akkad and Sumer, in the second half of the third millennium BC,[150] bringing this practice with them.

Texts from Ebla, probably the most powerful kingdom of the third millennium BC in northwestern Mesopotamia, reveal a pattern of religious rituals that connect the royal family and its deceased ancestors to the gods. The marriage of a royal couple in Ebla required the pair, accompanied by priests, scribes, and other officials, to set out on a ritual journey from the palace to the temples of various gods outside the city, and then to a special location to make offerings to the divinized kings of old. From there, the entourage traveled to the mausoleum of dead ancestors, which they reached on the seventh day. This apparently linked the royal family, embodied in the palace and the underground tombs beneath it, to the gods.[151] In other words, the time-consuming ritual connected palace and grave, a reminder to all that the living king was entwined with his royal ancestors at a cosmic level.[152]

This interpretation is confirmed by tomb artifacts from Ebla and other ancient cities from what is now northern Syria, such as Qatna and

Halab (Aleppo), seat of Yamkhad, the most powerful Amorite kingdom
in Mesopotamia until the rise of Babylon in the eighteenth century BC,
the time of Abraham. For example, a bone talisman found in the "Tomb
of the Lord of the Goats," probably the final resting place of Ebla's king
Immeya, a contemporary of Isaac and Jacob (reigned c. 1750–1725
BC), illustrates two scenes. The first shows the king at a meal, probably the *kispum* ritual for the newly deceased monarch, symbolizing his
acceptance into the company of the divinized dead.[153]

The talisman's reverse side depicts Immeya as a human-headed bull
venerated by other characters. Although this sounds weird to us in the
twenty-first century, it's consistent with texts from the Amorite kingdom of Mari, which was based on the Euphrates River near the modern
border between Iraq and Syria, that described the dead king's transformation into an *Aladlammu*, "a celestial guardian of the kingdom compa-
rable with the *rapi'uma* of the later Ugaritic tradition."[154]

Likewise, a cylinder seal from Yamkhad from about the same time
period shows three scenes in horizontal rows related to the cult of the
ancestors. The top row depicts the chief deities of the kingdom, featuring the chief god of Aleppo, Hadad (Baal) the storm-god, his consort,
and the plague-god and gatekeeper of the underworld, Resheph. The
bottom row shows the new king of the land enthroned, attended by
court officials. The middle register represents the *rapi'uma* (Rephaim)
summoned to the funeral ceremony, presumably to welcome the newly
deceased king.[155]

The bottom line is that evidence from older Amorite kingdoms in
northwestern Mesopotamia like Ebla, Mari, Yamkhad, and Qatna confirms "an astonishing continuity in the basic religious institution and
cult practice represented by the cult for the deified royal ancestors, the
Rapi'uma/Repha'im of the Ugaritic texts."[156]

In other words, Moses and the Israelites didn't invent the Rephaim
to justify the conquest of Canaan. While ritual texts explicitly describe
the veneration of the Rephaim (and the Ditanu/Titans) in the Amorite

kingdom of Ugarit around 1200 BC, the middle of the period of the judges in Israel, older grave goods, inscriptions, and palace art confirm that these religious practices, including the belief that the kings of the land would take their place among the Rephaim after death, extended back among the Amorites at least a thousand years earlier. Since this complex system of beliefs and rituals probably didn't spring into the imaginations of Ebla's priests minutes before they inscribed the ritual tablets, it's possible that the veneration of dead ancestors, kings, and Rephaim is much older, maybe extending back before 3000 BC.

Remember, the Rephaim were the spirits of the demigod Nephilim destroyed in the Flood. Amorite kings from Babylon to Ugarit claimed descent from those "mighty men who were of old," summoned them through rituals, offered sacrifices to them,[157] and apparently believed that these "warriors of Baal" were revivified—resurrected—by their creator-god El at his tabernacle (or threshing floor), which was on Mount Hermon.

Now, why is all of this relevant to Christians? Keep following this thread: Among the ritual texts from Ugarit is one (KTU 1.106) that specifies sacrifices to various divinities, including deified dead kings and Resheph, a deity connected to the dead as gatekeeper to the underworld.[158] Some of the sacrifices in this text were to be performed in the garden, which is *gn* in both Ugaritic and Hebrew. This festival took place in the month of *gn* ("Gannu"), March/April in our calendar, a time when gardens are coming into bloom.

Further, Resheph is designated *ršp gn* in two other Ugaritic texts, perhaps meaning "Resheph of the Garden."[159] This is a cognate (same meaning, different language) with the Eblaite phrase *rasap gunu(m)^{ki}*.[160] So, what's going on with sacrifices in gardens to a god of the underworld? It comes down to the purpose of the garden. In the Amorite world of the ancient Near East, gardens were not simply for growing pretty flowers; it was where the cult of the royal ancestors performed the rites to summon and feed the divinized kings of old. Understanding this concept helps us make sense of a number of confusing passages in the Old Testament.

I spread out my hands all the day
to a rebellious people,
who walk in a way that is not good,
following their own devices;
a people who provoke me
to my face continually,
sacrificing in gardens
and making offerings on bricks;
who sit in tombs,
and spend the night in secret places;
who eat pig's flesh,
and broth of tainted meat is in their vessels;
who say, "Keep to yourself,
do not come near me, for I am too holy for you."
(Isaiah 65:2–5)

Those who sanctify and purify themselves to go into the gardens, following one in the midst, eating pig's flesh and the abomination and mice, shall come to an end together, declares the LORD. (Isaiah 66:17)

What's wrong with gardens? Nothing, in the way we understand them today. But ancient Israel and Judah were surrounded by pagans who cultivated gardens specifically to worship the Rephaim, who were believed to be the ancestors of their kings.

It's clear from Isaiah that there was a cultic connection between gardens and tombs. Scholars have also noted that the pig was an animal associated with the underworld,[161] used by the Greeks in chthonian rituals[162] and by the Amorites (and other pagan cultures) in their sacrifices to the dead. In fact, some scholars believe that the use of pigs primarily as sacrificial offerings to the gods of the underworld and the dead[163] may be the reason for the taboo against eating pork.[164]

This cultic use of gardens may be the reason that chroniclers of the Old Testament note that two of worst kings of the line of David were buried in a garden rather than the tombs of their forefathers. Manasseh, son of Hezekiah, "was buried in the garden of his house, in the garden of Uzza."[165] Manasseh's son Amon was likewise buried in the garden of Uzza.[166]

All the previous kings of Judah, from David to Hezekiah, had been buried in the royal tombs in the City of David. Why did Manasseh break with tradition? It's consistent with his other changes. Unlike his father, who "did what was right in the eyes of the LORD,"[167] Manasseh is remembered as the most wicked king in Judah's history.[168]

He did what was evil in the sight of the LORD, according to the despicable practices of the nations whom the LORD drove out before the people of Israel. For he rebuilt the high places that Hezekiah his father had destroyed, and he erected altars for Baal and made an Asherah, as Ahab king of Israel had done, and worshiped all the host of heaven and served them. And he built altars in the house of the LORD, of which the LORD had said, "In Jerusalem will I put my name." And he built altars for all the host of heaven in the two courts of the house of the LORD. And he burned his son as an offering and used fortune-telling and omens and dealt with mediums and with necromancers. He did much evil in the sight of the LORD, provoking him to anger. (2 Kings 21:2–6)

In short, Manasseh went native and adopted the religion of the Amorites, which included, significantly, summoning the dead through mediums and necromancers. This is the first biblical record of a Judean king engaging in this occult practice, the visit by Saul to the medium of En-dor notwithstanding. This was so offensive to God that the author of 2 Kings wrote that Manasseh did things "more evil than all that the

Amorites did,"[169] which was bad enough to end God's patience with the House of David.

Manesseh's decision to be buried in the garden of Uzza (probably Uzziah, also known as Azariah, the great-grandfather of Hezekiah) appears to be part of his slide into full-blown paganism. Manasseh, and his son after him, apparently aspired to become Rephaim after death. This is supported by the message God delivered to Ezekiel during his vision of the Temple Mount:

> While the man was standing beside me, I heard one speaking to me out of the temple, and he said to me, "Son of man, this is the place of my throne and the place of the soles of my feet, where I will dwell in the midst of the people of Israel forever. And **the house of Israel shall no more defile my holy name**, neither they, nor their kings, by their whoring and **by the dead bodies of their kings at their high places,** by setting their threshold by my threshold and their doorposts beside my doorposts, with only a wall between me and them. They have defiled my holy name by their abominations that they have committed, so I have consumed them in my anger. **Now let them put away their whoring and the dead bodies of their kings far from me**, and I will dwell in their midst forever. (Ezekiel 43:6–9, emphasis added)

We don't know where the King's Garden was located, but it was apparently in close proximity to the Temple, probably in or adjacent to the City of David.

The pagan neighbors of ancient Israel had a long history of venerating dead royalty in special gardens set aside for that cult. What made this long-running practice so disgusting to God was that it corrupted the concept of His *original* garden, Eden. And with Manasseh and Amon, it had reached His holy mountain.

Not all scholars agree that the Ugaritic *gn* and Eblaite/Akkadian *gunu* should be translated "garden." However, the origin of the term is even more intriguing. Rather than "garden," respected scholar Edward Lipiński concluded that the term more accurately meant "camp," "enclosure," or "compound."[170] This is similar to a word from old Persian: "*Pairidēza*, borrowed into late Babylonian as *pardēsu*, into Hebrew as *pardēs*, and Greek as παράδεισος, appears to have meant originally 'rampart,' and hence a ramparted place, such as an enclosed royal garden." And, as you've undoubtedly noticed, it's where we get the English word "paradise."

This is not a coincidence. If Eden doesn't fit the definition of "paradise," an enclosed royal garden, we would truly like to see the place that does.

Pastor Carl Gallups makes a strong case in his book *Gods of Ground Zero* that Eden was understood to be paradise by Jews of the Second Temple period.[171] This is biblical. In Ezekiel 28, God condemns the king of Tyre by comparing him to the rebel in Eden, who was "an anointed guardian cherub" on "the holy mountain of God."[172] This places the garden on God's holy mountain, Zion. This means that Mount Moriah, where Abraham was tested, and the threshing floor of Araunah, which David bought for the site of the Temple, are located right where Eden was, and will be again.

We realize that placing Eden in the middle of Jerusalem might seem a little *too* obvious, but bear with us.

The Book of Genesis describes the garden's location:

A river flowed out of Eden to water the garden, and there it divided and became four rivers. The name of the first is the Pishon. It is the one that flowed around the whole land of Havilah, where there is gold. And the gold of that land is good; bdellium and onyx stone are there. The name of the second river is the Gihon. It is the one that flowed around the whole land of

Cush. And the name of the third river is the Tigris, which flows east of Assyria. And the fourth river is the Euphrates. (Genesis 2:10–14)

It's easy enough to identify the Tigris and Euphrates, the rivers that flow down from Turkey through Iraq and Syria, defining the Fertile Crescent. Likewise, the Gihon is simple enough, if we understand that the reference to Cush to be allegorical; as Jerusalem's only water supply, the Gihon Spring was vital to the holy city, and so probably the river meant by Moses in that passage.

That leaves only the Pishon. One intriguing explanation identifies it as the Nile, "from the Egyptian expression *p3 šny*, 'the encompassing one,' the river being conceptualised as an extension of the cosmic ocean surrounding the world."[173] This is plausible; after all, Moses was raised in the court of the king, presumably speaking and writing Egyptian.

If this is correct, the account in Genesis is a sort of cosmic model. A river flowed out of Eden to become the three major sources of fresh water in the world known to the Israelites (not to mention the cosmic ocean) and the crucial spring that supplied water to the city God had chosen as His own.

No doubt the river in the garden was the same one Ezekiel described in his vision of the future Temple. This, of course, locates the river of Eden beneath the Temple, the very throne of God, which will be on the site of Solomon's temple—Mount Moriah, the Temple Mount in Jerusalem.

At the risk of putting too fine a point on it: Eden, the original garden, is in Jerusalem.

By now, you've connected some dots in your mind that are making the story of Jesus' betrayal, death, and resurrection positively spine-tingling. He was betrayed in Gethsemane, a garden at the foot of the Mount of Olives. Not only that, "in the place where he was crucified there was a garden, and in the garden a new tomb in which no one had yet been laid. So because of the Jewish day of Preparation, since the tomb was close at hand, they laid Jesus there."[174]

Did you get that? Jesus was betrayed and crucified in a garden. The Infernal Council undoubtedly thought this was a great joke. In their minds, they'd desecrated Eden by killing the Son of the King! But then, at dawn of the third day, when the women went to the tomb, Mary Magdalene saw the resurrected Jesus—and *thought he was the gardener*.

Guess what? He is!

The Garden of Eden, *gan-bə ʿēḏen*, was a walled enclosure on the mountain of God[175] reserved for royalty—although in this case, we're talking about the King of Creation and His Divine Council. The Fallen lured the pagans of the ancient Near East into perverting the concept of the royal garden, turning them into cult places for sacrifice and worship where dead human kings were venerated alongside the Rephaim, the demonic spirits of the Nephilim destroyed in the Flood.

This will not end well for them. The Gardener will return, at the Mount of Olives, to *reclaim* His garden. You see, He is the landowner of the parable of the wicked tenants who planted a vineyard, fenced it, built a tower, and leased it out.[176] Although the parable applied to the chief priests and Pharisees of Jesus' day, it was also directed at the principalities and powers behind them. They have denied the landowner, God, the fruit of His garden, going even so far as to kill His son.

Even the chief priests and Pharisees realized the ultimate end of these rebels: "He will put those wretches to a miserable death and let out the vineyard to other tenants who will give him the fruits in their seasons."[177]

If you have accepted Jesus as your Lord and Savior, then we are among the tenants who will one day take over the care and cultivation of the garden of the King.

9

The Geography of Sheol

One of the burning questions in the minds of humans since the beginning of the time has been, "Where do I go when I die?" The pagans and Jews of the ancient Near East had definite ideas on the subject, although they're scattered through the Bible and across a multitude of texts recovered by archaeologists over the last two hundred years. By piecing together the evidence, we can assemble a rough idea of what they believed about the layout of the netherworld.

In ancient Mesopotamia, the underworld was a dismal place—damp, gloomy, and generally unpleasant. As we noted earlier, the quality of one's afterlife depended on the faithfulness of his or her descendants and how well they performed the monthly *kispum* rite. Abraham's distress at not having an heir was that he and Sarah would have to depend on a servant, Eliezer, to be the "son of the cup," the "pourer of water," to ensure their well-being in the netherworld. This tradition was so deeply ingrained in the cultures of the ancient world, from Babylon to Rome, that early Roman Christians built churches in cemeteries, including St. Peter's Basilica, and installed libation tubes in sarcophagi.

But what about the physical layout of the underworld? Were there actual gates? How about the landscape—were there hills, cliffs, pits, and other physical features described in pagan myth?

While the Bible tells us more about the netherworld than we've probably been taught, it leaves a lot to the imagination. In the Old Testament, the term for the land of the dead is Sheol. There is no consensus on the origin of the Hebrew word.[178] Unlike Greek myths of Hades, Sheol was not personified by the ancient Hebrews, although there are metaphorical references, such as the proverb that describes Sheol as "never satisfied"[179] and Isaiah's warning that "Sheol has enlarged its appetite and opened its mouth without measure,"[180] which is strikingly similar to the voracious hunger of the Canaanite death-god, Mot.

One of the most famous pagan myths of the patriarchal era, *The Descent of Inanna*, tells the story of the aftermath of one of the episodes of the *Epic of Gilgamesh*. In that story, the heroic king of Uruk spurned the sexual advances of the Queen of Heaven, rudely (but truthfully) pointing out that the men in Inanna's life usually came to an unhappy end. (Remember the story of Inanna's husband, Dumuzi, who was dragged down to the netherworld so she could escape the Great Below. Inanna, better known to us as Ishtar (Astarte in the Bible), didn't handle rejection well. The old saying, "Hell hath no fury like a woman scorned," applies double when the woman has godlike power. Imagine a spoiled, supernatural fourteen-year-old, and you have an idea of the character of Inanna: Raging hormones, violent temper, and virtually no restrictions on her abilities.

In a rage, Inanna flew up to heaven and demanded that the sky-god, Anu, release the Bull of Heaven to destroy Gilgamesh and his city. The king and his friend Enkidu finally managed to kill the bull, but not before it killed hundreds of innocent civilians. Enkidu then added insult to the goddess' injury by tearing off the bull's right thigh and throwing it in Inanna's face. (Interestingly, the right thigh of sacrificed bulls was given to the Temple priests, according to the Law of Moses.)[181]

Here's the thing: The Bull of Heaven was Gugalanna, consort of the Queen of the Great Below, Ereshkigal.[182] This adds dramatic tension to the plot of *The Descent of Inanna*: The Queen of Heaven claimed that she'd arrived at the gates of the underworld for the funeral rites of Eresh-kigal's husband—whose death was Inanna's fault. No wonder Ereshkigal "slapped her thigh and bit her lip."[183] What gall!

The relevant point of this chapter is that the realm of the dead was depicted as a place below the earth behind seven gates that could not be passed without the permission of the sovereign of the underworld. This is similar to the Egyptian concept of the passage to the land of the dead. Similar to *The Descent of Inanna*, two of the spells in the Egyptian *Book of the Dead* describe a series of seven doorways in "the house of Osiris in the west," guarded by triads of demonic creatures—a "doorkeeper," a "herald," and a "watcher."[184] These entities were often referred to by the Egyptian word *nṯr*, which, as we noted in an earlier chapter, is probably the term borrowed by Isaiah for his description of the rebel in Eden—the word meaning "dead god," but awkwardly translated "branch" in Isaiah 14:19 on the assumption that the prophet used the Hebrew word *netser*.[185]

You obviously noticed that the Egyptians, like the Hebrews, were familiar with the concept of Watchers, although their role in Egyptian religion as door-guardians of the underworld was much more specific than that of their counterparts in Jewish and Mesopotamian cosmology (where they were called *apkallu*).[186]

Like the Mesopotamian myths and the Egyptian *Book of the Dead*, the Bible describes Sheol as a place below the earth[187] where the dead are prevented from returning by some type of physical barrier.

As the cloud fades and vanishes,
so he who goes down to Sheol does not come up. (Job 7:9)

Will it go down to the bars of Sheol?
Shall we descend together into the dust? (Job 17:16)

97

I said, In the middle of my days
I must depart;
I am consigned to the gates of Sheol
for the rest of my years. (Isaiah 38:10)

So, during the era of the patriarchs and prophets, Hebrews saw Sheol as a place occupied by the dead where "bars" and "gates" kept them from returning to the living (in physical form, anyway). However, even then there was hope that the righteous would someday be raised from that dreary plane of existence.

The Lord kills and brings to life;
he brings down to Sheol and raises up. (1 Samuel 2:6)

For I know that my Redeemer lives,
and at the last he will stand upon the earth.
And after my skin has been thus destroyed,
yet in my flesh I shall see God,
whom I shall see for myself,
and my eyes shall behold, and not another.
My heart faints within me! (Job 19:25–27)

There was a category of malevolent dead known to occupy the netherworld, a group we've already met, who are mentioned in Isaiah 14:

Sheol beneath is stirred up
to meet you when you come;
it rouses the shades [*Rephaim*] to greet you,
all who were leaders of the earth;
it raises from their thrones
all who were kings of the nations. (Isaiah 14:9)

While Isaiah mocked the Rephaim spirits as "weak," sleeping on beds of maggots with worms for covers, it's clear from the text that these were once men of power. This is consistent with their depiction in the texts from Ugarit, where these "warriors of Baal" were summoned through necromancy rituals to the tabernacle of El (i.e., Mount Hermon).[188]

The prophet Ezekiel, writing about 125 years or so after Isaiah, suggested that there is a hierarchy in the underworld and that the spirits of the "mighty men who were of old" occupy a place of primacy.

Ezekiel 32 is one of the more fascinating chapters in the Bible. It gives us the only glimpse into the physical layout of Sheol and the placement of the spirits in it.

> They shall fall amid those who are slain by the sword. Egypt is delivered to the sword; drag her away, and all her multitudes. The mighty chiefs shall speak of them, with their helpers, out of the midst of Sheol: "They have come down, they lie still, the uncircumcised, slain by the sword." (Ezekiel 32:20–21)

The Hebrew phrase rendered "mighty chiefs," *elei gibborim*, could also be translated "chiefs" or "rulers of the Gibborim."[189] Their placement in the "midst of Sheol" suggests that they are fundamentally and substantially different from the run-of-the-mill dead, a callback to the long tradition among the Jews of the *gibborim* ("mighty men") of old— the Nephilim.

The context of Ezekiel 32 is a lament over Pharaoh and his people, whose lands would be ravaged by the Chaldean army of Nebuchadnezzar, king of Babylon. The Egyptians are described as going "down to the pit"[190] to lie among the dead from Assyria, "whose graves are set in the uttermost parts of the pit."[191] The location around the outer edges of Sheol suggests the Assyrians held a place of lower status, not surprising given that their army destroyed the northern kingdom of Israel. Likewise, Elam, Meshech-Tubal, Edom, the Sidonians, and "the princes of the north" will greet Pharaoh on his arrival in the netherworld.[192]

While Ezekiel's choices of the "uncircumcised" nations in Sheol are worth study, considering that Meshech, Tubal, and the princes of the north figure prominently in the prophecy of Gog of Magog just a few chapters later, it's out of bounds here. What's important is that several of these nations—Assyria, Elam, Meshech-Tubal, and the princes of the north—are described as having "spread terror in the land of the living."[193] The sense of the word translated "terror," *chittiyth*, isn't quite captured by the English. *Chittiyth* implies a supernatural fear, panic, like one would feel when suddenly confronted by, well, a ghost.[194]

Or in this case, the ghosts of giants.

> And they do not lie with the mighty, the fallen from among the uncircumcised, who went down to Sheol with their weapons of war, whose swords were laid under their heads, and whose iniquities are upon their bones; for the terror of the mighty men was in the land of the living. (Ezekiel 32:27)

Again, the English translation hides the meaning that was plain to the readers of Ezekiel's book 2,500 years ago. Let's consider an alternate translation:

> But they do not lie down with the fallen Gibborim of ancient times, who went down to Sheol, with their weapons of war, their swords placed under their heads, and their iniquities upon their bones, for the terror of the Gibborim was in the land of the living.[195]

Ezekiel was clearly saying the power of the nations he named was to cause terror *"in the land of the living"*—in other words, while they were alive. The prophet portrays the spirits of the dead as powerless to affect the living. Once they're in Sheol, they don't come back through the gates. This is contrary to the Amorite view of the Rephaim, the spirits of the *gibborim* of old, and, later, the Greek concept of the *heros*, demigods who were by definition, as the sons of gods and humans, Nephilim. Ezekiel essentially echoed Isaiah's description of the Rephaim as weak and powerless, thus condemning the cult of the royal dead that persisted from before the time of Abraham down to the prophet's day.

But the connection between the "mighty men" in the pit and the giants who walked the earth before the Flood is even more obvious than that. The bias of translators through the ages has obscured the prophet's intent. The phrase *gibbôrîm nōpĕlîm mēʿôlām*, literally "mighty fallen ones of old," which clearly alludes to the giants of Genesis 6:1-4, may be an explicit reference. Some scholars believe *nōpĕlîm* contains a mispointed vowel and should be read *nĕpîlîm*,[196] which would transform the verse into:

> But they do not lie down with the [mighty Nephilim] of ancient times, who went down to Sheol, with their weapons of war, their swords placed under their heads, and their iniquities upon their bones, for the terror of the [mighty ones] was in the land of the living.

The alternate translation doesn't change the meaning of the verse or the chapter, it just makes the meaning plainer: There are entities in the underworld who were separate and distinct from the human warriors who caused terror in the land of the living. These *gibborim*, spirits of the Nephilim of ancient times, held a central place in Sheol. Yet, echoing Isaiah, Ezekiel made it clear that these spirits no longer had the power to instill the kind of panicky terror they did when alive.

Neither did they have the power ascribed to them by the pagan Amorites or the later Greeks, who venerated such *heros* as Bellerophon, Perseus, and Herakles—who, you may be surprised to learn, was worshiped as Melqart, the chief god of Jezebel's home city, Tyre. (Which means the prophets of Baal slaughtered on Mount Carmel were actually prophets of Hercules!)

Not coincidentally, scholar Nicolas Wyatt points out that Bellerophon, called "the greatest hero and slayer of monsters, alongside Cadmus and Perseus, before the days of Heracles,"[197] is "a transparent transcription of West Semitic *Baʿal Rapiʾu*"[198] ("Lord of the Rephaim"). Bellerophon was the son of a mortal woman by the sea-god Poseidon. Like Satan, Bellerophon was punished for his arrogance, aspiring to claim a place on the holy mountain of the gods. Instead, he was cast down to earth to live out his days in misery on the Plain of Aleion ("Wandering"),[199] a name that's essentially the same as the Land of Nod ("Wandering"), where Cain dwelt after murdering his brother—perhaps not a coincidence. But we digress.

As demonic spirits, the *gibborim* of old still interacted with the living. As we've shown, the worship of these spirits continued for millennia. But they've been on a short leash. Demons only enter where an entry has been prepared, either through trauma or by invitation. Otherwise, they remain in "the midst of Sheol," kings among the dead.

A day is coming, however, when the gatekeeper will fling open the gates, and hell will literally break loose upon the earth.

Part Four

COMMUNING WITH THE DEAD

10

Stones of the Field and Threshing Floors

Behold, I make of you a threshing sledge,
new, sharp, and having teeth;
you shall thresh the mountains and crush them,
and you shall make the hills like chaff;
you shall winnow them, and the wind shall carry them away,
and the tempest shall scatter them.
And you shall rejoice in the LORD;
in the Holy One of Israel you shall glory.
                    —ISAIAH 41:15–16

An act called *necromancy*, speaking to the dead, was a common practice of pagans during both Old and New Testament eras. The word is based on the Greek *nekromanteía*, a compound of *nekros* ("corpse") and *manteía* ("divination"). In essence, it describes an attempt to speak to the dead and receive messages in return. Necromancy provided priests and kings the ability to ask favors or advice from gods, converse with long-dead sovereigns, powerful demons, and even woefully dependent ancestors, who relied upon food and drink offerings in order to maintain existence in the afterlife. Remember, the ancestors would respond quite harshly if living relatives failed in this task.

Necromancy required a sufficient and reliable gateway. Sometimes, these appeared at unexpected places. The story of Jacob's ladder is a case in point. Somewhere between Beersheba and Haran, Jacob happened upon a portal during his escape from the wrath of his brother Esau, discovering the gateway as he rested his head upon a rock in the wilderness. He described a two-way stairway used by angels, i.e., Jacob's ladder. Other similar portals might be created or discovered in nature. Reflective surfaces such as lakes, pools of water, rivers, and polished metals (obsidian being preferred when available, according to magicians like John Dee) also served as access points to summon the dead. Threshing floors, a created, yet practical, space where people gathered to winnow wheat and other grains, also provided a surprising window into other realms.

We'll take each portal in turn, explaining how it was used and examining the evidence for its place in society. Let's begin with Jacob's tantalizing discovery of a portal in the wilderness.

Rocks, Heaps, and Henges

Stones have been worshiped as progenitors and houses of gods and the dead for millennia. Mithras emerged from a stone that fell to earth. Dushara (worshiped by the Nabateans at Petra) lives in a rectangular stone called a *Betyl*, a word closely related to *Bethel* ("house of God"). Taken in cultural context, then, Jacob's experience of dreaming upon a stone and discerning a heavenly portal is relatable to this paradigm. Stones contain portals, if not the gods themselves.

Genesis 28:10–17 relates this dramatic story:

Jacob left Beersheba and went toward Haran. And he came to a certain place and stayed there that night, because the sun had set. Taking one of the stones of the place, he put it under his head and lay down in that place to sleep. And he dreamed, and behold, there was a ladder set up on the earth, and the top of it reached to heaven. And behold, the angels of God were ascending and descending on it! **And behold, the LORD stood above it** and said, "I am the LORD, the God of Abraham your father and the God of Isaac. The land on which you lie I will give to you and to your offspring. Your offspring shall be like the dust of the earth, and you shall spread abroad to the west and to the east and to the north and to the south, and in you and your offspring shall all the families of the earth be blessed. Behold, I am with you and will keep you wherever you go, and will bring you back to this land. For I will not leave you until I have done what I have promised you." Then Jacob awoke from his sleep and said, "Surely the LORD is in this place, and I did not know it." And he was afraid and said, "How awesome is this place! **This is none other than the house of God [Bethel], and this is the gate of heaven.**" (Genesis 28:10–17, emphasis added)

Genesis 28 is not describing a necromantic ritual. That would imply that Jacob performed some working to open the portal. In this instance, it was YHWH who opened it, allowing his servant to see into realms beyond our own. Mankind must never open these doors, for doing so is disobedience and puts us at risk, for we've no idea just what might lie beyond these portals. Here, Jacob sees angels ascending and descending along a ladder or stair; it is a powerful vision of God's throne room, for HE is standing above it. We often forget that part of the story, discussing only the angels walking along the portal, but our LORD was also there. While touring Israel in 2018, we were privileged to explore the mountainous region that Aaron Lipkin and many of his archaeologist colleagues believe is Jacob's "Beth-el"—the very place where the patriarch saw this magnificent vision.

The stone that Jacob used as a pillow did not contain God's throne room, but it was used to open Jacob's eyes. However, other cultures believe stones contain the presence of their god. When we were visiting Petra in 2018 and 2019, we filmed the temple where such a rock was worshiped as the home of a deity called Dushara. Mithras, a dying and rising god derived from Zoroastrianism and worshiped by Roman soldiers, is said to have been born from a rock. Ancient figures called *baetyls* (a word based on the earlier-mentioned Hebrew phrase, *beit-'el* or "house of God") can be seen at Petra and elsewhere throughout the Mesopotamian region and represent the god contained within the stone. These baetyls are rectangular blocks, sometimes carved with a rudimentary face or head, almost as though the god is emerging from the stone.

Groupings of rocks, such as dolmens, standing stones, and henges, provide access to these portals. Stonehenge is the most famous, but you can find them throughout Europe, the Middle East, and even in the United States. Mounds made of earth and stone, barrows, and cairns (piles of rocks) also represent or mark such portals, where gods and/or ancestors might be worshiped and appeased. Veneration of the dead is a universal story, found in every civilization and tribe.

Gilgal Refaim (Rujm el-Hiri) in Israel is another such monumental site. We visited this strange maze of stones in early 2019, following the trail through one of the doorways and winding our way to the center, where a dolmen-like cavern awaited. Inside the cramped interior, we discovered an open window, which may have communicated with a fixture on the landscape, a constellation, or, most likely, the position of the sun at the summer solstice.[200] The site stood in relatively poor condition, and our guides told us that it had been built in several stages. It sits in the middle of a plain surrounded by a number of dolmens, "a small part of more than 5,000 such structures recorded in the Golan."[201] The magnitude of the project astonished us, for its construction required the cooperation of a vast number of people, implying forfeiture of personal time, resources, and even forgoing military actions. At a time when tribal warfare over land and water was common, committing the larger portion of your able-bodied men to a building project sounds foolish, which makes us ask WHY? Why would a local leader suggest such a venture? Or, more accurately, what local god demanded it?

Threshing Floors

The imagery of threshing floors and winnowing grain evoked powerful reactions in the people living within the Old Testament-era Levant. Even today, rural communities still use ox-, horse-, or donkey-driven threshers (locally called a "thrasher" when Sharon was but a wee girl) to separate the grain from the husk and stalk. These circular installations represented life, death, and resurrection, serving as earthen observatories and portals. The winnowing wind that blew through the threshed byproduct would scatter the chaff and allow the heavier grain to fall to the ground. Both the circular threshing (performed by an ox or a donkey tied to a central post and sometimes pulling a sledge) and the subsequent winnowing evoke images of judgment. God crushes the grain to perfect it, and then blows away the refuse.

The grain itself represented life, sustenance for today and hope for tomorrow when planted (the grain "dies" to yield new "life"), providing a circular picture of birth, death, and rebirth. Like the *ouroboros* (a snake eating its tail), the threshing floor's very form echoed this pattern of life and death. And it served as a gateway to those who had died, to the rising and dying gods of the place. The threshing floor was a sacred space, ripe for necromancy and ritual.

Hosea 9:1–2 demonstrates a judgment against Israel for whoring upon threshing floors:

Rejoice not, O Israel!
Exult not like the peoples;
for you have played the whore, forsaking your God.

You have loved a prostitute's wages
on all threshing floors.
Threshing floor and wine vat shall not feed them,
and the new wine shall fail them. (Emphasis added)

These were communal spaces in the human sense, in that the floors were often clustered together, allowing locals to share news while working. But they were also communal in the spiritual sense, allowing contact with local deities. In fact, the Canaanite word for "grain" is *dagan*, which is very close to the name of their grain-god, Dagan (later called "Dagon" by the Philistines of Samson's day).[202] Around the time of Abraham and Isaac, Dagan was called *bēl pagrē* at the Syrian city of Mari, an epithet that's been translated "lord of corpse offerings, lord of corpses (a netherworld god), lord of funerary offerings, and lord of human sacrifices."[203] This has led some scholars to conclude that Dagan was at least a god with a strong connection to the underworld, if not part of the royal ancestor cult—and perhaps the recipient of human sacrifice.[204]

The circular space of the threshing floor was situated within a windy place, where breezes could reliably blow away the lighter chaff and allow the heavier grain to fall to the ground. This combines the grain-god with the storm-god (wind), which makes sense, for crops requires rain to grow, and winnowing requires wind. Storm-god imagery in the act of winnowing is obvious, for it is the wind that performs the ritualistic act of refinement (a symbol of judgment). Appeasing such a god of the grain could be the difference between life and death (physical death), and even though the Hebrews knew such carnal activities were forbidden by YHWH, they still engaged in the rites.

Baal, a storm-god, may also have been worshiped at threshing floors. Certainly, his minions, the Rephaim called "warriors of Baal" in the Rephaim Texts from Ugarit, were summoned through necromancy rituals to the threshing floors of the Canaanite creator-god, El:

They journeyed a day
and a second.
After sunrise on the third
the saviours [*rp'um*, the Rephaim][205]
arrived at the threshing-floors,
the divinities [*ilnym*, the *elohim*] at the plantations.
Then Danel the man of healing answered,
the hero, the devotee of Hrnm, replied:
"The saviours are at the threshing-floors,
the spirits are at the plantations."[206]
To his sanctuary the saviours [*rp'um*] hurried indeed,
to his sanctuary hurried indeed the divinities [*ilnym*].
They harnessed the chariots;
the horses they hitched.
They mounted their chariots,
they came on their mounts.
They journeyed a day
and a second.
After sunrise on the third
the saviours arrived at the threshing-floors,
the divinities at the plantations.[207]

There are several fascinating details to note in these texts. First, take note of the threshing floors of El's sanctuary, which was almost certainly the summit of Mount Hermon.[208] Second, Danel (a Ugaritic form of the name Daniel), a mythical hero mentioned in other Ugaritic texts, is described as the "man of healing" and "devotee of Hrnm." Another translation gives a different slant to the text:

And Daniel, the man of Rapiu said,
the hero, the Harnamite man replied...[209]

111

We mentioned Rapi'u earlier; he was the underworld god who ruled the land of Bashan. The reference to "Hrnm" or "Harnamite" is something scholars struggle with, although some believe it links the hero Daniel to Mount Hermon. The Ethiopic *Book of Enoch* names a Daniel as one of the fallen Watchers who descended to the mountain to create the giants, the Nephilim of Genesis 6 who are later called Rephaim. If so, the Canaanite name of the mountain, *hrnm*, may have been deliberately changed by the Hebrews to "Hermon," connecting it to *hrm*, the root behind the Hebrew *kherem*, which means "devoted to destruction."[210]

To Christians, the significance of the Rephaim arriving at the threshing-floors of El after sunrise of the third day is impossible to miss. It was then, at dawn of the third day, that the women arrived at the garden tomb of Jesus to find the stone rolled away. We believe this is not a coincidence, and the "third day" reference has roots deep in Mesopotamian pagan tradition.

Stay tuned, because we'll come back to this.

As portals, threshing floors also represented judgment and the seat of the assembly. In 1 Chronicles 21, judgment issues forth from a threshing floor. The background is this: Satan goes to David and tempts him into sin by numbering, or counting, the people of Israel. One wonders if Satan's temptation came about *after* he appeared to God (as he did in Job) and sought permission to test "the apple of God's eye." God is displeased with the census and tells Gad, the seer, that David may choose one of three punishments: three years of famine, three months of being destroyed by foes, or three days of "the sword of the LORD" (pestilence) brought about by the Angel of the LORD.

David chooses to let God decide which doom to pronounce: "Let me fall into the hand of the LORD."

And God sent an angel unto Jerusalem to destroy it: and as he was destroying, the LORD beheld, and he repented him of the evil, and said to the angel that destroyed, It is enough, stay now

thine hand. **And the angel of the** Lord **stood by the threshing floor of Ornan the Jebusite.** And David lifted up his eyes,
and saw the angel of the Lord stand between the earth and
the heaven, having a drawn sword in his hand stretched out
over Jerusalem. Then David and the elders of Israel, who were
clothed in sackcloth, fell upon their faces. (1 Chronicles 21:15–
16, emphasis added)

Note that verse 15 describes the angel as standing by the threshing
floor of Ornan, but verse 16 says He stands between earth and heaven.
The threshing floor here is a portal—a stairway, if you will, that connects our world to supernatural spaces. David repents at this and asks
God to set the angel against *him and his house*—not against the people
(who are innocent of any sin).

God's response? He told Gad to tell David to set up an altar on
that very site—at the threshing floor of Ornan! Religious historian Dr.
Tamara Prosic describes it this way:

David's purchase of a Jebusite threshing floor, in my view, does
not have anything to do with the economic value of the land,
legal purposes, or things of that kind. **Rather, it is a symbolic
act of a religious conversion of a cultic site** or, if you prefer, an
ideological de-semanticizing and re-semanticizing of a particular
"lived space." In other words, what was Jebusite, or rather, **what
was lived and experienced as a sacred space of a different religious tradition, as some other god's place, became Yahweh's.**
It is basically **a theological spatial usurpation**, which might be
expressed in economic terms, but the value of the land is primarily in its cultic significance.[211] (Emphasis added)

Prosic is correct, but her bias is showing, for she denies any rooted
ownership of the site prior to that of the Jebusites (really Amorites).

Rather, she sees this as an appropriation by YHWH. We, on the other hand, see this as **a reversal by the Creator**; a takeback of that which had always been His. And, as part of the war for the Promised Land, this was the ultimate smackdown, for this was also Mount Moriah, where Abraham offered up Isaac. This "threshing" place, a circular portal representing the passage from life to death to life again in the form of a rising and dying grain god, becomes the very ALTAR of God Almighty.

Note also the parallel between Job 5 and 1 Chronicles 21. Plague, pestilence, and judgment are mentioned in both. A threshing floor might be implied in Job 5:

> At destruction and famine you shall laugh,
> and shall not fear the beasts of the earth.
> For you shall be in league with the stones of the field,
> and the beasts of the field shall be at peace with you.
> You shall know that your tent is at peace,
> and you shall inspect your fold and miss nothing.
> You shall know also that your offspring shall be many,
> and your descendants as the grass of the earth.
> You shall come to your grave in ripe old age,
> like a sheaf gathered up in its season. (Job 5:22–26)

We see God's promise that Job will have many descendants and be protected against destruction (just as God's people will be protected during the end times). Job will make a contract or covenant with the "stones of the field" and with the beasts of the field. He is taken up as a sheaf in its season. Harvest always involved gathering of the grain and then separation of wheat from the chaff. Job makes the cut and will be gathered to God's throne. Does the threshing floor, then, represent the "council" place of the spirit realm, where judgment is rendered to determine wheat and chaff? Do the stones of the field relate to other portals or sacred spaces?

Returning to our story of David and his census, after seeing the Angel of the LORD standing upon the threshing floor, the king buys that very floor from Ornan the Jebusite, and this spot is where Solomon built the Temple. When Abraham brought Isaac there, it was a place of judgment and appeasement, where God met with man. During David's time, this same place provided a glimpse into the Divine Council and God's throne; and, as the site of His temple, it has served as a beacon to Jews and Christians alike throughout the centuries.

This temptation of David came right on the heels of the capture of Rabbah (capital city of the Ammonites) and the slaying of the giants. David took the crown off the Ammonite king's head and put it on himself. He then used saws and iron to "saw apart" the people of the city, and this led to war with the giants. No wonder Satan sought to end David's reign—but God had other plans. Hallelujah!

Dolmens

We explore the significance of dolmens in greater depth in the chapter, "Ruins of the Travelers," but for the purposes of this section, let's consider the dolmens' possible function as a communication doorway. The structure of a dolmen is simple: two, three, or four uprights are placed into the ground, and then are topped by a flat lintel or roof. The formation resembles a door or gateway—perhaps, a small shelter.

With our twenty-first century eyes, it's tempting to picture these stone structures as Fred Flintstone-style homes, but there is no archaeological evidence of habitation. Populating desert and mountainous areas alike, and scattered the world over, these have a universal sense of spiritual habitation, of ghosts and ancient voices. The simplest structures, two uprights and a lintel, remind one of the basic trilithons of Stonehenge.

The individual trilithons (meaning three stones) reveal a series of doorways built into the Stonehenge monument. This combines the circle of a threshing floor with the upright/lintel structure of the dolmen. This *portmanteau* in stone implies a supernatural aspect to dolmens. If not "little houses," then why take the manpower and time to build tens of thousands of them? It is our belief that dolmens provide locality for interactions with the dead.

Beyond the idea of a cemetery (for few bones have been excavated from these), dolmens are places of worship—magical boxes that provide an echo chamber to discern voices from beyond and a ritual site for provisional feasts, to offer food and water to the dead as appeasement or as required by relatives. These structures are often aligned in the same direction within a locality, as if the builders had the same motivation and goal, sometimes with the doors opening towards the east, where the sun and moon would rise[212] (signaling proper times of the year for planting or harvest). We do not believe them to be solely astronomical structures, though they may have served in this capacity, but that the opening *points towards the god's abode*, representing his command over life and death (planting and harvest as models for birth, death, and rebirth).

Dolmens once connected (and may still connect) our material realm to the spiritual plane, just as threshing floors link heaven and earth. Old Testament tribesmen surely saw these as sacred places to speak to the dead. Dolmens are sometimes grouped into expansive necropolises, or "cities of the dead." Scholars use the term "necropolis" despite the lack of burial evidence in most dolmens. *Menhirs*, or standing stones, are sometimes associated with these stone doorways, as are tower tombs. These portals exist the world over, but the greatest concentrations are in Korea with thirty-five thousand, Jordan with twenty-five thousand, and the Caucasus with three thousand.

As noted earlier, there are some five thousand dolmens on the Golan Heights alone, the ancient kingdom of Bashan. That place was believed by Canaanites of biblical times to be the entrance to the netherworld, ruled by a god called Rapi'u, the "king of eternity" (and note that Rapi'u is the singular form of *rapi'uma*—"Rephaim").[213] In the Ugaritic dialect,

Bashan literally meant "place of the serpent."[214] The only other concentration of dolmens this dense in the Levant is clustered around the base of what a growing number of scholars believes to be the ruins of ancient Sodom.[215]

Ancient man sought to appease, please, and gain secret knowledge from gods and deceased loved ones. Directional doorways pointing towards a certain constellation, the sunrise, or moonrise may have augmented and/or facilitated this communication. We'll discover much more about communing with the dead in the next chapter, where we cover the iconic places of pagan social media posts: high places, the woodlands, and reflective surfaces.

11

Treading the High Places

And it came to pass on the morrow, that Balak took Balaam, and brought him up into the high places of Baal, that thence he might see the utmost part of the people.

—NUMBERS 22:41 (ESV)

In our previous chapter, we explored rocks, threshing floors, and dolmens, taking particular care to perceive them through the eyes of an Old Testament-era citizen. To a man living at this time, the world was populated by numerous gods that required appeasement; some of these spirit beings might even be the poor man's ancestors. Finding a "telephone booth" where one might conduct conversations with this other side required more than just the right spot; it also required the correct device, such as an altar or even a human priest or medium. Despite YHWH's clear laws against attempting to summon or commune with the dead (necromancy), entire families, villages, and cities continued to seek approval from whatever baal controlled the area. It was a massive, spiritual shakedown racket—not only by the baals in question, but also by the mediums and priests.

Beyond the rocks, threshing floors, and dolmens, mountainous areas were favored, but bodies of water or their substitutes (reflective surfaces) would do, as well as woodlands. Wells and cisterns provided gateways to the underworld or otherworld, as if these drilled down into a subterranean telephone line. We'll begin up high and work our way down.

High Places

The Bible uses the phrase "high places" ninety-one times in the King James Version. Upon the slopes of nearby hills and mountains, residents of the Levant performed rituals of appeasement, sacrifice, and communication (necromancy), often at specific locales marked by stone monuments—and sometimes, spiral enclosures. The word translated to "high places" is *bamah*, a rich and contextual word that can mean battlefield, mountain, high place, cultic platform (or altar), and possibly funeral mound. According to Gesenius's *Hebrew Lexicon*, it can also mean fortress or castle that's built upon a mountain. Amos 4:13 uses *bamah* to refer to multiple high places, and reminds us that the LORD owns and controls them all:

> For behold, he who forms the mountains and creates the wind, and declares to man what is his thought, who makes the morning darkness, and **treads on the heights of the earth**—the LORD, the God of hosts, is his name! (Emphasis added)

We rather like the imagery of God Almighty "treading" upon the high places. It evokes far more than just a supreme spirit being walking across mountaintops, but implies a military sense combined with an echo of "treading out the grain" (as in threshing floors). This is most likely judgment language, for it follows a recounting of how YHWH had brought famine, pestilence, drought, blight, and the sword to Israel;

yet, despite these afflictions, they did not return to Him. Surely, "treading upon the heights" is a continuation of this language.

But upon what or *whom* is he treading? Far more than just the ground of the lofty space, the LORD is displacing the traditional rulers of these *bamah*. The encounter on Mount Carmel is a case in point. For three years, Israel had languished beneath the judgment of drought, and all because King Ahab and his Tyrian bride Jezebel worshiped Baal. Arriving in the throne room, the prophet Elijah confronts the stubborn king and lays down a gauntlet:

> When Ahab saw Elijah, Ahab said to him, "Is it you, you troubler of Israel?" And he answered, "I have not troubled Israel, but you have, and your father's house, because you have abandoned the commandments of the LORD and followed the Baals. Now therefore send and gather all Israel to me at Mount Carmel, and the 450 prophets of Baal and the 400 prophets of Asherah, who eat at Jezebel's table. (1 Kings 18:17–19)

Note that Elijah accuses Ahab of following "the Baals." Plural. Perhaps Ahab was hedging his bets, so to speak, making sure that he worshiped the correct god—not only one that pleased his overbearing wife, but also any with local power. Mount Carmel is nearly eighteen hundred feet high with a promontory that looks westward to the Mediterranean Sea. Ruins excavated in the region indicate a god with numerous names: *Melqart*, the city god of Tyre and the Phoenician version of Heracles; *Karmelos*; and even *Zeus*, based on a Greek inscription upon a stone foot discovered in the artifacts collected by the nuns at the Carmelite Monastery. The inscription on the foot, from a statue that may have stood within a temple or votary, says:

To Heliopolitan Zeus (god of) Carmel
(by) Gaius Julius Eutychas colonist (of) Caesarea

Ironically and perhaps not unintentionally, the object is a foot, relating it to a god treading upon the mountain. It also connects Carmel to Heliopolis (Baalbek), built by the Romans to honor Jupiter (the Roman version of Zeus) and his Syrian consort, Atargatis (Jupiter's local "queen," i.e., Astarte) along with their son, known at Baalbek as Mercury, but might also refer to any number of sons born from a union between Jupiter and a conquest, Heracles (or Hercules) being one of them.

But let's return to Elijah, who had dared Ahab to pit his priests against YHWH. This high place had power, and Elijah took the battle into the lion's den. After those caught up in the Baal frenetics had scored themselves with lances (the practice of "furrowing the chest" would have produced a great deal of blood) to appease the Baal of Carmel, they received no response. Surely, these priests believed themselves in a position of strength; after all, they stood upon Baal's holy ground. HE had the power here, not the God of Jacob. HE tread upon these heights. They petitioned their "rising and dying" storm-god (Elijah suggested he might be sleeping," which refers to the six-month snooze taken by all rising and dying gods). However, all their bloodshed, weeping, and wailing availed nothing.

Enter Elijah. First off, he *repaired* the altar of the Lord, implying that someone had previously been worshiping YHWH on Carmel. The text isn't clear, but as part of the repair, Elijah ordered twelve stones be placed upon it to represent the twelve sons of Jacob. This connects our high place with the idea of stones or heaps of stones, which often represent a portal. No, Elijah wasn't practicing necromancy; he was following his LORD's commands. By erecting this structure and making it a part of the original altar, Elijah made a bold statement: YHWH of Jacob is the true God of this mountain, and we are about to commune with Him.

Step two: put on wood—oh, but soak it first:

"Fill four jars with water and pour it on the burnt offering and on the wood." And he said, "Do it a second time." And they did it a second time. And he said, "Do it a third time." And they did it a third time. And the water ran around the altar and filled the trench also with water." (1 Kings 18:33b–35)

Twelve jars total, one for each stone.

What? Why do this? Remember that the entire region had suffered from a three-year drought, which meant most water sources had dried up, unless their origin came from a mountain spring (underground origin). The passage doesn't tell us where the priests went to collect the precious water, but everyone watching (and you can bet this showdown had quite an audience) must have gasped! It might be that the LORD performed a miracle by providing the water (proclaiming Himself the God of fresh water). Regardless, the wood was too wet to light by any conventional means. Now, here's the good part: As with Baal, YHWH is expected to provide ignition, a spark from the spirit realm to confirm His position as the head of all gods: the great Storm God (an epithet ascribed to Zeus and Jupiter, who both wielded lightning bolts).

Elijah speaks to God. He communes with Him, quietly, reverently. He does not score his chest with a blade. He does not dance and scream and wail and plead:

Elijah the prophet came near and said, "O LORD, God of Abraham, Isaac, and Israel, let it be known this day that you are God in Israel, and that I am your servant, and that I have done all these things at your word. Answer me, O LORD, answer me, that this people may know that you, O LORD, are God, and that you have turned their hearts back." (1 Kings 18:36)

One of our favorite musical pieces is Mendelssohn's oratorio *Elijah*. It's all Scripture, which means you learn biblical truths as you memorize it. We've probably listened to this magnificent oratorio fifty times or more. As the prophet prays, the music shifts from jagged and frenetic to elegant and confident. It's almost a musical whisper. Immediately, the LORD replies with a flash! He proves His position as God of Lightning; the entire offering—bull pieces, wood, stones, even the dust, *and* all the water—vanish! Everyone falls on his face in fear and terror. Imagine seeing such a marvel and then realizing the miracle was the work of the very God whose altar you'd destroyed and whose land you'd stolen. Not only did the humans tremble, but we'll bet the very foundations of the spirit realm took note.

Boom! Mic drop. YHWH has spoken: "Baal, get off my mountain!"

Carmel isn't the only mountain with spiritual associations. There is another with a reputation as a major portal to the unseen realms, and it's one most prophecy scholars know well: Mount Hermon. Not only is Hermon the very summit upon which two hundred *bene ha elohim* ("sons of God," or what we would call "angels") descended; it is also the site of Christ's transfiguration (another smackdown with the fallen realm—another victory in the real "Game of Thrones"!).

What do we know about Mount Hermon as a place of pagan worship and communication with the dead? In 1869, while surveying Hermon for Great Britain's Palestine Exploration Fund (PEF), Sir Charles Warren discovered an ancient temple with an enclosure upon the mountain's summit, called by the locals *Qasr Antar*. As a trained surveyor and mathematician with the Royal Engineers, Warren documented the site with meticulous care, offering the PEF intricately drawn sketches of the layout and design. To reach the summit required an anticlockwise circumambulation, much like complex labyrinths, which forced the pilgrim to engage in slow contemplation as he approached the god awaiting at the center. This circular motion is reminiscent of the pathway formed by oxen that tread out the grain in a threshing floor. On page 212 of the report, Warren writes:

On the northern and western peaks no ruins could be found or any sign that they had been used as places of worship; but **on the southern peak there is a hole scooped out of the apex**, the foot is surrounded by an oval of hewn stones, and at its **southern end is a Sacellum, or temple**, nearly destroyed: the latter appears to be of more recent date than the stone oval, and·the mouldings on its cornice appear to be Roman. The oval is formed of well-dressed stones, from two to eight feet in length, two-and-a-half feet in breadth, and two feet thick; they are laid in a curved line on the uneven ground, their breadth being their height, and their ends touching each other. In some places it almost appears as though there had been two courses of these stones one on the other; many of them are still *in situ* while others are only just overturned; but in some place to the west the stones have been completely removed, and the position they occupied can only be ascertained by the cutting in the rock made to receive them…. The Oval appears to have been something of an ellipse, its longer axis from northwest to southeast being one hundred and thirty feet, its shorter axis being about one hundred feet: within, the peak rises for about eighteen feet, and **at the apex is a hole cut out like a cauldron**, nine feet in diameter and about six feet deep; at the bottom is shingle and rubbish, and the true bottom is probably deeper. The rock is cut and scarped in several places. To the south, and just outside the oval, is the ruin of a rectangular building. whose entrance was to east, the angle of the side is 72 degrees; it is 36ft. 3in. long, and 33ft. 3in. broad; the shorter sides being to east and west. The rock is cut down to receive it; at the north-east angle the rock has been scarped down so as to leave a passage two feet wide between it and the building.[216]

There are several points we can discern from this description.

1. Approaching the facility requires circumambulation in an anticlockwise direction, climbing as you proceed.

2. There is a sacred temple at the start of this threshing floor-style oval with Roman aspects to its architecture, indicating use even into the Roman era.

3. As you near the center of the oval, you ascend slightly, about eighteen feet, according to Warren.

4. The ultimate goal is reached when you perceive a "cauldron," or depressed area within this eighteen-foot-high mound. The purpose of this cauldron is to receive water libation, (discussed in more detail in the section on the *yarid* ritual in the chapter, "The Pourer of Water") But the idea is also observed in the encounter on Mount Carmel. God's insistence that twelve jars of water be poured onto the altar must have made sense to the pagans, who believed libation was required as appeasement to their mountain god.

Caves and Caverns

Rocky openings into the sides of mountains, both natural and man-made, became temples and sites for worship and communion in the Old Testament era. Panias, the Grotto of Pan, that sits near the base of Mount Hermon is one example, but these doorways to the underworld form a universal labyrinth of sacred spaces. Remember that when we use the word "sacred" in this context, it refers to the idea that these belong to spiritual beings, most likely demons or fallen angels, but also ancestors. Caves have a long association with the dead and occult rites, beginning in Genesis 19, when Moab and Ammon are conceived within a cave.

Consider the context of this drama. Lot and his wife and daughters flee Sodom, following an angel (yes, they recognized him as a spirit being from the other realm). The wife turns back and becomes a pillar of salt. The two daughters have known only life in Sodom, where men lusted after strange flesh (that of angels) and worshiped every god except the Creator. As they flee their home, they see their mother die. Later, Zoar is one of the cities linked with God's planned judgment against Sodom and Gomorrah, but because Lot pleads to seek shelter in Zoar, it is (presumably) spared. Lot takes his daughters up into "the mountain," where they live in a cave. Perhaps he and his daughters had grown fearful of cities; perhaps the locals blamed Lot for the calamity. Or it may be that God decided to level Zoar as well and told Lot to escape. Who knows? Scripture is silent on this, but we do know that Lot took his children to a mountain cave. Why there? Did it seem safe, or was there a local legend about a connection to a powerful entity that might preserve them? Again, we can only speculate.

Whatever the reason, the girls conclude that their father's lineage will end with them unless they get him drunk and lie with him. It's quite possible that the daughters had seen sex rites enacted or had heard them discussed back at home, in Sodom. One might even suggest that they heard whispers in that dark cave, a lying voice that encouraged their debauchery. No matter. Whatever the cause, the products of these illicit liaisons are Ammon and Moab—two tribes that would prove troublesome for centuries to come.

Other caves in Scripture are:

- The cave of Machpelah, where Abraham buried his beloved Sarah after purchasing it from Ephron the Hittite.
- The cave at Mikkedah, where the five kings (the king of Jerusalem, the king of Hebron, the king of Jarmuth, the king of Lachish, and the king of Eglon) hid from Joshua.
- David escaped to the cave of Adullam while fleeing from Saul.
- David chose not to kill Saul, who was relieving himself in a cave somewhere in the wilderness of Engedi.

- When Jezebel was killing prophets (after the showdown on Carmel), Obadiah hid one hundred faithful prophets in an unnamed cave.

Those were just a few places where caves helped hide someone, but can we find evidence for communication from "another realm" in the Old Testament accounts? Take a look at 1 Kings 19. This chapter follows on the heels of the showdown on Carmel, and Elijah is running for his life. In fact, he runs forty days and nights, all the way to Mount Horeb, where he enters a cave:

> And he came thither unto a cave, and lodged there; and, **behold, the word of the LORD came to him**, and he said unto him, "What doest thou here, Elijah?" (1 Kings 19:9, emphasis added)

Elijah isn't communing with the dead, but he is conversing with YHWH. In fact, this conversation leads to one of the most dramatic scenes in the entire Old Testament (again, we refer you to Mendelssohn's *Elijah* oratorio to hear an amazing musical version of this encounter). After complaining that he's the only loyal prophet left in all the land, Elijah is told by God to go up to the mount and wait:

> And behold, the LORD passed by, and a great and strong wind tore the mountains and broke in pieces the rocks before the LORD, but the LORD was not in the wind. And after the wind an earthquake, but the LORD was not in the earthquake. And after the earthquake a fire, but the LORD was not in the fire. And after the fire the sound of a low whisper. (1 Kings 19:11b–12)

Picture the scene. All the storm-god elements are here: wind, earthquake, and fire. But these showy attributes are not how our Lord chooses to speak to His beloved. He speaks in *a low whisper*. It's like a gentle kiss on the cheek after being pummeled by natural disasters. Our Lord speaks to us with love, not with threats and violence. Yes, He can and will bring judgment to those who refuse His sweet words, but He prefers to converse with us as a Father.

Next up, we'll examine the pagan portals within woodlands and water.

12

Word of Tree and Whisper of Stone

For I have a word that I would say to you,
a message that I would repeat to you:
a word of tree
and a whisper of stone,
a word unknown to men,
and which multitudes of the earth do not
understand:
the coupling of the heavens with the earth,
of the deeps with the stars.
—BAAL CYCLE, KTU 1.1 II 1–3[217]

In our initial chapter on communal meeting places with the dead, we examined threshing floors as representing a portal connecting our material realm to those unseen and outside the natural. Seen to unseen; material to immaterial; earth to heaven. The above quote is from the Ugaritic *Baal Cycle*. Of course, "baal" is not a proper name, but a title meaning "owner" or "lord." The *Baal Cycle* is actually about a "lord," or "baal," named Hadad, who is a storm-god. What we find so compelling about the line "word of tree and whisper of stone" is that it seems to imply a communal tie between the unseen realm and nature. We've also taken a brief look at rocks and how they might serve as anchors to heavenly stairways or birthing places for gods such as Mithras and Dushara. We've seen how mountaintops and caves provide natural meeting places for humans and nonhumans, but even the common ash or elm might speak with a god's seductive voice. Adam and Eve could certainly discuss how hanging out near a tree can get you in trouble. With this in mind, let's take our final tour of spiritual meeting halls with a look at woodlands, megalithic structures, and bodies of water.

Into the Woods

There are numerous "green gods" that prefer woodland habitation. Fertility gods and goddesses who control the elements and make crops thrive or wiither; goatlike satyrs and sprites abound in folklore, amidst tales of fairies and even elves. The Bible speaks of Asherah poles, which YHWH condemned, and these were probably made from ash trees, felled and then carved with phallic and fertility symbols, around which the priests and acolytes performed their rituals. The maypole is a remnant of this rite. Woodland gods and pastoral spirits promise the birth of healthy children and bountiful harvests. In return, they expect obedience and offerings, sometimes in blood.

One well-known god of the woods is Herne the Hunter, who dominates tales in England. In her novel, *The Mists of Avalon,* Marion Zimmer Bradley uses Herne as a spirit guide for Arthur in her version of the famous Grail story, told from a very pagan and female-centric point of view. Herne was also a major character in the 1980s revision of Robin Hood, starring Michael Praed in the title role. Often, Robin communed with the mysterious entity, who was half man, half stag, and this spiritual connection to the woodlands added a supernatural element to a well-known tale.

Herne is another version of a more widely worshiped being called Cernunnos, whose name derives from the Pillar of the Boatmen, a Roman column erected in Lutetia (modern-day Paris) in honor of Jupiter, but features images to other gods as well, including a horned man in a seated position. This being is listed on the pillar as Cernunnos. He is a god of fertility and the woodlands, associated with animals and plants (according to the pillar's imagery) and wearing torcs or rings on his antlers. Other depictions show him wearing a torc round his neck and holding another in his right hand. His name refers to his horned state (*cern* being etymologically related to the proto-Indo-European word *krn*). He is also associated in imagery with the "ram-horned serpent," and less frequently with bulls, dogs, and rats. The god's horns represent power, virility, and aggression.

In ancient Mesopotamia, horned gods abounded, usually representing a bull-like (bovine) physiology. The Bible speaks of the "bulls of Bashan," referring to spirit beings, not actual cattle.[218] A bull's horns may be seen in the crescent moon (the god Nanna or Sin), and in the god Kronos, also a name based on *krn*.[219] God specfically forbade woodland rites, condemning them. Here are just a few examples of this practice in the Old Testament:

- "You shall not plant any tree as an Asherah beside the altar of the LORD your God that you shall make." (Deuteronomy 16:21)
- "He also removed Maacah his mother from being queen mother because she had made an abominable image for Asherah. And Asa cut down her image and burned it at the brook Kidron." (1 Kings 15:13)
- "And Ahab made an Asherah. Ahab did more to provoke the LORD, the God of Israel, to anger than all the kings of Israel who were before him." (1 Kings 16:33)
- "And they abandoned all the commandments of the LORD their God, and made for themselves metal images of two calves; and

they made an Asherah and worshiped all the host of heaven and served Baal." (2 Kings 17:16)

- "He removed the high places and broke the pillars and cut down the Asherah. And he broke in pieces the bronze serpent that Moses had made, for until those days the people of Israel had made offerings to it (it was called Nehushtan)." (2 Kings 18:4)

Now, this last verse is very interesting, because it references the bronze serpent called by the people *Nehushtan*. In the chapter on Inanna, we'll relate a story about her consort Dumuzi, who may have been the god known by this very name (after he was turned into a reptilian creature). It's unclear if these serpentine images were associated with the Asherah poles, but if so, one can picture a *caduceus*. Associating snakes with trees also evokes Genesis 3, when the Nachash tempted Adam and Eve into sinning.

A Glass Darkly

Paul's well-known description of our limited ability to perceive God's domain and His plans for us reveals a great deal about communication with the other side. Mirrors and reflective surfaces have long been understood as portals to other realms. Beginning with Genesis 1:2, we see a picture of such a liminal space, covered with a gatekeeper:

And the earth was without form, and void; and darkness was upon the face of the deep. And the Spirit of God moved upon the face of the waters.

Regardless of whether or not you believe in the "gap theory" (which implies an undetermined space of time between verses 1 and 2 of Genesis chapter 1), this verse certainly describes a victorious scene. We have darkness upon water. The word for "darkness" is *choseck*, which refers to a secret place, obscurity, or darkness. No light penetrates this place, but something hovers over the top of it. The waters or "deep" in the original Hebrew is *tehowm*, called in the Sumerian "abzu" and in the Greek "abyss." We're told it's "the Spirit" (*ruwach*) that hovers over this abyss, and it may mean it's guarding something. If so, the Spirit is the gatekeeper to a vast prison.

Enki, the Sumerian lord of the earth, is known as the god of fresh waters. Tiamat is goddess of the sea. This entity is called "Yam" (a male deity) in Canaanite and "Leviathan" in the Bible. Since these live within the water, it makes sense that one might seek them through water rituals. Libation rituals are common throughout Mesopotamian religions. Previously, we mentioned the inundation of the altar on Mount Carmel and the libation cauldron carved out at the top of Mount Hermon.

Another way to seek the small-*g* gods through water rites was scrying. Using a bowl of water, the priest, priestess, or shaman would sit beneath the stars, sometimes within a threshing floor, beneath a full moon. If a bowl of water wasn't used, then a highly reflective stone or metal might be employed to reflect the light. This same idea is repeated in the sacred wells of Sardinia, which we visited in 2018. During certain seasons of the year, the light of the moon or sun would strike the water inside an underground cavern (representing a womb), and this light would then reflect through a staircase and be observed by the priest. Peasant women of the Caucasus regions use this method to catch "moon milk," representing semen from the heavenly god. They use a water-filled bowl, sit upon the threshing floor beneath the full moon, and catch the light (milk). If they can achieve this, it guarantees fertility for themselves and for their crops.

Scrying is also used for divination. The most famous scryers are Nostradamus and John Dee. The former would stare into a bowl of water, waiting for visions of the future, and then would write them down in obscure verse. Dee used an obsidian mirror (volcanic glass) to see into the other realms. Fairy tales such as *Sleeping Beauty* encourage children to believe in such magic. The "mirror, mirror on the wall" ritual opens communication with the spirit of the glass. *Alice Through the Looking Glass* is another example of a tale that demonstrates the magic of these liminal spaces.

The border between our realm and that of the gods is guarded by one or more gatekeepers, powerful beings with keys to vision. Thanatos is such a gatekeeper. We see his ride in Revelation chapter 6, and this fallen angel brings not only plague and pestilence, but the god Hades himself follows in his wake. Thanatos opens the very gates to hell.

In Sharon's fiction series *The Redwing Saga*, she makes use of this idea of reflective surfaces through several tropes: mirrors, obsidian glass, and water. She writes the following in the Prologue to Book 5, *Realms of Fire*:

As Charles progressed deeper into the dusty attic, his lantern fell upon a series of surfaces: wood, metal, cloth, even the odd jewel. Then, to his surprise, the buttery beam produced what looked like a companion beacon. A second, brighter light that shimmered seductively from the northeast corner.

It's a reflection! the boy realised.

A velvet drape covered most of the tall mirror, but a tiny hole, the size of a penny, allowed the light to shine forth like a radiant eye. A deep chill ran along his long arms, and Charles paused, suddenly overwhelmed with dread.

There's something in there.

Swallowing his fear, the child reached for the velvet cloth that shrouded the mirror. His fingers went numb, and a seductive voice whispered into this thoughts.

Hello, boy. The answers to all your questions lie within. Unveil me and behold the Face of Destiny!

Charles paused, praying the voice was his imagination.

Come find me, boy.

Warning bells clanged inside his mind, and Charles longed for the safety of his father's arms. He started to leave, but as he turned to go, the thick velvet draping slid away, as though a ghostly hand removed it. The cloth pooled on the wooden planks near his feet.

The mirror was unlike any the boy had ever seen. Rather than silver, the black surface was formed of polished obsidian, and its beveled edges etched with shapes that had the regularity of language. Charles reached out to touch the forbidding glass, intending to trace the unfamiliar words, but to his utter shock, his hand passed into it, as through an open window—or doorway.

The glass rippled, and the boy's reflection disappeared, replaced by crimson eyes set into a dazzling face.

"*Hello, boy,*" an enormous Dragon whispered out of swirling grey mists. "*Let's play.*"

Using fiction, Sharon teaches the dangers of these liminal spaces. As with Alice through the looking glass, it's a child who encounters the seductive nature of the glass. A voice speaks to him from the other side, promising power and knowledge. The voice tries to lure him into sin and, by extension, into forever abandoning the path God has designed for him.

Children are certainly at risk in our world. Demons and seductive spirits entice from the black mirrors of computer screens and televisions. They speak in loving whispers, promising the freedom that "*You can be anything you want* [be it male or female or something in between]. *You might even be a superhero child of the gods who's lost his or her memory. Your DNA just needs an upgrade.*"

Is it possible that the acolytes who sought liminal gatekeepers during biblical times also heard seductive spirit voices? We'd say it's likely, and the Asherah poles and other woodland rites fulfilled every debauched "freedom" within their fallen hearts. Woodlands, waters, and stone...no wonder the earth groans for Christ's return.

Part Five

GODDESS OF THE DEAD

13

Spirit of the Age

The devil made me do it." That's the phrase we hear over and over again. But who is THE DEVIL of our age? It's assumed this subtle spinner of lies is a fallen angel—perhaps the serpent, or more properly, the "Nachash" of Genesis 3. Or is he the accuser of the brethren, the Satan? Is Satan a name or a job title? Is Nachash another such job title, or perhaps a classification of *elohim*, a word that describes citizens within the unseen realm? Who's out there tempting mankind and wooing us away from following Christ's narrow path?

Hint: It's more than one.

Second hint: Not all of them appear as a male.

Understand our point here. We're not proposing that the Antichrist or Leviathan, that old dragon, is female. But it's our belief that, beginning in the late-eighteenth century, a system of neotheology emerged in Europe and the Americas that isn't "neo" at all. It is a pseudoscientific doctrine whispered to men and women by an old, old deity. This hidden hand intends to seduce our children, enslave teens and adults with promises of magic and sexual delights, and force our military forces to wage endless war.

Third hint: She's in the Book of Revelation.

Let us introduce you the real puppet master behind the marionette thrones of the modern world, the true whisperer in the ears of CEOs, inventors, sovereigns, and even factory workers. She loves war, sex, violence, and power. Boy does she love power. And it is HER spirit that governs our present age. She is evil in a diaphanous gown.

Her name is INANNA.

Don't worry if you've never heard the name before, because Inanna has managed to keep her existence a secret.

The reference book, *Dictionary of Deities and Demons of the Bible*, has become a much-used research tool for both of us. Published in 1999, this collection of scholarly opinions and definitions runs the gamut of spirit entities from A–Z, and it's rare when we fail to find an entry on a topic. Inanna is one of the few major goddesses of the ancient world without her own section. Instead, the editors chose to combine her with another, much more familiar goddess: ISHTAR.

Yes, we've all heard of Ishtar. She's often mentioned in conjunction with or as a cognate for other goddesses such as Astarte, Isis, Aphrodite, Venus, Ashtoreth, Minerva, Neith, Metis, Cybele, and Brigit, to name but a few. Innana's domains are both heaven and earth, but her most famous appellation is "Queen of Heaven," bride of the shepherd boy, Dumuzi.

Dumuzi, a Sumerian god, is a cognate for the Akkadian god Tammuz (a name probably familiar to most of you). He is a shepherd, while Inanna is a grain goddess. A least, that's how she is often portrayed, but, as we'll soon discover, she's much more, and she's riding herd on the new age.

Let's start by getting a grip on the gods of ancient Sumer. This will help us understand Inanna's role in our world.

VENERATION

In the Beginning Were:

Nammu, sometimes called "Engur" (meaning "deep"), is a primordial goddess who represents the original *waters*. Nammu is a cognate for the Babylonian *apsu* ("fresh water") and "tiamat" ("salt water"). If *apsu* sounds familiar, it's because it is the etymological root for the Greek work "abyss."

Nammu gives birth to Anu and Ki. An (or Anu) is the supreme god, lord of the sky (the Greek equivalent was Ouranos). Ki, goddess of the earth, is Anu's sister-wife consort. These two engendered the Annunaki. Bet you've heard that word before, right?

Both the epic poem, *Inanna's Descent into the Underworld* and the *Epic of Gilgamesh* describe the Annunaki as the seven judges of the underworld who sit before the throne of Inanna's sister, Ereshkigal. The Annunaki were thought to be chthonic or subterranean beings. Perhaps their current domain is Tartarus. However, some list the Annunaki as rulers of the *upper world*:

According to the scholar S. Greengus, cited in *Dictionary of Demons and Deities in the Bible*:

> In Old-Babylonian times, the Babylonian tradition of the Gilgamesh-Epic situates the "cedar-forest", well guarded by the demon Huwawa, in Lebanon (and Saria/Hermon); it is called "the hidden dwelling place of the Anunnaki", i.e. the gods of the upper world.[220]

Perhaps the Annunaki ruled *both* the upper and lower realms. They may represent the Watchers, who descended to Mount Hermon and "ruled the upper world," but were then thrust down to Tartarus for their crimes.

Nammu, the original goddess, is also credited with giving birth to *all other gods*, meaning ALL deities arise from "the deep." Nammu is even listed as the creatrix of *men* in some ancient Sumerian texts. This makes her equivalent to the God of the Bible—which, of course, is nothing more than Genesis told with a seditious twist by the fallen realm's overworked PR firm, *Devils, Incorporated*. The *waters* (or *abzu*) give birth to the original creation: a chaotic soup of fresh and salt water, which is a concept beloved by evolutionists the world over. These waters then give rise to the heavens and the earth, and from these arise mankind.

No, Moses wasn't retelling the Sumerian myths; he was setting the story straight by revealing the *truth*—the Lord's version of events.

- An and his sister-wife Ki engender Enlil and Enki
- Enlil sires Nanna, god of the Moon. He's called Sîn in Semitic languages. As in the Sinai desert. And the wilderness of Sin.
- Nanna, the moon-god, is father to Utu, god of the Sun and the law (or justice) and Inanna, Queen of Heaven.

Nanna and his kids form a very interesting triad: sun, moon, Venus. You will see this unholy trinity represented over and over in ancient bas reliefs, stelae, and scroll seals. Nanna's children have essentially overshadowed their father in the past two millennia. At one time, the moon was considered preeminent to the sun, but beginning with Rome, the sun (the lawgiver) took precedence. One might say the moon was forced into occultation, overwhelmed by *Sol Invictus,* as in a lunar eclipse.

But all this time, Venus has continued to shine as the "evening star." Inanna has maintained her position in the heavens. And this queen wants to rule over her brother, her father, *and* the Annunaki, those judges in the underworld.

So, Who Is Inanna?

Inanna (sometimes spelled Inana) is the goddess of love, beauty, sex, desire, fertility, war, justice, and political power. Think about that. She is essentially the controller of all aspects of human life. As "Queen of Heaven," she rules over the stars and is worshiped with special cakes. In Jeremiah 7:18, we read:

> The children gather wood, and the fathers kindle the fire, and the women knead their dough, to make cakes to **the queen of heaven**, and to pour out drink offerings unto other gods, that they may provoke me to anger. (Emphasis added)

They also poured out drink offerings and burned incense. Jeremiah 44:15–19 talks about special worship, performed by the very stubborn women of Israel who appear to influence their husbands and fathers, and even the kings:

> Then all the men which knew that their wives had burned incense unto other gods, and **all the women that stood by, a great multitude**, even all the people that dwelt in the land of Egypt, in Pathros, answered Jeremiah, saying, As for the word that thou hast spoken unto us in the name of the LORD, **we will not hearken unto thee. But we will certainly do whatsoever thing goeth forth out of our own mouth**, to burn incense unto **the queen of heaven**, and to pour out drink offerings unto her, as we have done, **we, and our fathers, our kings, and our princes**, in the cities of Judah, and in the streets of Jerusalem: for then had we plenty of victuals, and were well, and saw no evil. (Emphasis added)

This first portion makes it clear that the Queen of Heaven, called Astarte or Inanna, was worshiped by women and men; however, the cessation of her rites is blamed for an entire host of calamities:

> But since we left off to burn incense to **the queen of heaven**, and to pour out drink offerings unto her, we have wanted all

things, and have been consumed by the sword and by the famine. (Emphasis added)

Jeremiah goes on to tell us that the women then sneaked off and restored the queen's rites:

And when we burned incense to **the queen of heaven**, and poured out drink offerings unto her, did we make her cakes to worship her, and pour out drink offerings unto her, **without our men**? (Emphasis added)

This is a startling picture of the world in which we live. The women's rights movement, which began in the late nineteenth century with the suffragettes, kicked off the return of Inanna. Hers is the hand that *robs* the cradle, for she demands not only cakes, libations, and incense; she wants our children. More on that in the next chapter, but for now, let's continue to explore the personality of this Sumerian deity.

In the Sumerian *Hymn to Inanna*, she is described as the great warrior who controls battles, who *turns women into warriors* and enters the battle like a whirlwind:

The Anuna gods bow down in prostration, they abase themselves. You ride on seven great beasts as you come forth from heaven. Great An feared your precinct and was frightened of your dwelling-place. He let you take a seat in the dwelling-place of great An and then feared you no more, saying: "I will hand over to you the august royal rites and the great divine rites."[221]

She causes the other gods to cower:

At her loud cries, the gods of the Land become scared. Her roaring makes the Anuna gods tremble like a solitary reed. At her rumbling, they hide all together. She controls the mountains, the winds, the waters: Who opposes the mistress who raises her head and is supreme over the mountains? She stirs confusion and chaos against those who are disobedient to her, speeding carnage and inciting the devastating flood, clothed in terrifying radiance.[222]

She is pictured as the holder of the shepherd's crook, possibly meaning she controls the shepherd, Dumuzi.

She makes perfect the great divine powers, she holds a shepherd's crook, and she is their magnificent pre-eminent one.[223]

She is described as a great bull, which puts her in the same class as her father (the horns of the crescent moon):

...the mistress is a great bull trusting in its strength; no one dare turn against her...the foremost among the Princes, a pitfall for the disobedient, a trap for the evil, a...for the hostile, wherever she casts her venom.[224]

She's praised as the goddess who marches up and down the earth and defeats all other gods:

The mistress who, having all the great divine powers, deserves the throne-dais; Inanna, who, having all the great divine powers, occupies a holy throne-dais; Inanna, who stands in E-ana as a source of wonder—once, the young woman went up into the mountains, holy Inana went up into the mountains. My lady stands among wild bulls at the foot of the mountains, she possesses fully the divine powers. Inana stands among stags in the mountain tops, she possesses fully the divine powers.[225]

147

The poem "Descent of Inanna" describes her as something terrifying to behold:

My queen, a maid, As tall as heaven,

As wide as the earth, As strong as the foundations of the city wall, Waits outside the palace gates.

She has gathered together the seven *me*. She has taken them into her hands. With the *me* in her possession, she has prepared herself:

On her head she wears the *shugurra*, the crown of the steppe. Across her forehead her dark locks of hair are carefully arranged. Around her neck she wears the double strand of beads. Her body is wrapped with the royal robe. Her eyes are daubed with the ointment called, "Let him come, let him come." Around her chest she wears the breastplate called "Come, man, come!"

On her wrist she wears the gold ring. In her hand she carries the lapis measuring rod and line."[226]

You'll note in the above quote that Inanna is the keeper of the *me*. What is *me*?

Hint: It's not a personal pronoun. We'll explore that and much more in the next chapter.

14

The *Me*, Myself, and I

So what is a *me*, anyway? If the term is new to you, you're not alone. Very few outside the small circle of Mesopotamian studies have heard of it. The *me* (plural, *mes*) refers to a set of rules and guidelines—a how-to guide on all aspects of society. One might even say the *mes* represent legal authority, dominion within the seen and unseen realms.

Enki, Lord of the Earth, once owned and controlled the *mes*, and he parceled them out to whichever god or goddess he felt deserving. But his niece, the lovely Inanna, who is often portrayed in some of the literature as a whining, ambitious young goddess, is envious of this power and decides to take all of the *mes* for herself. To accomplish this, she puts on her best finery and sets sail in her "boat of heaven" for Enki's abode, the *e-abzu*—that is, the abyss. When she arrives and is announced, Uncle Enki finds her quite pleasing to the eye, perhaps impressionable and naive (she is after, all, just a female). He orders his servant to prepare a feast in her honor:

Come, my messenger, Isimud, give ear to my instructions,
a word I will say to thee, take my word.

The maid, all alone, has directed her step to the Abzu,
Inanna, all alone, has directed her step to the Abzu,
Have the maid enter the Abzu of Eridu,
Have Inanna enter the Abzu of Eridu,
Give her to eat barley cake with butter,
Pour for her cold water that freshens the heart,
Give her to drink date-wine in the "face of the lion",
…for her…make for her, at the pure table, the table of heaven,
    speak to Inanna words of greeting.[227]

The elipses (…) are inserted when a translation lacks content, due to incomplete source material, which means we cannot know for certain what is missing. What we can derive from the extant text are Enki's basic thoughts: Inanna's a maid, she's all alone, and she looks thirsty. Remember, also, that these might be seen by her worshipers as only deserving, for part of Inanna's temple worship included barley cakes and libations. Inanna's fans might have seen this tale as indicative of Enki's intent: either he worshiped her, or else he was luring her into his web. Either way, it looks like Uncle Enki plans to get lucky. After all, she was a maiden and easily swayed, right? Surely her capacity for wine was less than his.

But the Lord of Earth was wrong. Enki lost the ensuing drinking contest, and while jolly with beer and wine, he handed over the mes to Inanna:

O name of my power, O name of my power,
To the pure Inanna, my daughter, I shall present...
The exalted scepter, staffs, the exalted shrine, shepherdship,
    kingship.[228]

Once Enki rouses from his stupor, he notices the *mes* are missing and asks his servant what happened. When Enki learns Inanna now has these symbols of kingship, he fires up the underworld and orders the thief's precious boat of heaven to be stopped at all costs. Entire cadres of warriors are released: the great sea monster; the fifty *lahama*, or gods of the subterranean waters; the guardians of Unug; and the Id-Surungal. By this point, we have the plot of a great Marvel movie. But nothing can stop her. Inanna and her boat full of *mes* powers make it through all seven gates.

Through cunning and trickery, Inanna stole authority over all aspects of society. In addition to ruling heaven, she now sits upon the earth as queen with the power of lordship, godship, the exalted and enduring crown, the throne of kingship, the exalted scepter, the exalted shrine, shepherdship, heroism, the right to plunder, the power over lamentations, and rejoicing, as well as the numerous priestly offices, truth, and the right to descend into the netherworld and ascend from it (which may explain why she later does that very thing and tries to take the underworld throne as her own).

Inanna controls the flood, sexual intercourse, and prostitution, the legal tongue and the libelous tongue, art, the holy cult chambers, music, eldership, heroship and power, enmity, straightforwardness, the destruction of cities, rejoicing of the heart, falsehood, the rebel land, goodness and justice, the craft of the carpenter, metal worker, scribe, smith, leather worker, mason, and basket weaver, wisdom and understanding, purification, fear and outcry, the kindling flame and the consuming flame, weariness, the shout of victory, counsel, the troubled heart, judgment and decision, exuberance, musical instruments.[229]

Inanna also now owns the secret to kindling fire and all the recipes for making things, including weapons for war. She controls the taps to production and hence to commerce, because without products to sell and demand for them, there'd be no commercial activities, no bankers, no stock market. It all derives from the work of a man's hands. She is also a judge, because she controls justice, judgment, and decisions. In other words, she decides who buys and who sells. Sound familiar?

Remember, she just tricked Enki, Lord of the Abyss, into handing over his power. Here's a familiar prophecy from Revelation 13, beginning with verse 11:

> Then I saw another beast rising out of the earth. It had two horns like a lamb and it spoke like a dragon. It exercises all the authority of the first beast in its presence, and makes the earth and its inhabitants worship the first beast, whose mortal wound was healed. It performs great signs, even making fire come down from heaven to earth in front of people, and by the signs that it is allowed to work in the presence of the beast it deceives those who dwell on earth, telling them to make an image for the beast that was wounded by the sword and yet lived. And it was allowed to give breath to the image of the beast, so that the image of the beast might even speak and might cause those who would not worship the image of the beast to be slain. Also it causes all, both small and great, both rich and poor, both free and slave, to be marked on the right hand or the forehead, so that no one can buy or sell unless he has the mark, that is, the name of the beast or the number of its name. This calls for wisdom: let the one who has understanding calculate the number of the beast, for it is the number of a man, and his number is 666. (Revelation 13:11–18)

Okay, here's a *major* speculation moment: What if the lamb-like beast rising out of the earth with the power to inflict all these laws is a reference to Inanna (who is gender fluid—sometimes male, sometimes female) and her stolen *me* powers. She'd have these powers because she "speaks with the voice of a dragon" (Enki). Of course, if she is allowed to ride herd on the lords of the underworld (the Annunaki and Enki, their leader), then, she will eventually learn a very hard lesson. Might it be these ancient small-*g* gods are using Inanna to set up their final kingdom?

Let's now take a look at how Inanna has used her magic powers.

VENERATION

Warfare

Inanna is often portrayed in her hymns and poems as capricious, spoiled, and conniving. One did not want to get on this goddess' bad side, which probably made her priests and priestesses very obedient, lest she seek revenge on them or their city. In this, she is like other despotic rulers, and she seems to have a thirst for blood:

> In her joyful heart she performs the song of death on the plain. She performs the song of her heart. She washes their weapons with blood and gore.... Axes smash heads, spears penetrate and maces are covered in blood.[230]

The Queen of Heaven is said to promote transgender identity as part of her daily routine, which can be a huge advantage in battle. Quoting from Hymn C:

> When she had removed the great punishment from her body, she invoked blessings upon it; she caused it to be named the *pilipili*. She broke the spear and as if she were a man...gave her a weapon.[231]

Also:

> The male *gisgisagkec*, the *nisub* and the female *gisgi* ritual officiants, after having...punishment, moaning.... The ecstatic, the transformed *pilipili*, the *kurgara* and the *sagursag* ... Lament and song.... They exhaust themselves with weeping and grief, they...laments.[232]

Though the original text of Inanna's hymn is incomplete and several of the words are mysterious, you get an idea of what's inherent within

153

its lines. We have male and female participants, a transformed *pilipili*, which previously is associated with punishment. We see the acolytes weeping and wailing with grief. The text does have holes, but one might conclude that, pictured here, are people who are miserable about their lives. A young woman with the heart of a man is transformed by Inanna into a fierce warrior. The *pilipili* may be a class of performers or worshipers in her temple. Others are *lualeddi*, *kurgara*, and *sagursag*.

It's entirely possible that Inanna transforms each of these into their opposites or somewhere in between.

Imagine, then, that you're the human ruler of Inanna's city, Erech, and you intend to do battle with another kingdom. Wouldn't it be helpful if Inanna could emasculate the enemy troops? Or add sexual weakness and impotence to the enemy king? Based on the language in the "Hymn to Inanna C," this headstrong goddess was seen as preeminent in the counsel. As such, every army from the generals on down to the smallest soldier would seek her pleasure and approval. Even her fellow gods bowed down to Inanna:

The great gods kissed the earth and prostrated themselves. The high mountain land, the land of the cornelian and lapis lazulli bowed down before you, but Ebih did not bow down before you, and did not greet you. Shattering it in your anger, as desired, you smashed it like a storm. Lady Preeminent through the power of An and Enlil ... Without you, no destiny at all is determined, no clever counsel is granted favor.

To run, to escape, to quiet and to pacify are yours, Inanna. To rove around, to rush, to rise up, to fall down and to…a companion are yours. To open up roads and paths, a place for peace for the journey, a companion for the weak are yours, Inanna. To keep paths and ways in good order, to shatter earth and to make it firm are yours. To destroy, to build up, to tear out and to settle, are yours, Inanna. To turn a man into a woman, and a woman into a man are yours, Inanna…. Assigning virility, dignity, guardian angels, protective dieties and cult centers are yours, Inanna.[233]

It's clear from this hymn that Inanna was worshiped as a supreme deity, one to whom all the other gods bowed down. She is even described as seeking vengeance on the Ebih, which she "shatters like a storm." Inanna, a grain-goddess, is then equated with the storm-god, which makes a bit of sense. The storm-gods of Mesopotamia tended to also serve as grain-gods. It's an understandable connection. Without rain, no plants can grow, and the wind is required to separate chaff from wheat. In fact, it's Inanna's love of plants and growing things that causes her to deride Dumuzi, because he was nothing but a dirty shepherd boy. Despite her initial rejection, however, she falls for him, and their union is celebrated in *Ploughing with the Jewels*, where the idea of ploughing is a euphemism for the marriage bed. It is also thought by some scholars that the specific activities described in *Ploughing with the Jewels* might also be a formula for ritualistic sex rites in Inanna's temples.

Speaking of her temples, worshiping this demanding goddess featured sexual activities of all types (remember, she turns men into women and women into men), but a priest or priestess was also expected to offer his blood. The *kurgarra*, mentioned earlier, may have been a reference to male self-mutilation using a knife as part of the ceremony to remove his male parts, hence fulfilling her magical rites of gender transformation.

Finally, Inanna is associated with Tanit, a serpent goddess. As mentioned in our previous chapter, Inanna's name within various cultures changes to Astarte, Ishtar, and very likely Isis. Scholar Eahr Joan associates these three as representing the same deity, which by extrapolation, we can connect to Inanna (in that her Semitic name is Astarte). While on the island of Sardinia in 2018, we visited numerous sacred wells, and each bore the same overall shape, rather like a keyhole, with a rounded top and a trapezoidal bottom portion. This is the sign of Tanit, said to represent the *ankh,* or life. But what we found fascinating about Eahr's paper on Tanit is this:

> According to J. Kien's *Reinstating the Divine Woman in Judaism,* the source of Tannit's name is *tannin,* translated as "serpent" or Serpent Lady. Tannit/Tannin as Serpent Lady also relates to Isis. The overriding discovery of Isis as a self-renewing snake goddess was that of life itself. As the goddess of rebirth or self-renewal, the ankh was one of her most well-known hieroglyphs and amulets. The womb oval over a vertical cruciform (cross) is analogous to Tanit's symbol. Additionally, Kien draws the correlation between Tanit and Asherah, given that the serpent Nehushtan at the First Temple in Jerusalem was Asherah's major "life-creating" animal.[234]

Both Asherah (Astarte/Inanna) and Tanit are identified with trees, the palm tree in particular.

The story of the *Rape of Inanna* takes place in a garden, where Enlil has commanded a raven to create a palm tree, using Enlil's secret formula. Inanna finds the tree pleasant for shade and lies down for a nap. Whilst asleep, a naked gardener defiles her. Needless to say, our volatile goddess isn't happy when she awakes and discovers what's been done to her. But Tanit is also identified with the consort of Baal:

> The Sign of Tanit is also an identifying appellation for Phoenician goddess Ashtoret, ** "face of Baal" and chief consort.[235]

If Inanna can be identified with Ashtoreth, is it possible that Dumuzi can be identified with Baal? It's a big leap, but there are clues to Dumuzi's importance in *Inanna's Descent into the Underworld.*

We'll explore that, as well as Inanna's place in the Book of Revelation, next.

15

The King Under the Earth

Dead things are formed from under the waters,
and the inhabitants thereof.
—JOB 26:5

Often during this book, we've referred to the *Rephaim*, the dead, small-*g* gods who sleep beneath the stony, dry places, awaiting their call to return to life—their call to a great meal, perhaps a metaphor for warfare and the consumption of mankind. What, you may ask, has this to do with Inanna and the idea of a sacred female aspect to ancient rulership? First of all, let me remind you that Inanna is neither male nor female, for she behaves as both, and she has the power to do the same for her followers: turning the man into a woman, and the woman into a man. Therefore, any study of Rephaim must include the so-called goddesses as actors. And if Inanna can be connected through some thread of cultural syncretism to Asherah, then Inanna/Asherah is very powerful indeed, because Asherah is known by another name: Athirat, "She Who Treads on the Sea." In this case, "the sea" means the god Yam. Athirat is also the mother of Shalim and Shachar, "dusk" and "dawn," respectively. As such, she is the queen of morning and evening, much as Inanna is called both the morning star and the evening star.

Don't despair if you're unable to keep track of names, dominions, and powers. The fallen realm deliberately obscures the true identities behind avatars. It's as though they're playing a massive, multiplayer video game, each one assuming a variety of identities and characters and trading powers and abilities in exchange for favors and alliances. It's really not much different than our own, human geopolitical system—only, in this case, it's a *theopolitical* system with diplomatic missions, embassies, treaties, deal-making, back-stabbing, warfare, and conquest.

We even see this female/male role reversal in certain types of Christianity. Mary is worshiped as "Queen of Heaven," which equates her with Inanna and Astarte. Mary is said to be a perpetual virgin, another epithet of Inanna, despite the fact that Inanna had a husband and was reputedly raped by the naked gardener beneath the palm tree. Mary is so powerful that she has been called a co-redemptrix, meaning salvation relies upon her participation—as though she somehow enabled Jesus to offer up His life. Strangely enough, this depiction of Mary as a participant in Calvary's miracle is a strange twisting of *Inanna's Descent into the Underworld.*

The reason Inanna travels to the "land of no return" is supposedly to attend her brother-in-law's funeral. Ereshkigal, sister to Inanna, is queen of the underworld, and her husband, "the Wild Bull of Heaven," has been slain. Inanna doesn't bother to mention that it was SHE who precipitated this by sending the bull to slay a lover who'd spurned her advances.

His name is Gilgamesh.

Let's begin this tale with the setup. Gilgamesh was an historic king of Uruk (sometimes spelled "Erech"). Remember, Inanna is the patron goddess of Erech, and all authority moved to this city when she tricked Enki into granting her the *mes.* Apparently, Gilgamesh was quite a looker, and Inanna made it clear that she desired him—however, Gilgamesh had other ideas:

When Gilgamesh placed his crown on his head, a princess Ishtar raised her eyes to the beauty of Gilgamesh. "Come along, Gilgamesh, be you my husband, to me grant your lusciousness."[236]

Gilgamesh's response is to list her lovers and what happened to each. Here's one example:

See here now, I will recite the list of your lovers. Of the shoulder …. his hand, Tammuz, the lover of your earliest youth, for him you have ordained lamentations year upon year You loved the colorful "Little Shepherd" bird and then hit him, breaking his wing, so now he stands in the forest crying "My Wing."[237]

He also lists the "mighty lion" who ended up in seven pits, a "mighty stallion," whipped and lashed and goaded; another "shepherd, the Master Herder" whom she turned into a wolf; and he even mentions the "naked gardener," Inhullanu—yet Gilgamesh blames the sexual encounter on Inanna, rather than on Inhullanu.

Inanna's response is anything but measured, but it is typical for her:

Father, Gilgamesh has insulted me over and over, Gilgamesh has recounted despicable deeds about me, despicable deeds and curses.

Anu addressed Princess Ishtar, saying: "What is the matter? Was it not you who provoked King Gilgamesh? So Gilgamesh recounted despicable deeds about you, despicable deeds and curses."

Ishtar spoke to her father, Anu, saying: "Father, give me the Bull of Heaven, so he can kill Gilgamesh in his dwelling. If you do not give me the Bull of Heaven, I will knock down the Gates of the Netherworld, I will smash the door posts, and leave the doors flat down, and will let the dead go up to eat the living and the dead will outnumber the living."[238]

Needless to say, An capitulates to Inanna's demands, warning her that the consequence would be seven years of famine in her land. Of course, the plan fails, because the bull is a bust. Gilgamesh and his look-alike brother Enkidu emerge victorious:

After they had killed the Bull of Heaven, they ripped out its heart and presented it to Shamash [the sun god]. They withdrew bowing down humbly to Shamash. Then the brothers sat down together. Ishtar [Inanna] went up onto the top of the Wall of Uruk-Haven, cast herself into the pose of mourning, and hurled her woeful curse: "Woe unto Gilgamesh who slandered me and killed the Bull of Heaven."

Gilgamesh and his friends respond:

When Enkidu heard this pronouncement of Ishtar, he wrenched off the Bull's hindquarter and flung it in her face: "If I could only get at you I would do the same to you I would drape his innards over your arms."

Ishtar [Inanna] assembled the (cultic women) of lovely-locks, joy-girls, and harlots, and set them to mourning over the hindquarter of the Bull.[239]

The entire plot thickens, as the council of gods meet to determine what's to be done about the dust-up in Uruk (Erech). Shamash, the sun god (and Inanna's brother), backs Gilgamesh; in fact, he says he instructed them to kill the bull. The council compromises with a decree that Enkidu must die, but Gilgamesh may live. You see, not only did these two slay the bull of heaven; they also killed Humbaba, the protector of the Cedar Forests (possibly the guardian and/or deity of Mount Hermon), making their acts sedition against members of the council.

Poor old Enkidu departs, wailing that he will now join the dead as a ghost, and he relates a dream given to him regarding his fate, to enter the world of the dead:

> On entering the House of Dust, everywhere I looked there were royal crowns gathered in heaps, everywhere I listened, it was the bearers of crowns, who, in the past, had ruled the land, but who now served Anu and Enlil cooked meats, served confections, and poured cool water from waterskins. In the House of Dust that I entered there sat the high priest and acolyte, there sat the purification priest and ecstatic, there sat the anointed priests of the Great Gods. There sat Etana, there sat Sumukan, there sat Ereshkigal, the Queen of the Netherworld. Beletseri, the Scribe of the Netherworld, knelt before her, she was holding the tablet and was reading it out to her Ereshkigal.[240]

Enkidu's dream brings us to part two of this soap opera, in which Inanna uses the death of the Bull of Heaven to accomplish her earlier threat. Remember how she warned An that she would "smash the door posts and leave the doors flat down, and will let the dead go up to eat the living and the dead will outnumber the living"? One wonders if this wasn't the plan all along. Inanna (Ishtar) is a brilliant little schemer.

In *Inanna's Descent into the Underworld*, the conniving goddess puts on her best finery and all the symbols of her power and majesty and travels to visit her sister, Ereshkigal, the widow of the slain Bull of Heaven. Claiming she's there to pay her respects and attend the funeral, Inanna slips through each of seven gates through a slender crack, left open by the gatekeeper (who'd been commanded to do so by his mistress, Queen Ereshkigal, who's no fool). At each of these seven gates, the gatekeeper insists that Inanna remove one item of clothing, forcing the haughty queen to arrive at the underworld throne room naked and stripped of her authority. Despite this, Inanna dares to stake a claim on her sister's throne. Perhaps Inanna/Ishtar saw this as phase one in taking command of the dead in preparation for unleashing them upon the living. Regardless, it's clear that the Queen of Heaven and Earth (remember, she holds the *mes*) wants to be Queen under the Earth as well. Instead, her witchy sister turns Inanna into a sack of rotting flesh and hangs her on a hook.

Now, here is where we move into another echo of Mary and the idea of a co-redemptrix or salvific aspect to her powers. Inanna is rescued by the *kurgarra* and the *galatur*. Here's the lowdown:

> Ninshubur [Inanna's servant] went to Eridu and the temple of Enki. When she entered the holy shrine, She cried out,: "O Father Enki, do not let your daughter be put to death in the underworld. Do not let your bright silver be covered with dust of the underworld. Do not let your precious lapis be broken into stone for the stoneworker. Do not let your fragrant boxwood be cut into wood fro the woodworker. Do not let the holy priestess of heaven be put to death in the underworld."
>
> Father Enki said; "What has happened? What has my daughter done? Inanna, Queen of All the Lands Holy Priestess of Heaven What has happened? I am troubled, I am grieved."
>
> From **under his fingernail Father Enki brought forth dirt.** He fashioned the dirt into a *kurgarra*, a creature neither male nor female. From under the fingernail of his other hand he brought forth dirt. He fashioned the dirt into a *galatur*, a **creature neither male nor female.** (Emphasis added)[241]

In clear rebuttal of the truth that YHWH lovingly fashioned mankind with His hands as male and as female, this sideways reference to a "dirt-based" life form demonstrates the fallen realm's disdain for Adam and Eve and all their descendents. These golem creatures rescue Inanna, and she is brought back to life *three days later.*

That is not coincidental, but deliberate. In another reversal of our loving Savior's sacrifice, Inanna chooses to escape from the underworld, but leaves another in her place. Christ died in *our place,* but the Queen of Heaven demands someone else substitute for her. It seems hell has a quota, and if one leaves, another must fill in the gap. Bureaucracy of the nether realms is truly evil.

Remember Dumuzi? When Inanna roams the city in search of a good substitute, she finds everyone weeping and lamenting and scoring their flesh in mourning—that is, all but one. She finds her husband, the shepherd boy, wearing her symbols of authority (dressed in the *mes*) and sitting on her throne.

Boom. Down you go, Dumuzi. Nice knowing you.

Now, there are two versions of what happens to our shepherd boy. Either he convinces his sister Gestin-ana to stand in for him six months out of the year *or* he gets away:

> Dumuzi wept, his face turned green.
> Toward heaven, he lifted up his hands: "O, Utu, you are my
>   wife's brother, I am your sister's husband,
> I am the one who carries fat to your mother's house, I am the
>   one who carries milk to Ningal's house,
> Turn my hands into the hands of a snake,
> Turn my feet into the feet of a snake,
> Let me escape my demons, let them not seize me!"[242]

Utu (Shamash, the sun-god) granted Dumuzi's plea and turned him into a snake. What does this mean? If he's given a snake's *hands* and a snake's *feet,* then it sounds like Dumuzi was transformed into a *dragon,* doesn't it? Does this mean Dumuzi sits as the new king of the underworld for half of the year in the form of a serpentine being?

One source names him the snake-god *Ishtaran.*[243] Other sources say Dumuzi was transferred to the underworld, but during six months of the year, his sister takes his place. Dumuzi then becomes a rising and dying god. Ritualistic mourning for Dumuzi (also called Tammuz) would take place in the sixth month.

The cult of Dumuzi/Tammuz was particularly associated with women, who were the ones responsible for mourning his death. As part of this mourning period, the women planted miniature gardens (an interesting call-back to Inanna's garden story, but also an echo of Eden) with fast-growing plants such as lettuce and fennel, which would then be placed out in the hot sun to sprout before withering in the heat. This same custom occurred ancient Greece, associated with the festival of Adonia in honor of Adonis, the Greek version of Tammuz.

Interestingly, the same women who mourned the death of Tammuz also prepared cakes for his consort Ishtar, the Queen of Heaven. These cakes were baked in ashes. Even the priests of Israel engaged in these practices. In Ezekiel 8 beginning in verse 7, the prophet is shown a vision of the temple and its dark secrets:

And he brought me to the entrance of the court, and when I looked, behold, there was a hole in the wall. Then he said to me, "Son of man, dig in the wall." So I dug in the wall, and behold, there was an entrance. And he said to me, "Go in, and **see the vile abominations that they are committing here.**" So I went in and saw. And there, **engraved on the wall all around, was every form of creeping things and loathsome beasts, and all the idols of the house of Israel.** And before them stood seventy men of the elders of the house of Israel, with Jaazaniah the son of Shaphan standing among them. Each had his censer in his hand, and the smoke of the cloud of incense went up. Then he said to me, "**Son of man, have you seen what the elders of the house** of Israel are doing in the dark, each in his room of pictures? For they say, 'The LORD does not see us, the LORD has forsaken the land.'" He said also to me, "You will see still greater abominations that they commit." **Then he brought me to the entrance of the north gate of the house of the LORD, and behold, there sat women weeping for Tammuz.** Then he said to me, "Have you seen this, O son of man? You will see still greater abominations than these." And he brought me into the inner court of the house of the LORD. And behold, at the entrance of the temple of the LORD, between the porch and the altar, were about **twenty-five men, with their backs to the temple of the LORD, and their faces toward the east, worshiping the sun toward the east.** Then he said to me, "Have you seen this, O son of man? Is it too light a thing for the house of Judah to commit the abominations that they commit here, that they should fill the land with violence and provoke me still further to anger? **Behold, they put the branch to their nose.** Therefore I will act in wrath. My eye will not spare, nor will I have pity. And though they cry in my ears with a loud voice, I will not hear them." (Emphasis added)

Here, we see a picture of syncretism in action. The priests of the temple have absorbed a variety of traditions and created their own secret altars—rooms filled with pictures—within it. Images of serpentine, loathsome, and creeping things may refer to Dumuzi's transformation as well as to other foreign gods. There is also a peculiar phrase used to describe their acts of contrition: They "put the branch to their noses." Apparently, this is an idiomatic saying originating in Akkad, which may refer to holding a branch or twig from a living tree to one's nose:

There is an Akkadian expression (*laban appi*) that refers to a gesture of humility used to come contritely before deity with a petition. When this act is portrayed in art, the worshiper has his hand positioned in front of his nose and mouth, and is sometimes shown with a short cylindrical object in his hand. From the Sumerian tale called *Gilgamesh in the Land of the Living* there is some evidence that what is held is a small branch cut off a living tree. This would suggest that in Ezekiel the people are putting on a show of humility. It must be admitted, however, that these connections are very hazy and the significance may lie somewhere else entirely.[244]

This passage is a picture of what's going on today. Behind the facade of civilization, propriety, uprightness, and righteousness lurk rooms filled with secret pictures and ceremonies. Walls of abominations. Darkened chambers abounding in devilish acts, featuring worshiping idols and symbols, and wailing for dead gods. The veil that has covered these acts is slowly being lifted. The deeds done in darkness are coming into the light.

The secret king (or queen) behind the world's wickedness is emerging from the Underworld, and s/he prepares to mount the heavenly throne. Armageddon is the end game, but the Infernal Realm somehow believe they can avoid the inevitable by ensnaring foolish humans in their sinister webs. Veneration of the dead is real, and even Ezekiel felt its effects.

Next up, our final section on the female side of the fallen realm—and how Inanna's spirit continues to impact our world today.

16

The Once and Future King

> Hearest thou this great voice that shakes the world,
> And wastes the narrow realm whereon we move,
> And beats upon the faces of the dead,
> My dead, as tho' they had not died for me?—
> O Bedivere, for on my heart hath fall'n
> Confusion, till I know not what I am,
> Nor whence I am, nor whether I be King.
> Behold, I seem but King among the dead.
> —ALFRED LORD TENNYSON, *IDYLLS OF THE KING*,
> "THE PASSING OF ARTHUR"

Recently, we had the chance to travel to England and Scotland as part of the research for Sharon's bestselling fiction series, *The Redwing Saga*. One of the biggest surprises of that trip came when we visited Glastonbury, England. We've both conducted extensive research into the Arthurian myths—not only Arthur and his knights, but also the idea of a wounded "Fisher King," and how the land itself is spiritually connected to the mysterious king's fate and promised return. We'd gone there to visit the famous Glastonbury Tor, but while in the town, we discovered something quite unexpected: the influence not of Arthur, but of Guinevere. Or more accurately, of the feminine side of the Fisher King. It's an insidious rebranding of the old gods and goddesses—the ancient dead—and it is pervasive throughout the Glastonbury area. This will soon make sense, but let's begin with a quick look at the Arthur story.

There are many versions of Arthur and his knights, but here are the basics: A great king, Arthur, arises to unite the various squabbling tribes of England. This great king marries Lady Guinevere. She falls in love with his best knight, Sir Lancelot du Lac. The king's half-sister, Morgan le Fay (a sorceress), decides to take control of the kingdom and so seduces Arthur and bears his child, Mordred. No surprise, Mordred grows up hating his father.

Eventually, the affair between Guinevere and Lancelot is exposed, and Arthur is forced to condemn his wife to death for treason. Sir Lancelot saves Guinevere, but the two of them can never be together (Lance also loves Arthur, which makes it a very strange triangle). With his marriage and the Round Table, the assembly of Arthur's closest and noblest knights, in shambles, Arthur grows ill; some stories list him as wounded "in the thigh" (in other words, his manhood is weakened), and this lack of virility affects the land (because the king and the land are one).

Arthur is now "the Fisher King," a limping ghost of himself who's forgotten who he is really is. To save the land and the king, the Knights of the Round Table are tasked with finding the Holy Grail, the chalice Jesus is supposed to have used at the Last Supper. Only the grail can save Camelot, and by extension, all of England. Sir Percival is the lucky guy who stumbles upon the grail, and the king, once given a sip from the sacred chalice, rallies. Of course, by now, Mordred is all grown up and wants the throne as his. In the final battle with his son, Arthur is mortally wounded, but the Ladies of Avalon arrive and take him to their secret island. The legend has it that the Isle of Avalon is where Arthur now sleeps, awaiting the day when England needs him most, when he will rise again.

Arthur becomes a rising and dying god, "the once and future king" with two advents, and the world is awaiting the second: Arthur's big return to set the world to rights.

Sound familiar? It should. Arthur is essentially a gnostic form of Christ. Guinevere is a thinly veiled Mary Magdalene, and the knights of the Round Table are the disciples. In fact, one version of the story describes this table as intentionally designed to look like the one in Leonardo Da Vinci's famous painting, "The Last Supper." In such a scenario, it's hard to say whether Lancelot would be John the Beloved or Judas Iscariot—perhaps he's both.

Now, why are we even discussing this tale in a book about veneration of the Rephaim and the return of the ancient dead? Because, at Glastonbury, the entire town is built around Guinevere/Magdalene, rather than Arthur.

The Chalice Well, which draws thousands of visitors a week, purports to arise from an underground spring used by Joseph of Arimethea as the hiding place for the infamous Holy Grail. The waters of the bubbling stream emerging from the Lion's Mouth are rust-colored, the color due to the presence of the blood-filled cup hidden beneath the earth. Of course, the iron oxide present in the water might have something to do with it, but try explaining that to a true believer—and lots of them were present at the well that day.

Not far from the well sits Glastonbury Abbey, where it is claimed that Arthur is buried, as though he is waiting for the right moment to arise and claim his throne. The people of the town are genuinely friendly, although many are misguided in their understanding of reality. England has a rich tradition that claims Christ walked on those very lands, and that London is the new Jerusalem. Their myths teach that Joseph of Arimethea was Christ's uncle, and that he not only secreted the grail in the well, but gnostics claim that he also hid Mary Magdalene. Of course, Dan Brown's books make the claim that Magdalene was the grail, the *Sang Real*, or holy (royal) blood. In a way, it's an echo of a Sumerian myth of Inanna and Dumuzi. As we've already learned, Inanna is the daughter of the moon god, Nanna (called *Sin* in Semitic languages). Her consort is Dumuzi, a shepherd boy who ends up in a very dark place (the underworld). Other rising and dying gods are Adonis, Ishtar (Inanna, who ascends from the netherworld after three days), Persephone (another version of Dumuzi's sister), Osiris/Horus, Baal (who is consumed by Mot in the Baal Cycle, but then triumphs), and also the Hadad Cycle (where Hadad evades a group of monsters by feigning death while hiding out in a bog for seven years), Attis, Dionysus, Marduk (who in *The Death and Resurrection of Bel-Marduk* is held prisoner and then released, sort of like dying and rising), Orpheus, Apollo, Mithras (a bull-slayer who may be patterned after Prometheus), Baldr (so of Odin), and Odin, to name but a few.

This idea of a renewal to life after lying beneath the earth or hidden within a cave (or in Hadad's case, a bog) is repeated across continents and civilizations. It is the idea of a golden age to which we long to return, one overseen by a benevolent king (or queen) who rules with grace and mercy. Often, these gods are born of virgins, die tragic—even sacrificial—deaths, and rise with the change of seasons. These are usual fertility gods and/or goddesses, whose dying means death to the land (as in winter), but whose rebirth equates to spring. One such god is Cernunnos, the horned hunter who is part man, part stag. He dies on the summer solstice and rises on the winter. He is equated with Pluto as Lord of the Underworld, which also puts him into the same class as Apollo and perhaps Dumuzi.

Our visit to Glastonbury opened our eyes regarding how much paganism has crept into our everyday lives. Every shop in the city center proudly displayed their charms, palmistry supplies, magick tricks, powders, potions, spells, and sacred jewelry. They sold amulets, crystals, bottles of Chalice Well water (or you could just buy an empty vial at the little shop and fill one yourself), books on witchcraft and Wicca, Druidism and devilry, wizardry and warlockism. A certain amount of this was kitsch, but as we listened to some of the locals (particularly the women), we noticed a disturbing strain of sincerity in their conversations. It was as though these faithful truly believed in the power of the Grail Water and the sacred feminine associated with it. One might say that Guinevere overruled Arthur by a margin of ten to one. And so it is in our current day and age.

Our society has turned topsy-turvy, where men are women and women are men, where children are little more than playthings, and a "do-as-thou-wilt" attitude rules the day. In many ways, Aleister Crowley's magical working on the shores of Loch Ness in 1900 didn't so much bring up the twelve dukes of hell so much as it unlocked the doors to a hellish ride of banshees on broomsticks. The idea of Women in Charge, courtesy of our old friend Inanna, emerged from Crowley's cauldron full-blown, and may have paved the way for two world wars. Remember that Inanna is also a goddess of war.

Part Six

THE ANCIENT DEAD

17

Life after Eden

Life after Eden must have been a crushing disappointment for early humans, especially the first couple. Forget about the burden of living under the curse—toiling to coax enough food from the ground to survive, the pain of bringing new life into the world, and all the rest. The realization that they had disappointed their Creator, condemning their children and their children's children until the end of time to life apart from Yahweh must have been nearly unbearable.

The Bible gives us very little on the rest of their lives. We only know the names of three of their children: Cain, Abel, and Seth. There must have been others, and at least two of them were girls, because Cain and Seth both married and had children of their own. (See? The old question, "Where did Cain find his wife?" isn't that hard to answer.)

It's understood that secular archaeologists and historians won't agree with much of what we believe about human history. That's okay. Bible-believing Christians don't reject science when we interpret data through a biblical lens. Science is the process by which we collect and record information to test theories about the way things are. Analysis is what we do with that information after it's collected. It's not the science we often question, it's the analysis.

Scholars do agree, however, that civilization emerged in the Fertile Crescent around 10,000 BC. (Note: We're using dates that are generally accepted by scholars so we don't get bogged down arguing about the timeline.) Agriculture, cities, writing, trade, science, and organized religion all developed in a broad arc that stretched from Egypt through the Levant and down into Mesopotamia.

This civilization is called the Ubaid culture by scholars. That's not what the people who lived in it called it, of course; we don't know what they called themselves, because they never invented writing. The Ubaid civilization got its name from Tell al-`Ubaid, a small settlement mound in southeast Iraq where famous archaeologists Henry Hall and Sir Leonard Woolley dug up the first bits of pottery from those people between 1919 and 1924.

Archaeologists who study the Ubaid culture agree that it spread from Eridu in southeast Iraq, eventually going as far as what is today northwest Iran, northern Syria, southern Turkey, and the Levant (Syria/Lebanon/Jordan/Israel). The Ubaid civilization was typified by large, unwalled villages; rectangular, multiroom, mud-brick houses; high-quality pottery; and the first public temples. Crop irrigation developed by about 5000 BC, so cereals and grains could grow in the dry climate that again dominated the region. The first city in Mesopotamia, and therefore the oldest city in the world, appeared around 5400 BC. Although agricultural settlements like Jericho (c. 9000 BC) and Jarmo, east of modern-day Kirkuk in Iraq (c. 7100 BC) are older, Eridu, located in what is today southeastern Iraq, was remembered by later Sumerians as the first city, with a degree of specialization among its citizens not seen before in other settlements.

The Sumerian King List, dated to about 2100 BC, records it this way:

After the kingship descended from heaven, the kingship was in Eridu. In Eridu, Alulim became king; he ruled for 28,800 years.[245]

Interestingly, the Bible may support this account.

Cain went away from the presence of the Lord and settled in the land of Nod, east of Eden. Cain knew his wife, and she conceived and bore Enoch. **When he built a city, he called the name of the city after the name of his son, Enoch. To Enoch was born Irad,** and Irad fathered Mehujael, and Mehujael fathered Methushael, and Methushael fathered Lamech. (Genesis 4:16–18, emphasis added)

Some scholars, such as Egyptologist David Rohl, believe it's possible that the "he" in the second sentence refers to Enoch, not Cain. That would follow the normal rules of grammar. The last word, Enoch, might be a later addition to the sentence, an editor's attempt to clarify the sentence. It also might be a clumsy attempt at identifying the city-builder, sort of like writing, "He called the name of the city after the name of his son, Enoch did." In either case, the builder of the city would be Enoch, and the city was named for *his* son, Irad—hence, Eridu.

To speculate a little further, we can apply a rudimentary translation to the name of the first king of Mesopotamia, Alulim of Eridu, and come up with "fourth man" (*A* = prefix + *lu* = "man" + *lim*, a contraction of *limmu* = "four"). Again, this is speculative and possibly way off base, so don't take it as gospel. But if it's correct, then Alulim might have been Irad, the "fourth man," or fourth generation, after creation—Adam, Cain, Enoch, Irad—and the first king of the first city on Earth, Eridu, the city that bore his name.

Regardless of its origins, what's most interesting about Eridu is that, besides being the oldest city in Mesopotamia and possibly the world, it was also the home of the oldest and largest ziggurat in Mesopotamia. This was the temple of one of the most important gods of the ancient Near East. He was known as Enki to the Sumerians and Ea to the later Akkadians and Babylonians. Enki was the god of the sweet waters needed for life. He was normally depicted with two streams of water flowing from his shoulders that represented the Tigris and Euphrates rivers, the main sources of fresh water in Mesopotamia.

Along with An (or Anu) the sky-god and Enlil, the king of the gods, Enki was one of the three most important gods in Sumer. He arrived very early in Sumer from Dilmun, probably the island of Bahrain in the Persian Gulf. In fact, the Sumerians believed Enki personally created Eridu, elevating it from the marshy ground on what was then the shore of the gulf. He was the god of magic, craftsmanship, and wisdom. Although Enlil was the king of the gods, Enki was the keeper of the *mes* (sounds like "mezz"), decrees of the gods that formed the fundamental concepts and gifts of civilization—everything from religious practices to social interaction to music.

The Babylonian creation myth, the *Enuma Elish*, describes how everything on earth came into being through the defeat of the chaos goddess Tiamat by Marduk, son of Enki and the chief god of Babylon. However, the older Sumerian story credits Enki with giving life to all things, including mankind, and names Enlil the slayer of Tiamat.

The differences in the story are at least partly due to the ebb and flow of power over the centuries. Each city in Mesopotamia had a patron god or goddess. The importance of a deity was, as you'd guess, tied to the political fortunes of its city. Just as Eridu was the home of Enki, Enlil was chief deity at Nippur, Inanna (Ishtar) was supreme at Uruk, the sun god Utu was the patron deity of Sippar, and so on. To give you an idea of the incredible amount of time we're dealing with, Enki ruled in Eridu for about 3,500 years before Marduk replaced Enlil at the head of the

Mesopotamian pantheon, an event linked to Babylon's emergence as the region's dominant power in the eighteenth century BC.

That's about the same amount of time that's passed between Moses leading the Israelites out of Egypt and you reading this sentence.

This essay is not in any way a thorough review of life, culture, or religion in ancient Mesopotamia, but there is one more aspect of life in the ancient Near East to call to your attention. It's something we usually only hear about from fringe pseudo-scholars who blame the phenomenon on extraterrestrials. Scholars—archaeologists and sociologists—have known at least since the late 1940s that people throughout Mesopotamia, before they learned how to write, figured out how to turn their children into coneheads.

It appears, based on human remains dated to between about 10,000 BC and 3500 BC, that cranial deformation was widespread in the Ubaid culture, and Eridu—the world's first city, possibly built by Cain or his son—was ground zero for head-shaping. An archaeological dig at Eridu just after World War II discovered about a thousand bodies that were buried during the Ubaid. Of the 206 sets of remains the archaeologists exhumed, "all of the crania had been deformed in one fashion or another."[246]

Got that? That's 206 out of 206. Not a few, and not just the elites. It appears that everybody from every strata of the Eridu culture had a deformed skull.

Now, instead of asking why, the lead archaeologist decided "earth pressure" after burial was the cause—even though none of the skulls were cracked or broken, which would be expected if the deformations had occurred after death.

Evidence of head-shaping has been found at sites all over Iraq, southwestern Iran, eastern Turkey, the valleys of the Zagros mountains, and the western shores of the Persian Gulf, dated from 7500 BC. to about 4000 BC. After that, the practice seems to disappear.

Hmm. If we place a global flood sometime between 4000 and 3500 BC...

The big question is why this was even a thing. Please understand that we're not suggesting that these were genetic mutations or part-human Nephilim, the angel-human hybrids mentioned in Genesis 6 (although the Nephilim would have been around during at least part of this time). But who wakes up one morning in 7000 BC and decides to wrap something around baby's skull to see if it makes his head pointy? What inspires that? And why was Eridu the starting point for this?

A study published in the academic journal *Paléorient* in 1992 concluded that the practice of head-shaping, which is found around the world, must have originated in the Near East because it was so widespread there. However, the researchers believed the deformation was not necessarily intentional, but probably "incidental to patterns of head-gear."[247]

Really? For more than six thousand years, our ancestors *accidentally* forced their babies to wear head-gear so tight that it deformed their skulls?

Here's another bit of data to chew on. At Eridu and nearby sites in ancient, pre-flood, southern Sumer, and only there, archaeologists have found about 120 terracotta figurines scholars call "ophidian." That's fancy talk for "snake-like." The figurines are slender bipeds adorned with button-like protuberances, more often female than male, and often in poses that are exclusively mammalian—for example, a female lizard-like figure suckling an infant.

The aforementioned scholars pointed out in their paper that there had been no serious study of those figurines and what they meant to the ancients, and no scholarly literature on the origins of human cranial deformation as of their writing in 1992. Why might that be?

While there hasn't been much scholarly attention paid to the snake-like figurines, several papers have been published within the last ten years on head-shaping in the ancient Near East. Still no conclusions on why or how it got started, but it's clear that the people who lived in the region—descendants of the refugees from Eden—made a habit of this odd practice.

We'll never know for sure, but we can speculate: The people who formed the earliest human civilizations copied a look that someone, somewhere, had seen and decided was a physical ideal. It's not likely that this was a simple fashion statement. However it started, this was apparently a practice that was believed to convey some advantage. Is it possible that the citizens of the prehistoric Near East were trying to curry favor with a god? And if so, was it Enki, the god who ruled the *abzu*—the abyss?

18

Abode of the Gods

One of the most curious incidents in the Bible is the construction of the Tower of Babel. For generations, well-meaning Bible teachers have presented the story of Babel as an object lesson on the dangers of pride. Those foolish people were so primitive (or arrogant) they thought they could build a tower high enough to reach heaven!

With all due respect to those teachers, that's an insult to the intelligence of our ancestors, if you think about it. And it's a disservice to people in church who want to know why Yahweh was so offended by this project. *Is God really that insecure?*

Babel was not about God taking down people who'd gotten too big for their britches. The clue to the sin of Babel is in the name—and its location. Remember, the Hebrew prophets loved to play with language. We often find words in the Bible that sound like the original but make a statement—for example, Beelzebub ("lord of the flies") instead of Beelzebul ("Ba'al the prince"). Likewise, the original Akkadian words *bāb ilu*, which means "gate of god" or "gate of the gods," is replaced in the Bible with "Babel," which is based on the Hebrew word meaning "confusion."

Now, there's a bit of misinformation that must be corrected about the Tower of Babel: Babel was not in Babylon.

It's an easy mistake to make. The names sound alike, and Babylon is easily the most famous city of the ancient world. It's also got a bad reputation, especially to Jews and Christians. Babylon, under the megalomaniacal King Nebuchadnezzar, sacked the Temple in Jerusalem and carried off the hardware for temple service. It makes sense to assume that if God personally intervened, Babel *must* have been at Babylon.

But there's a problem with linking Babylon to the Tower of Babel: Babylon didn't exist when the tower was built. It didn't even become a city until about a thousand years after the tower incident—and even then, it was an unimportant village for about another five hundred years.

Traditions and sources outside the Bible identify the builder of the tower as the shadowy figure named Nimrod. Our best guess is that he lived sometime between 3500 and 3100 BC, a period of history called the Uruk Expansion. This tracks with what little the Bible tells us about Nimrod. In Genesis 10:10, we read "the beginning of his kingdom was Babel, Erech, Accad, and Calneh, in the land of Shinar."

The land of Shinar is Sumer and Erech is Uruk. Uruk was so important to human history that Nimrod's homeland is *still* called Uruk, five thousand years later! We just spell it differently—Iraq.

Accad was the capital city of the Akkadians, which still hasn't been found, but was somewhere between Babylon and ancient Assyria. Babylon itself was northwest of Uruk, roughly three hundred miles from the Persian Gulf in what is today central Iraq. But it wasn't founded until around 2300 BC, at least seven hundred years after Nimrod, and it wasn't Babylon as we think about it until the old Babylonian empire emerged in the early part of the second millennium BC.

So where should we look for the Tower of Babel?

The oldest and largest ziggurat in Mesopotamia was at Eridu, the first city built in Mesopotamia. Scholars put its founding at around 5400 BC. In recent years, scholars have learned that the name "Babylon" was interchangeable with other city names, including Eridu. So "Babylon" didn't always refer to the city of Babylon in ancient texts.

Eridu never dominated the political situation in Sumer after the reigns of its first two kings, Alulim and Alalgar. But as the home city of Enki, god of fresh water, wisdom, and magic, Eridu was so important to Mesopotamian culture that more than three thousand years after Alalgar, Hammurabi the Great was crowned not in Babylon, but in Eridu—even though it had ceased to be a city about three hundred years earlier.

Even as late as the time of Nebuchadnezzar, 1,100 years after Hammurabi, the kings of Babylon still sometimes called themselves *LUGAL. NUN^{ki}*—King of Eridu.

Why? What was the deal with Eridu?

Archaeologists have uncovered eighteen levels of the temple to Enki at Eridu. The oldest levels of the *E-abzu*, a small structure less than ten feet square, date to the founding of the city. The spot remained sacred to Enki long after the city was deserted around 2000 BC. The temple was still in use as late as the fifth century BC, nearly five thousand years after the first crude altar was built to accept offerings of fish to Enki, the god of the subterranean aquifer, the *abzu*.

Now, this is where we tell you that *abzu* (*ab* = water + *zu* = deep) is where we get our English word "abyss." And the name "Enki" is a compound word. *En* is Sumerian for "lord," and *ki* is the word for "earth." Thus, Enki, god of the *abzu*, was "lord of the earth."

Do you remember Jesus calling someone "the ruler of this world"? Or Paul referring to "the god of this world"? Who were they talking about?

Satan. The lord of the dead.

Here's another piece to our puzzle: Nimrod was of the second generation after the Flood. His father was Cush, son of Ham, son of Noah. In Sumerian history, the second king of Uruk after the Flood was named Enmerkar, son of Mesh-ki-ang-gasher.

Now, get this: An epic poem from about 2000 BC called *Enmerkar and the Lord of Aratta* preserves the basic details of the Tower of Babel story, including the confusion of language among the people of Sumer.

We don't know exactly where Aratta was, but guesses range from northern Iran to Armenia, which is an interesting possibility. Not only is Armenia near the center of an ancient kingdom called Urartu, which may be a later form of the name Aratta; it's where Noah landed his boat—the mountains of Ararat. So it's possible Nimrod/Enmerkar was trying to intimidate the people who settled near where their great-grandfather landed the ark.

The point is this: Wherever Aratta was, Enmerkar muscled this neighboring kingdom to compel its king to send building materials for a couple of projects that were near and dear to Enmerkar's heart.

Some background: The poem *Enmerkar and the Lord of Aratta* refers to Enmerkar's capital city Uruk as the "great mountain." This is intriguing, since Uruk, like most of Sumer, sits on a plain where there are no mountains whatsoever. More relevant to this book is that the great city Uruk was home to two of the chief gods of the Sumerian pantheon: Anu, the sky-god, and his granddaughter Inanna, the goddess of war and sex. (And by sex, we mean the carnal, extramarital kind.)

While Anu was pretty much retired, having handed over his duties as head of the pantheon to Enlil, Inanna played a very active role in Sumerian society. For example, scholars have translated ritual texts for innkeepers to pray to Innana, asking her to guarantee that their bordellos turn a profit.

Apparently, part of the problem between Enmerkar and the king of Aratta was a dispute over who was Inanna's favorite. One of the building projects Enmerkar wanted to tackle was a magnificent temple to Inanna, the *E-ana* ("House of Heaven"). He wanted Aratta to supply the raw materials. This not was not just because there isn't much in the way of timber, jewels, or precious metals in the plains of Sumer, but also because Enmerkar wanted the lord of Aratta to acknowledge that he was Inanna's chosen one. And so Enmerkar prayed to Inanna:

My sister, let Aratta fashion gold and silver skillfully on my behalf for Unug [Uruk]. Let them cut the flawless lapis lazuli from the blocks, let them ...... the translucence of the flawless lapis lazuli .... build a holy mountain in Unug. Let Aratta build a temple brought down from heaven—your place of worship, the shrine E-ana; let Aratta skillfully fashion the interior of the holy *jipar*, your abode; may I, the radiant youth, may I be embraced there by you. Let Aratta submit beneath the yoke for Unug on my behalf.[248]

Notice that Inanna's temple was, like Uruk, compared to a holy mountain. And given the type of goddess Inanna was, the "embrace" Enmerkar wanted was more than just a figure of speech. Honestly, some of the messages between Enmerkar and Ensuhkeshdanna about Inanna were the kind of locker-room talk that got Donald Trump into trouble during the 2016 presidential campaign.

But as we've noted elsewhere in this book, that's consistent with Inanna's role in human history. The goddess has been known by many names through the ages: Inanna in Sumer, Ishtar in Babylon, Astarte in Canaan, Atargatis in Syria, Aphrodite in Greece, and Venus across the Roman world. And the image we were taught of Aphrodite/Venus in high school mythology class was way off.

Since this is a family-friendly book, we won't dig too deeply into the history and characteristics of Inanna. But it's safe to say Inanna wasn't a girl you'd bring home to meet your mother.

In fact, she wasn't always a girl at all. You see, while Inanna was definitely the goddess with the mostest when it came to sex appeal, she was also androgynous. She was sometimes shown with masculine features like a beard. On one tablet (although from much later, in the first millennium BC, almost three thousand years after Nimrod), Inanna says, "When I sit in the alehouse, I am a woman, and I am an exuberant young man."[249] Her cult followers included eunuchs and transvestites, and she was apparently the first in history to perform sex reassignment procedures—much less make it a religious act:

> She [changes] the right side (male) into the left side (female),
> She [changes] the left side into the right side,
> She [turns] a man into a woman,
> She [turns] a woman into a man
> She ador[ns] a man as a woman,
> She ador[ns] a woman as a man.[250]

It's wonderfully ironic. The twenty-first-century progressive ideal of gender fluidity was personified more than five thousand years ago by the Sumerian goddess Inanna, a woman who craved sex and fighting as much (or more) than men, taking on all comers in love and war, and better than men at both. Her personality is celebrated by modern scholars as complex and courageous, transcending traditional gender roles, turning Inanna into an icon of independent man/woman/other-hood.

There is an ongoing debate among scholars as to whether the priesthood of Inanna was involved in ritual sex. The concept of divine marriage was common in ancient Mesopotamia, but generally the participants were a god and his consort. It appears that the rituals were intended to please the god so he'd be receptive to the requests from a city or kingdom under his protection.

However, as a *harimtu*, which might mean "temple prostitute" or may simply refer to a single woman, Inanna herself participated in the rite with a king. And since she was the dominant partner in the ritual coupling, gender roles might not have been as clearly defined in the ancient Near East as we would assume.

Inanna had no shortage of male lovers, however. The Sumerian hero Gilgamesh, who ruled Uruk two generations after Enmerkar, is remembered partly for having the courage to reject the goddess. As he pointed out in the story, every one of the men in her life suffered horrible consequences—for example, Dumuzi the Shepherd, who was dragged down to the netherworld at Inanna's request so she could escape the Great Below. Dumuzi's sister pleaded for him, so Inanna agreed to allow her to take his place for half the year, thus making Dumuzi the first of the "dying and rising gods" in the ancient Near East.

Since you've read the Old Testament, you remember that one of the abominations God showed the prophet Ezekiel was women at the north gate of Solomon's Temple weeping for Dumuzi, called Tammuz in the Bible.

Well, for daring to remind Inanna about the fate of Dumuzi and the other fools who'd succumbed to her charms, she flew up to heaven in a rage and demanded that her grandfather Anu unleash the Bull of Heaven on Gilgamesh. That didn't go well for the Bull of Heaven, you'll recall, which was killed by the king of Uruk and his buddy, Enkidu. That was the excuse Inanna used to try to usurp the power of her older sister, Ereshkigal, the queen of the underworld.

Sadly for Gilgamesh, his best friend was killed by the gods as punishment for spoiling Inanna's revenge. That set the hero on his own quest—obsession, really—to find the secret of immortality, a subject we'll explore in another chapter.

We shared all of that with you to make a point: *This is who Enmerkar/ Nimrod wanted to make the patron goddess of his city!* (Replacing Anu, ironically.) Could it be that veneration of the violent, sex-crazed, gender-bending Inanna was responsible for Yahweh's decision to stop Babel, Nimrod's artificial holy mountain?

Probably not, actually. Inanna has enjoyed a very long career. And why not? Selling humans on the concept of sex as worship is easy. Looking at the values of our society, it's no stretch to say that Inanna is the spirit of the age. Gender fluidity is the flavor of the month among progressives in the West. The values of Inanna—immediate gratification and sex with whoever, whenever—are considered more open-minded, tolerant, and loving than the virtues of chastity, fidelity, and faithfulness introduced by Yahweh long after Inanna was first worshiped as the Queen of Heaven.

If Yahweh had genuinely intervened to put a stop to the cult of Inanna, she would be long forgotten. No, the transgression of Nimrod was much more serious. Besides building a fabulous temple to Inanna and devoting the seat of his kingdom to the goddess of prostitutes, Nimrod also wanted to expand and upgrade the home of the god Enki, the *E-abzu*—the House of the Abyss.

> Let the people of Aratta bring down for me the mountain stones from their mountain, build the great shrine for me, erect the great abode for me, make the great abode, the abode of the gods, famous for me, make my me prosper in Kulaba, make the *abzu* grow for me like a holy mountain, make Eridug (Eridu) gleam for me like the mountain range, cause the *abzu* shrine to shine forth for me like the silver in the lode. When in the *abzu* I utter praise, when I bring the *me* from Eridug [Eridu], when, in lordship, I am adorned with the crown like a purified shrine, when I place on my head the holy crown in Unug Kulaba [Uruk], then may the ...... of the great shrine bring me into the *jipar*, and may the ...... of the *jipar* bring me into the great shrine. May the people marvel admiringly, and may Utu (the sun god) witness it in joy.[251]

That's the issue Yahweh had with Nimrod right there. The tower project wasn't about hubris or pride; Nimrod tried to build the "abode of the gods" right on top of the *abzu*—the abyss!

Could he have succeeded? Ask yourself: Why did Yahweh find it necessary to personally put a stop to it? There are many magnificent pagan temples in the ancient world, many of them copying the pyramid-like shape of the ziggurats, from Mesopotamia to Mesoamerica. Why did God stop this one?

We can only speculate, of course, but God had a good reason or we wouldn't have a record of it in the Bible. Calling building a tower at Babel a sin of pride is easy, but it drains the story of its spiritual and supernatural context.

The evidence is compelling. It's time to correct the history we've been taught since Sunday school: Babel was not at Babylon, it was at Eridu. The tower was the temple of the god Enki, Lord of the Earth, the god of the abyss. Its purpose was to create an artificial mount of assembly, the abode of the gods, which humans could access.

We mentioned earlier that archaeologists at Eridu have found eighteen construction layers at the site of Enki's temple. Some of those layers are below an eight-foot deposit of silt from a massive flood. The most impressive layer of construction, called Temple 1, was huge, a temple on a massive platform with evidence of an even larger foundation that would have risen up to almost the height of the temple itself.

But Temple 1 was never finished. At the peak of the builders' architectural achievement, Eridu was suddenly and completely abandoned.

> ...the Uruk Period...appears to have been brought to a conclusion by no less an event than the total abandonment of the site.... In what appears to have been an almost incredibly short time, drifting sand had filled the deserted buildings of the temple-complex and obliterated all traces of the once prosperous little community.[252]

Why? What would possibly cause people who'd committed to building the largest ziggurat in Mesopotamia at the most ancient and important religious site in the known world to just stop work and leave Eridu with the E-abzu unfinished? Could it be...

> "Come, let us go down and there confuse their language, so that they may not understand one another's speech." So the LORD

dispersed them from there over the face of all the earth, and they left off building the city. (Genesis 11:8–9)

To the Sumerians, Enki was the supernatural actor with the most influence on human history. He was the caretaker of the divine gifts of civilization, the *mes* (at least until he was tricked by Inanna), and he retained enough prestige for powerful men to justify their reign by claiming kingship over his city, Eridu, for 2,500 years after the city around the temple complex was abandoned.

For one moment in human history, Enki induced a human dupe— Nimrod, the Sumerian King Enmerkar—to build what he hoped would be a new abode of the gods, the *bāb ilu*, to rival Yahweh's mount of assembly.

Not only that, it was to be built above what was believed to be the abyss—the very place where the rebellious Watchers, called *apkallu* by the ancient Mesopotamians, were confined.

That was something Yahweh could not allow.

19

Gilgamesh

For mankind, whatever life it has, be not sick at heart,
be not in despair, be not heart-stricken!
The bane of mankind is thus come, I have told you,
what was fixed when your navel-cord was cut is thus come,
    I have told you.
The darkest day of mortal man has caught up with you,
the solitary place of mortal man has caught up with you,
the flood-wave that cannot be breasted has caught up with you,
the battle that cannot be fled has caught up with you,
the combat that cannot be matched has caught up with you,
the fight that shows no pity has caught up with you!
        —Epic of Gilgamesh

The oldest work of epic poetry on earth is the story of the legendary Sumerian King Gilgamesh. It's part coming-of-age story and part Hollywood buddy film, and the plot revolves around the realm of the dead and how our hero can avoid spending the rest of eternity there.

The question is how much of the story is rooted in truth.

More than five thousand years ago, the mighty king of Uruk embarked on a single-minded quest to get his hands on the secret of immortality. After the death of his best friend, Enkidu, thanks to the schemes and temper of Inanna, Gilgamesh, obsessed with overcoming his own mortality, tracked down the Sumerian Noah, Utnapishtim the Far-away, for advice.

Some background: Gilgamesh reigned two generations after Enmerkar, whom we believe was the biblical Nimrod. Both men ruled from the city of Uruk in what is today southeastern Iraq—which, you might have noticed, is just a different spelling of the city's name. The legendary kings of Uruk probably lived when that city ruled nearly the entire Fertile Crescent, the land between the Euphrates and Tigris rivers in what is now Iraq, Syria, and southern Turkey. Scholars call this period the Uruk Expansion, between about 4000 BC and 3100 BC. Logically, Nimrod and Gilgamesh would fit somewhere in that time frame.

The Sumerian King List names Lugalbanda as Enmerkar's successor as king of Uruk, and he was succeeded in turn by Gilgamesh. We don't know whether Gilgamesh was Enmerkar/Nimrod's grandson, but scholars generally consider him a historical character. A team of German archaeologists mapped Uruk in 2001 and 2002 using cesium magnetometry, and among their discoveries was a building under what was the bed of the Euphrates River in the third millennium BC that *might* be the burial crypt of the legendary king.[253]

We don't know whether Gilgamesh was actually Nimrod's grandson, but he had his predecessor's ambition and then some. Where Nimrod tried to conquer the known world and build a home for the gods in his kingdom, Gilgamesh set his sights on becoming immortal.

Evidence suggests that the king may have resorted to bringing back knowledge that had been lost beneath the waters of the Great Flood. According to the *Book of 1 Enoch*, a group of angelic beings, called Watchers by the Hebrews, descended from heaven to the summit of

Mount Hermon in the days of the patriarch Jared (or, as we noted earlier, in the days of the *yarid* ritual.[254] There was more to the invasion of the Watchers than producing monstrous hybrid offspring; the rebellious angels brought information mankind was not meant to possess: sorcery, charms, the cutting of roots and plants (probably for mixing potions), metalworking and the making of weapons, makeup (and presumably the art of seduction), and reading fortunes in the movement of the stars. In short, the Watchers lured humanity into evil, and "all the earth was filled with the godlessness and violence that had befallen it."[255]

Until the early twenty-first century, it was generally believed by scholars that the Watchers were a creation of the Hebrews during the Old Testament period. In 2010, scholar Amar Annus changed our understanding of the Watchers with a well-researched academic paper showing that their Mesopotamian forebears knew those supernatural beings as *apkallu*, servants of the god Enki, lord of the abyss.[256]

Gilgamesh was referred to on a Mesopotamian cylinder seal "master of the *apkallu*,"[257] and by the time of Hammurabi the Great, who was probably a contemporary of Isaac and Jacob, Gilgamesh was viewed as the one who had returned to mankind the pre-Flood knowledge of the *apkallu*. In fact, it appears that the sages and priests of Babylon believed it was precisely that arcane knowledge that Made Babylon Great Again.

Interestingly, the Old Babylonian text of the Gilgamesh epic establishes another link between Gilgamesh and the Watchers. To make a name for himself, Gilgamesh and his drinking buddy Enkidu decided to kill Huwawa (or Humbaba), the monster who guarded the Cedar Forest in the west. In a sense, the pair aimed for a sort of immortality by performing a great deed.

Hear me, O elders of Uruk-the-Town-Square!
I would tread the path to ferocious Huwawa,
I would see the god, of whom men talk,

whose name the lands do constantly repeat.
I will conquer him in the Forest of Cedar:
let the land learn Uruk's offshoot is mighty!
Let me start out, I will cut down the cedar,
I will establish forever a name eternal!²⁵⁸

The Old Babylonian text of the epic, dated to the time of Abraham, locates the cedar forest on the peaks of "Hermon and Lebanon."²⁵⁹ After killing Huwawa, the two friends "penetrated into the forest, opened the secret dwelling of the Anunnaki."²⁶⁰

This is significant for a couple of reasons. First, the mission of Gilgamesh and Enkidu may have been far darker than it appears on the surface. The late Dr. David Livingston, founder of Associates for Biblical Research, pointed out that "Huwawa" may have sounded a lot like "Yahweh" in ancient tongues. If Livingston was right, then the *real* mission of Gilgamesh was to achieve eternal fame and glory by killing the guardian of the secret home of the gods—Yahweh.²⁶¹

Secondly, the Anunnaki, who were originally the great gods of Mesopotamia, had become the gods of the underworld by the time of Abraham.²⁶² Marduk, after defeating the chaos-dragon Tiamat, decreed that the Anunnaki (or at least half of them), should relocate permanently to the nether realm.²⁶³ The Hittites, who lived north of Mesopotamia in what is now Turkey, identified the Anunnaki as primordial deities of the underworld, possibly "an earlier generation of gods who had retired or were banished by the younger gods now in charge."²⁶⁴ So, the text of Gilgamesh cited above shows that at the time of Abraham, underworld deities called the Anunnaki (or the "Anuna gods," as in *The Descent of Inanna*) are connected to Mount Hermon, the threshing floors of the Canaanite creator-god El.

In Derek's book *Last Clash of the Titans*, he showed from ancient sources that El was identified with Dagan ("lord of the corpse") and Kronos, king of the Titans.²⁶⁵ Like the "angels when they sinned," who were *tartarōsas* ("thrust down to Tartarus"),[266] Kronos was banished to the abyss, connecting the old god and his titanic colleagues to the even older Anunnaki and the Watchers of Genesis 6.

Interestingly, El's abode was described as "the source of the rivers, at the midst of the springs of the two deeps."[267] This is reflected in a psalm that takes on new meaning in this context:

> My soul is cast down within me;
> therefore I remember you
> from the land of Jordan and of Hermon,
> from Mount Mizar.[268]
> Deep calls to deep
> at the roar of your waterfalls;
> all your breakers and your waves
> have gone over me. (Psalm 42:6–7)

The word translated "deep" is *tehom*, which means "the abyss," the deepest parts of the earth. As we noted earlier, Mount Hermon was believed to be El's mount of assembly. Apparently, it was believed that the two deeps of the world—a fountain that emerged from Banias, which is the Grotto of Pan at the base of Hermon, and the celestial ocean that produced the rain—met at Mount Hermon.[269]

Remember that Bashan, the kingdom of Og below the southern slopes of that mountain, was thought to be the entrance to the netherworld, ruled by Rapi'u, the king of eternity, a deity linked in Ugaritic texts with Molech, the dark god who demanded the sacrifice of children. The underworld connections of Hermon were known far and wide in the ancient Near East—or at least as far as Babylon. To us, the distance between Lebanon and Iraq doesn't seem all that far, but four thousand years ago, without motorized transport, mobile phones, GPS, and the Internet, putting religious significance on a place that took several months of walking to reach is worth noting.

The *Epic of Gilgamesh* is ultimately a story about the inevitability of death. The hero of the story, despite his desperate, superhuman efforts to avoid "the bane of mankind" (he was two-thirds god, according to the story), eventually died anyway. Upon his death, apparently as a consolation prize, he was made ruler of the dead.

> Gilgamesh, in the form of his ghost, dead in the underworld, shall be the governor of the Netherworld, chief of the shades![270]

This has special significance because of the importance of the ancestor cult among the Amorites, who founded the old kingdom of Babylon. For more than a thousand years, Amorites in the ancient Near East venerated their dead, especially the dead ancestors of their kings.[271] Although Gilgamesh was a Sumerian king who had departed this world a millennium before the great kings of Babylon, it seems he epitomized the venerated royal dead and played an important role in the ancestor cult and magical healing rituals of Babylon.[272]

Earlier in this book, we quoted Canaanite texts that appear to be rituals for summoning the Rephaim, which were the spirits of the Nephilim destroyed in the Flood, and something called the Council of the Didanu, an assembly of underworld gods. Note that the Hebrew word *rephaim* is often rendered "shades," "spirits," or "the dead" in the Bible (for example, Isaiah 14:9 and 26:14, 19; Job 26:5; and Proverbs 2:18, 9:18, and 21:16).

Remember, *Didanu* was the name of an ancient Amorite tribe from which the kings of Babylon, old Assyria, and Canaan claimed descent, and it was the word from which the Greeks got the name of their former gods, the Titans.[273]

Let's take a moment to stop and summarize here:

- Gilgamesh, a legendary (but probably historical) post-Flood king of Uruk in the fourth millennium BC, was obsessed with finding the key to immortality.

- He died anyway sometime around 3000 BC, give or take a few centuries.
- Amorites more than a thousand years later linked Gilgamesh with the "shades" (the Rephaim?), the *apkallu* (the Watchers/Titans), and the Anunnaki, the gods of the underworld.
- If the Hittites were correct in identifying the Anunnaki as "former gods" who'd been overthrown and banished to the netherworld, then they, too, can be identified as the Hebrew Watchers and Greek Titans.
- The Anunnaki and the Watchers (and thus the Titans) were linked to Mount Hermon. Mount Hermon is also where Gilgamesh and Enkidu killed the monstrous Huwawa.
- By comparing their stories with the Bible, we can identify the Titans, the Anunnaki, and the *apkallu* as the Watchers of Genesis 6, "the angels who did not stay within their own position of authority" who are "kept in eternal chains under gloomy darkness until the judgment of the great day."[274]

According to the epic, when Gilgamesh died, he was laid to rest in a tomb of stone in the bed of the Euphrates River. As noted above, a structure that resembles the description of his tomb was discovered in 2003. But there is a dark footnote to the story—evidence that Gilgamesh didn't go to his eternal rest alone:

His beloved wife, his beloved children, his beloved favorite and junior wife, his beloved musician, cup-bearer and ......, his beloved barber, his beloved ......, his beloved palace retainers and servants and his beloved objects were laid down in their places as if ...... in the purified (?) palace in the middle of Uruk.[275]

Scholars have debated the meaning of that text for the last hundred years, but tombs of the wealthy at the Sumerian city of Ur, at least five hundred years after the time of Gilgamesh, included as many as sixty-five servants and retainers who were buried with the deceased.[276] Contrary to the idealistic view of the discoverer of the Royal Tombs of Ur, famed archaeologist Sir Leonard Wooley, those buried with Sumerian queen Puabi did *not* "go gentle into that good night"—they were, we now know (thanks to modern CT scans), bashed in the back of the head with a sharp object, probably a battleaxe.[277]

It's possible that this was a tradition that extended back to the kingdom of Uruk ruled by Gilgamesh, and by Nimrod before him. Is it possible that Gilgamesh, like the people around him, was so afraid of the next phase of his existence that he compelled those who surrounded him in life to travel with him to the Great Below?

There is one thing we can take away from the story of Gilgamesh and the legacy he left behind: While he may not have established the practice of worshiping the royal dead, his cult is one of the oldest documented examples of venerating a long-dead king believed to have the power to help the living. Texts from ancient Ur establish that the last Sumerian kings of Mesopotamia called Gilgamesh their "divine brother."[278] Whether or not he was one of the Nephilim, as his "two-thirds god" ancestry implies, the cult of Gilgamesh was similar in substance to the veneration of the Rephaim by the Amorites who supplanted the Sumerians in Mesopotamia.

Ironically, the transhumanists of today are following in the five thousand-year-old footsteps of Gilgamesh. They promise to overcome what they see as "the bane of mankind" through technology, but, like the companions of Gilgamesh and the retainers of Puabi, those who trust in science to overcome death will eventually fall before "the flood-wave that cannot be breasted."

In the next section, we'll look at how the ancient practice of communing with the dead has been transformed into a thoroughly modern phenomenon for the Space Age.

Part Seven

TECHNOLOGY OF THE DEAD

20

Planets of the Dead

Humans have wondered about the stars since forever. That's understandable; they're beautiful and mysterious, as out of reach as mountain peaks. And perhaps for the same reasons, the earliest speculation about the stars revolved around gods, not extraterrestrials.

As with mountains, humans have associated stars with deities since the beginning of human history. Three of the most important gods in the ancient Near East, from Sumer to Israel and its neighbors, were the sun, moon, and the planet Venus. To the Sumerians, they were the deities Utu, Nanna, and the goddess Inanna; later, in Babylon, they were Shamash, Sîn, and Ishtar. The Amorites worshiped Sapash, Yarikh, and Astarte (who was also the war-god Attar when Venus was the morning star).

Yahweh not only recognized that the nations worshiped these small-g gods, He allotted the nations to them as their inheritance—punishment for the Tower of Babel incident.

When the Most High agave to the nations their inheritance,
when he divided mankind, he fixed the borders of the peoples

according to the number of the sons of God. (Deuteronomy 32:8)

And beware lest you raise your eyes to heaven, and when you see the sun and the moon and the stars, all the host of heaven, you be drawn away and bow down to them and serve them, things that the LORD your God has allotted to all the peoples under the whole heaven. (Deuteronomy 4:19)

In other words, God placed the nations of the world under small-*g* "gods" represented by the sun, moon, and stars, but He reserved Israel for Himself. The descendants of Abraham, Isaac, and Jacob were to remain faithful to Yahweh alone, and through Israel He would bring forth a Savior.

But the gods Yahweh allotted to the nations went rogue. That earned them a death sentence.

God has taken his place in the divine council;
in the midst of the gods he holds judgment:
"How long will you judge unjustly
and show partiality to the wicked? *Selah* ..."
I said, "You are gods,
sons of the Most High, all of you;
nevertheless, like men you shall die,
and fall like any prince." (Psalm 82:1–2, 6–7)

To be absolutely clear, those small-*g* gods are not to be confused with capital-*G* God, Yahweh, Creator of all things including those "sons of the Most High." We know the consensus view among Christians is to treat the gods of Psalm 82 as humans, usually described as corrupt Israelite kings or judges. With all due respect to the scholars who've held that view over the centuries, it's wrong. The most obvious error is that verse 7—"nevertheless, like men you shall die"—makes no sense if God is addressing a human audience.

Humanity has looked to the stars as gods for at least the last five thousand years. And end-times prophecy, from the perspective of pagans, is really about the return of the old gods, spirits defined as rebel angels[279] and demons[280] by the prophets and apostles of God.

The Infernal Council has been playing a very long game. Once upon a time, Christians generally held a biblical worldview. While the influence of the spirit realm on our lives wasn't perfectly understood, at least it was acknowledged. And while the Church of Rome can be fairly criticized for keeping the Bible out of the hands of laypeople for nearly a thousand years, at least the learned scholars and theologians made a fair effort to interpret their world through a biblical filter.

In our modern, enlightened age, however, the principalities and powers have nudged and prodded humanity through the Enlightenment and Modernism into Postmodernism, shifting us from a supernatural worldview to one that only accepts an external creator in the form of "ancient aliens," which allows us to account for the supernatural while simultaneously denying the existence of God.

In 1973, science fiction author Arthur C. Clarke wrote, "Any sufficiently advanced technology is indistinguishable from magic." By substituting advanced science for the supernatural, ancient-aliens evangelists have created a godless religion perfect for the twenty-first century. It offers mystery, transcendence, and answers to the big questions: Where do we come from? Why are we here? Where do we go when we die?

Best of all, believers in ET don't need to change the way they think or act, except maybe to promise to our benevolent space brothers that we'll live peacefully with our galactic neighbors. And, as surprising as it may seem, the followers of Eric von Däniken and Zecaria Sitchin aren't the first to concoct a religion that includes a belief in extraterrestrial life.

Consider, for example, Emanuel Swedenborg, an eighteenth-century Swedish scientist, philosopher, and mystic. He was undoubtedly brilliant, but sometimes the brilliant are blinded by their own light. His theology encompassed the following concepts:

- The Bible is the Word of God; however, its true meaning differs greatly from its obvious meaning. Furthermore, he and only he, via the help of angels, was in the position to shed light upon the true meaning and message of the Scriptures.
- Swedenborg believed that the world of matter is a laboratory for the soul, where the material is used to "force-refine" the spiritual.
- In many ways, Swedenborg was quite universal in his concepts, for he believed that all religious systems have their divine duty and purpose, and that this is not the sole virtue of Christianity.
- Swedenborg believed that the mission of the Church is absolutely necessary inasmuch as, left to his or her own devices, humanity simply cannot work out its relationship to God.
- He saw the real power of Christ's life in the example it gave to others and vehemently rejected the concept of Christian atonement and original sin.[281]

Swedenborg believed he heard directly from angels who lived elsewhere in the solar system. To this day, the Swedenborg Foundation offers a modern translation of the mystic's 1758 work *Life on Other Planets*, a book that "details Swedenborg's conversations with spirits from Jupiter, Mars, Mercury, Saturn, Venus, and the moon, who discuss their lives on other planets and how their cultures differed from those of earthly life."[282] Swedenborg's teachings on spiritism and angelic extraterrestrial intelligences (ETIs) and those who believe them are still around, although they've rebranded the faith as the New Church. (Maybe "Swedenborgianism" didn't test well in focus groups.) It's a small sect, with maybe ten thousand adherents worldwide, but the point is that the messages Swedenborg received are very much like the telepathic contact some claim to receive from ETIs today—and like the messages whispered into the minds of the demonically oppressed and possessed.

Of course, Swedenborg, who died in 1772, wasn't the last word in the rise of mystic scientism. Joseph Smith, who founded Mormonism about fifty years after Swedenborg's death, incorporated belief in the existence of many worlds in the doctrines of the Church of Jesus Christ of Latter-day Saints. Smith taught that God was flesh and blood,[283] formerly a mortal man who'd earned godhood and, apparently, the right to create multiple earths.

And [Moses] beheld many lands; and each land was called earth, and there were inhabitants on the face thereof.

And it came to pass that Moses called upon God, saying: Tell me, I pray thee, why these things are so, and by what thou madest them?

And behold, the glory of the Lord was upon Moses, so that Moses stood in the presence of God, and talked with him face to face. And the Lord God said unto Moses: For mine own purpose have I made these things. Here is wisdom and it remaineth in me.

And by the word of my power, have I created them, which is mine Only Begotten Son, who is full of grace and truth.

And worlds without number have I created; and I also created them for mine own purpose; and by the Son I created them, which is mine Only Begotten.

And the first man of all men have I called Adam, which is many.[284]

Mormonism was just one among the waves of new spiritual movements that washed across the United States in the nineteenth century. Beginning with the Second Great Awakening in the 1790s, a reaction to the rationalism and deism of the Enlightenment, a series of revivals, cults, and camp meetings followed European settlers westward as the country grew and prospered. The raw, unspoiled nature of the frontier contributed to a desire to restore Christianity to a purer form, free from the formality and hierarchy of the churches of Europe.

The Second Great Awakening, which swelled the numbers of Baptists and Methodists especially, peaked by the middle of the nineteenth century, but other spiritual movements followed close behind. And here's where the Venn diagram begins to overlap ancient cults of the dead with a modern, "scientific" worldview.

The spiritualist movement, which emerged from the same region of western New York state that produced Joseph Smith, the so-called Burned-over District, first appeared in the late 1840s. Sisters Kate and Margaret Fox, ages twelve and fifteen, claimed to communicate with spirits of the dead through coded knocks or "rappings." They convinced their seventeen-year-old sister, Leah (or brought her in on the gag), who took charge of the younger two and managed their careers for years.

The Fox sisters not only enjoyed long careers as mediums, but they left a legacy that continues to this day in the work of television mediums like John Edward, Theresa Caputo, and Tyler Henry—despite the fact that Margaret and Kate admitted in 1888 that they'd invented the whole thing:

> That I have been chiefly instrumental in perpetrating the fraud of Spiritualism upon a too-confiding public, most of you doubtless know. The greatest sorrow in my life has been that this is true, and though it has come late in my day, I am now prepared to tell the truth, the whole truth, and nothing but the truth, so help me God!… I am here tonight as one of the founders of Spiritualism to denounce it as an absolute falsehood from beginning to end, as the flimsiest of superstitions, the most wicked blasphemy known to the world.[285]

The Fox sisters used a variety of techniques, one of which was simply cracking their toe joints[286] to produce the sounds that fooled gullible audiences into believing that spirits answered their questions. But even after their confession was published by a New York City newspaper, the spiritualist movement never skipped a beat. To this day, "many accounts of the Fox sisters leave out their confession of fraud and present the rappings as genuine manifestations of the spirit world."[287]

Isn't that remarkable? Humans are so desperate for contact with the dead that the spiritualist movement lives on into our enlightened age even though its founders admitted their act was as real as professional wrestling. Well-known believers have included such powerful intellects as Sir Arthur Conan Doyle, the creator of Sherlock Holmes. In fact, Doyle wrote *The History of Spiritualism* in 1926, and he pegged March 31, 1848—the very first time Kate and Margaret Fox claimed to hear from spirits—as the date the movement began.

By the fourth quarter of the nineteenth century, the Spiritualist movement was joined on the spiritual scene by the new Theosophist movement, a blend of Eastern and Western mystical traditions that found fertile ground among urban elites. Following the lead of their founder, Helena Petrovna Blavatsky, Theosophists saw Spiritualism as unsophisticated and provincial. For their part, "Spiritualists rejected Theosophy as unscientific occultism."[288]

Blavatsky is an enigmatic character, partly because it's difficult to confirm much of what she said and wrote about herself. According to official histories, she was the daughter of a Russian-German nobleman who traveled widely across Europe and Asia in the 1850s and 1860s. By cobbling together traditions cribbed from Eastern sources, Blavatsky was guided by her "ascended masters" to lay the foundation for the modern UFO phenomenon and ET disclosure movement.

Entire books have been devoted to the life and claims of Madame Blavatsky, and we don't have time or space here to dig deeply into the material. Briefly, Blavatsky acknowledged the existence of Spiritualist phenomena, but denied that mediums were contacting spirits of the dead. She taught instead that God is a "Universal Divine Principle, the root of All, from which all proceeds, and within which all shall be absorbed at the end of the great cycle of Being."[289] That's a very Eastern worldview. Madame Blavatsky wove Hindu and Buddhist concepts into her philosophy, and it's claimed that she and Henry Steel Olcott, with whom she founded the Theosophical Society in New York City in 1875, were the first Western converts to Buddhism. The success of Theosophy in the United States and the United Kingdom did much to spread Eastern mysticism in the West. The New Age movement owes a huge debt to Helena Blavatsky.

Through her most famous books, *Isis Unveiled*, published in 1877, and her magnum opus, *The Secret Doctrine*, published in 1888, Blavatsky attracted international attention to her society and its goal of uniting the world in brotherhood by blending the philosophies of East and West through the study of comparative religion, philosophy, and science.[290]

In *The Secret Doctrine*, which Blavatsky claimed was channeled from a prehistoric work called *The Book of Dzyan* (which critics accused her of plagiarizing without credit from a number of sources, including the Sanskrit Rigveda), she wrote:

Lemuria was the homeland of humanity, the place of the first creation. Further, there were to be seven Root Races ruling the Earth in succession, of which humanity today was only the fifth. The fourth of these races were the Atlanteans, who were destroyed by black magic. Lemuria would rise and fall to spawn new races until the Seventh Root Race, perfect in every way, would take its rightful place as master of the world.[291]

Who, you ask, were the Atlanteans, and what is Lemuria? In the nineteenth century, this odd marriage of Spiritualism and Modernism gave rise to competing claims that the human race was either evolving or devolving. Spiritualists more or less accepted Darwinian evolution because it supported their belief in the continued development of the spirit after death. Blavatsky and her followers, on the other hand, believed that humanity had left behind a golden age that collapsed when Atlantis fell beneath the waves, similar to the belief of ancient Greeks in a long-ago golden age when Kronos ruled in heaven.

Lemuria, like Atlantis, was another lost continent believed to be submerged somewhere in the Pacific or Indian Oceans. It got its name in 1864, when zoologist Philip Sclater noticed that certain primate fossils existed in Madagascar and India, but not in Africa or the Middle East. To solve the puzzle, Sclater theorized that a lost continent that once connected Madagascar and India accounted for the similar lemur fossils—hence Lemuria.

No kidding.

While belief in the existence of Lemuria was abandoned by mainstream scientists when plate tectonics and continental drift caught on, the lost continent was kept alive by the imagination and teachings of pseudoscientists and spiritual deceivers like Helena Blavatsky.

Mysterious symbols, tragic history, and memories of a glorious, golden past transmitted to Blavatsky by disembodied Masters via "astral clairvoyance" apparently stirred something in the hearts of those who read *The Secret Doctrine*. Through the force of her powerful will, Madame Helena Blavatsky convinced thousands that the history they'd been taught was a lie, and that humanity's future was to return to the golden age that was lost when Atlantis slipped beneath the waves.

To put it simply, in Theosophy, Helena Blavatsky gave the world a religious faith in human evolution as an integral part of cosmic evolution. The ultimate goal was perfection and conscious participation in the evolutionary process. This process was overseen by the Masters of the Ancient Wisdom, a hierarchy of spiritual beings who'd been guiding humanity's development for millennia.

From a Christian perspective, it's easy to recognize the deception embodied by the doctrines of Theosophy. While Blavatsky's critics believed she invented her faith out of whole cloth, a discerning follower of Jesus Christ sees through the lies. Humanity is not the product of random evolutionary chance; the "golden age" was the pre-Flood era during which the "mighty men who were of old" spread their terror throughout the earth, and there is no spiritual discipline that will enable us to become one with God and the cosmos.

The appeal of the old lie, "Ye shall be as gods," is why the Infernal Council keeps rolling it out. It deceived Adam and Eve, the kings of the Amorites, and even the son and grandson of Hezekiah, who, like the pagan Amorites, aspired to join the assembly of the Rephaim or the council of the Ditanu (Titans) after death.

And now these messages from beyond the grave have been rebranded as communications from beyond the stars—thanks to the wickedest man in the world and an atheist author of horror fiction.

21

The Great Old Ones

Howard Phillips Lovecraft (1890–1937) is one of the giants of twentieth-century literature, although he wasn't recognized as such until after his death. And because he wrote horror fiction, he wasn't the kind of writer who got invited to fancy society parties. Lovecraft and his friends, most of whom he knew through volumes of letters that some believe were more influential than his published work, wrote to entertain, usually by crafting terrifying tales and conjuring monstrous images of overpowering, inhuman evil.

H. P. Lovecraft was a sickly child who missed so much school in his youth that he was basically self-educated. He never completed high school, giving up on his dream of becoming an astronomer, because of what he later called a "nervous breakdown." It's possible that whatever intellectual gift Lovecraft was given came at the expense of social skills. It's also possible that he was tormented by the same demons—psychological or spiritual—that drove both of his parents to spend the last years of their lives in an asylum. Lovecraft lived as isolated an existence as he could manage most of his life, and he admitted "most people only make me nervous—that only by accident, and in extremely small quantities, would I ever be likely to come across people who wouldn't."[292]

As a child, Lovecraft was tormented by night terrors. From the age of six, young Howard was visited by what he called night-gaunts—faceless humanoids with black, rubbery skin, bat-like wings, and barbed tails, who carried off their victims to Dreamland. The nocturnal visitors were so terrifying that Howard remembered trying desperately to stay awake every night during this period of his life. These dreams, which haunted him for more than a year, apparently had a powerful influence on his fiction.

From a Christian perspective, it's a shame that Lovecraft's mother, who raised Howard from age three with his aunts after his father was committed to a psychiatric hospital, failed to recognize the phenomenon for what it was—demonic oppression of her only child. But by the late nineteenth century, the Western world didn't have room in its scientific worldview for such things. In fact, despite his personal experience with what many would call the spirit realm, Lovecraft claimed to be an atheist throughout his life.

In spite of his disbelief, the fiction of H. P. Lovecraft has been adapted and adopted by occultists around the world. The man who died a pauper not only found an audience over the last eighty years, Lovecraft has inspired an army of authors who have preserved and expanded the nightmarish universe that sprang from his tortured dreams.

Although Lovecraft claimed he didn't believe in the supernatural, he was more than happy to use the spirit realm as grist for his writing mill. He apparently saw potential in the doctrines of nineteenth-century occultist Helena Petrovna Blavatsky for stories that would sell. And they did—but mostly after his death. During his lifetime, Lovecraft was barely known outside the readership of pulp magazines.

While Lovecraft may have rejected the idea of lost continents like Atlantis or Lemuria as the forgotten motherland of humanity, a popular pseudoscientific theory in the late nineteenth century, the concept served him well as an author. The notion that certain humans gifted (or cursed) with the ability to see beyond the veil were communicating with evil intelligences vastly greater than our own also made for compelling horror. Lovecraft viewed the universe as a cold, unfeeling place, so in his fiction those entities, unlike the kindly "ascended masters" of Blavatsky's Theosophical teachings, had no use for humanity—except as slaves or sacrifices. The horror of discovering that one is at the mercy of immense, ancient beings incapable of mercy is a common theme in Lovecraft's tales, and he gave those ideas flesh and bone with carefully crafted prose that infused them with a sense of dread not often distilled onto the printed page.

It's fair to say that Lovecraft's style of gothic horror has had a powerful influence on horror fiction and film over the last seventy-five years. Stephen King, Roger Corman, John Carpenter, and Ridley Scott, among others, drew on Lovecraft's style, if not lifted directly from his Cthulhu mythos, a series of stories that began with his 1928 classic, "The Call of Cthulhu." Maybe that's not the kind of legacy left by Ernest Hemingway or F. Scott Fitzgerald, but compare the number of people who have seen *The Thing, Alien*, or any movie based on a King novel (*The Shining, The Stand, It*, etc.) to the number of people who've actually *read* Hemingway or Fitzgerald, and a good case can be made that Lovecraft was far more influential on pop culture than the literary greats who were his contemporaries.

And, as we'll see, Lovecraft's influence has bled over into the metaphysical realm. Maybe it's fitting that the principalities and powers aligned against their Creator would find an atheist a most useful tool.

While Lovecraft was beginning his career as a writer, across the ocean, another man fascinated with the influence of old gods on our world was hearing voices from beyond. Edward Alexander "Aleister" Crowley, born 1875 in Warwickshire, England, traveled to Cairo in 1904 with his new bride, Rose Kelly. While there, Crowley, who'd been a member of the Order of the Golden Dawn about five years earlier, set up a temple room in their apartment and began performing rituals to invoke Egyptian deities. Eventually, something calling itself Aiwass, the messenger of Hoor-Paar-Kraat (known to the Greeks as an aspect of Horus, Harpocrates, the god of silence), answered. Over a period of three days, April 8–10, 1904, Crowley transcribed what he heard from the voice of Aiwass.

> The Voice of Aiwass came apparently from over my left shoulder, from the furthest corner of the room....
>
> I had a strong impression that the speaker was actually in the corner where he seemed to be, in a body of "fine matter," transparent as a veil of gauze, or a cloud of incense-smoke. He seemed to be a tall, dark man in his thirties, well-knit, active and strong, with the face of a savage king, and eyes veiled lest their gaze should destroy what they saw. The dress was not Arab; it suggested Assyria or Persia, but very vaguely. I took little note of it, for to me at that time Aiwass and an "angel" such as I had often seen in visions, a being purely astral.
>
> I now incline to believe that Aiwass is not only the God or Demon or Devil once held holy in Sumer, and mine own Guardian Angel, but also a man as I am, insofar as He uses a human body to make His magical link with Mankind, whom He loves.[293]

That eventually became the central text for Crowley's new religion, Thelema, which in turn is the basis for Ordo Templi Orientis (OTO), a secret society similar to Freemasonry that, like Blavatsky's Theosophical Society and the Freemasons, believes in universal brotherhood. The primary difference between Thelema and Theosophy is in the nature of the entities sending messages from beyond. Blavatsky claimed to hear from ascended masters who shepherded humanity's evolution; Crowley claimed he was guided by gods from the Egyptian pantheon: namely, Nuit, Hadit, and Ra-Hoor-Khuit.

The irony of all this is that Lovecraft, who denied the existence of

Crowley's gods and Blavatsky's mahatmas, may have drawn his inspiration from the same supernatural, spiritual well.

A key thread woven through the fiction of H. P. Lovecraft was a fictional grimoire, or book of witchcraft, called the *Necronomicon*. The book, according to the Lovecraft canon, was written in the eighth century AD by the "Mad Arab," Abdul Alhazred (Lovecraft's childhood nickname—"all has read"—because of his love for the book *1001 Arabian Nights*). Perhaps significantly, inspiration for the invented grimoire came to Lovecraft in a dream (Jason Colavito, "Inside the Necronomicon," *Lost Civilizations Uncovered* [2002], http://jcolavito.tripod. com/lostcivilizations/id25.html, retrieved 8/6/17) and through his many letters to friends and colleagues (by one estimate, Lovecraft wrote about a hundred thousand), he encouraged others to incorporate the mysterious tome in their works. Over time, references to the *Necronomicon* by a growing number of authors creating Lovecraftian fiction led to a growing belief that the book was, in fact, real. One of those who believed in the book was occultist Kenneth Grant.

Grant was an English ceremonial magician and an acolyte of Crowley, serving as Crowley's personal secretary toward the end of his life. After Crowley's death, Grant was named head of the OTO in Britain by Crowley's successor, Karl Germer. However, Grant's promotion of an extraterrestrial "Sirius/Set current" in Crowley's work infuriated Germer, who expelled Grant from the organization for heresy. (Declan O'Neill, "Kenneth Grant: Writer and occultist who championed Aleister Crowley and Austin Osman Spare," *The Independent* [March 4, 2011], http://www. independent.co.uk/news/obituaries/kenneth-grant-writer-and-occultist-who-championed-aleister-crowley-and-austin-osman-spare-2231570. html, retrieved 8/5/17).

Lovecraft's fiction inspired some of Grant's innovations to Thelema. Grant said Lovecraft "snatched from nightmare-space his lurid dream-readings of the *Necronomicon*." Instead of attributing the *Necronomicon* to Lovecraft's imagination, Grant took it as evidence of the tome's existence as an astral book. (Daniel Harms and John Wisdom Gonce, *The Necronomicon Files*: The Truth Behind Lovecraft's Legend [Boston, MA: Weiser Books, 2003], pp. 109–110.) Furthermore, Grant believed others, including Crowley and Blavatsky, had "glimpsed the akashic *Necronomicon*" (Ibid.)—a reference to the Akashic records, a Theosophist concept describing a collection of all human thoughts, deeds, and emotions that exists on another plane of reality accessed only through proper spiritual discipline.

Kenneth Grant was perhaps the first to notice the strange parallels between the writings of H. P. Lovecraft and Aleister Crowley. In *The Dark Lord*, an extensive analysis of Grant's magickal system and Lovecraft's influence on it, researcher and author Peter Levenda documented a number of these similarities.

> In 1907, Crowley was writing some of the works that became seminal to the doctrines of Thelema, known as The Holy Books. These include Liber Liberi vel Lapidus Lazuli, Liber Cordis Cincti Serpente, and other works written between October 30 and November 1 of that year, and Liber Arcanorum and Liber Carcerorum, written between December 5th and 14th that same year. Lovecraft would have had no knowledge of this, as he was only a seventeen-year old recluse living at home on Angell Street in Providence, Rhode Island, dreaming of the stars.
>
> Instead, he later would write of an orgiastic ritual taking place that year in the bayous outside New Orleans, Louisiana, and on the very same day that Crowley was writing the books enumerated above. The story Lovecraft wrote is entitled "The Call of Cthulhu" and is arguably his most famous work. He wrote the story in 1926, in late August or early September, but placed the action in New Orleans in 1907 and later in Providence in 1925.
>
> How is this relevant? Lovecraft's placement of the orgiastic ritual in honor of the high priest of the Great Old Ones,

Cthulhu, and the discovery of a statue of Cthulhu by the New Orleans police on Halloween, 1907 coincides precisely with Crowley's fevered writing of his own gothic prose. In the Liber Liberi vel Lapidus Lazuli, for instance, Crowley writes the word "Tutulu" for the first time. He claims not to know what this word means, or where it came from. As the name of Lovecraft's fictional alien god can be pronounced "Kutulu," it seems more than coincidental, as Kenneth Grant himself noted.

However, this is only the tip of an eldritch iceberg. In Crowley's Liber Cordis Cincti Serpente—or "The Book of the Heart Girt with a Serpent"—there are numerous references to the "Abyss of the Great Deep," to Typhon, Python, and the appearance of an "old gnarled fish" with tentacles...all descriptions that match Lovecraft's imagined Cthulhu perfectly. Not approximately, but perfectly. Crowley's volume was written on November 1, 1907. The ritual for Cthulhu in New Orleans took place on the same day, month and year. (Peter Levenda, *The Dark Lord: H. P. Lovecraft, Kenneth Grant, and the Typhonian Tradition in Magic* [Lake Worth, FL: Ibis Press, 2013], pp. 97–98.)

Now, this could be nothing more than a strange coincidence. Your authors, however, are not coincidence theorists. Levenda, an excellent researcher and a gifted author (and more on just how gifted shortly), and Kenneth Grant before him, also concluded otherwise.

Both men—the American author and the English magician—were dealing with the same subject matter, and indeed Lovecraft had dated the first appearance of the Cthulhu statue to the same year, month and day that Crowley began writing these sections of the Holy Books. There is no hard evidence that either man knew of the other, although the author believes that references to an English satanist in Lovecraft's "The Thing on the Doorstep" could be an allusion to Crowley. In any event, to suggest that these two men cooperated or collaborated in any deliberate way would be the height (or depth!) of conspiracy theory.

It may actually be more logical to suggest—as an explanation for some of these coincidences—that darker forces were at work. In fact, it is possible that the same forces of which Lovecraft himself writes—the telepathic communication between followers of Cthulhu and the Great Old Ones—was what prompted him to write these fictional accounts of real events. Either Lovecraft was in some kind of telepathic communication with Crowley, or both men were in telepathic communication with…Something Else. (Ibid, pp. 102–103.)

As Christians, we're inclined to go with "Something Else." If the apostle Paul knew his theology—and he did—then we must consider the influence of principalities and powers on our natural world. And that's the most likely source of the odd, highly improbable Crowley-Cthulhu connection.

In the early 1970s, Grant would break with the American OTO and form his own Thelemic organization, the Typhonian OTO. The "Sirius/Set current" that Grant identified in the '50s referred to the Egyptian deity Set, god of the desert, storms, foreigners, violence, and chaos. To grasp the significance of Grant's innovation to Crowley's religion, a brief history of Set is in order.

Set—sometimes called "Seth," "Sheth," or "Sutekh"—is one of the oldest gods in the Egyptian pantheon. There is evidence that he was worshiped long before the pharaohs, in the predynastic era called Naqada I, which may date as far back as 3750 BC. To put that into context, we estimate the that the Tower of Babel incident probably occurred between 3500 and 3100 BC. Writing wasn't invented in Sumer until about 3000 BC, around the time of the first pharaoh, Narmer (whom some researchers identify as Nimrod).[294]

Set was originally one of the good guys. He protected Ra's solar boat, defending it from the evil chaos serpent Apep (or Apophis), who tried to eat the sun every night as it dropped below the horizon. During the Second Intermediate Period, roughly 1750 to 1550 BC, Semitic people called the Hyksos (actually Amorites) equated Set with Baal, the Canaanite storm-god, and scholars have concluded that Ba'al-Set was the lord of Avaris, the Hyksos capital.

But the worship of Baal-Set continued even after the Hyksos were driven out of Egypt. Two centuries after Moses led the Israelites to Canaan, Ramesses the Great erected a memorial called the Year 400 Stela to honor the four hundredth year of Set's arrival in Egypt. In fact, Ramesses' father was named Seti, which literally means "man of Set."

Set didn't acquire his evil reputation until the Third Intermediate Period, during which Egypt was overrun by successive waves of foreign invaders. After being conquered by Nubia, Assyria, and Persia, one after another between 728 BC and 525 BC, the god of foreigners wasn't welcome around the pyramids anymore. No longer was Set the dangerous rabble-rouser whose appetite for destruction kept Apophis from eating the sun; now Set was the evil god who murdered his brother, Osiris, and the sworn enemy of Osiris' son, Horus.

By the time of Persia's rise, Greek civilization was beginning to flower, and they identified Set with Typhon, their terrifying, powerful serpentine god of chaos. There's the link between Set and Typhon, and this is the entity Kenneth Grant believed was the true source of power in Thelemic magick. That's why the "Sirius/Set current" led to the Typhonian OTO, and that's the destructive, chaos-monster aspect of Set-Typhon we need to keep in view when analyzing the magickal system Grant created by filtering Crowley through Lovecraft.

Grant's anxiety—as expressed in *Nightside of Eden* and in his other works—is that the Earth is being infiltrated by a race of extraterrestrial beings who will cause tremendous changes to

221

take place in our world. This statement is not to be taken quite as literally as it appears, for the "Earth" can be taken to mean our current level of conscious awareness, and extraterrestrial would mean simply "not of this current level of conscious awareness." But the potential for danger is there, and Grant's work—like Lovecraft's—is an attempt to warn us of the impending (potentially dramatic) alterations in our physical, mental and emotional states due to powerful influences from "outside." (Ibid., p. 75.)

By the 1970s, Lovecraft's work had found a new audience, and his stories were being mined by Hollywood (for example *The Dunwich Horror*, starring Dean Stockwell and Sandra Dee, and several episodes of Rod Serling's *Night Gallery*). Then in 1977, a hardback edition of the *Necronomicon* suddenly appeared (published in a limited run of 666 copies—see what they did there?) (Colavito, op. cit.) edited by a mysterious figure known only as "Simon," purportedly a bishop in the Eastern Orthodox Church. According to Simon, two monks from his denomination had stolen a copy of the actual *Necronomicon* in one of the most daring book thefts in history.

Apparently, the good bishop wasn't above earning a few bucks by publishing a stolen heretical text.

A mass-market paperback edition followed a few years later. That version has reportedly sold more than a million copies over the last four decades. Kenneth Grant validated the text, going so far as to offer explanations for apparent discrepancies between Crowley and the *Necronomicon*.

Crowley admitted to not having heard correctly certain words during the transmission of Liber L, and it is probable that he misheard the word Tutulu. It may have been Kutulu, in which case it would be identical phonetically, but not qabalistically, with Cthulhu. The Schlangekraft recension of the *Necronomi-*

con (Introduction, p.xix) suggests a relationship between Kutulu and Cutha. ("Remembering Kenneth Grant's Understanding of The Necronomicon Tradition," *Warlock Asylum International News* [Feb. 18, 2011]. https://warlockasyluminternationalnews. com/2011/02/18/ remembering-kenneth-grants-understanding-of-the-necronomicon-tradition/, retrieved 8/30/19).

The "Schlangekraft recension" refers to the Simon *Necronomicon*, which was just one of several grimoires circulating in the '70s that claimed to be the nefarious book. The others were either obvious fakes published for entertainment purposes, or hoaxes that their authors admitted to soon after publication. Simon, on the other hand, appeared to be serious.

By the way, we note that Cutha, a city in ancient Babylonia, was the city sacred to Nergal, the plague-god and gatekeeper of the underworld known in western Mesopotamia as Resheph and to the Greeks and Romans as Apollo. Since *lu* was Sumerian for "man," is the name Cthulhu—*cutha-lu*—a reference to the "man of Cutha"? If so, it links one of the great figures of horror fiction with the *actual* horror of an ancient god of the dead.

Well, maybe. But here's the thing: People involved with producing the "Simonomicon" have admitted to making the whole thing up, and the man behind the book was the aforementioned Peter Levenda.

The text itself was Levenda's creation, a synthesis of Sumerian and later Babylonian myths and texts peppered with names of entities from H. P. Lovecraft's notorious and enormously popular Cthulhu stories. Levenda seems to have drawn heavily on the works of Samuel Noah Kramer for the Sumerian, and almost certainly spent a great deal of time at the University of Pennsylvania library researching the thing. Structurally, the text was modeled on the wiccan Book of Shadows and the Goetia, a grimoire of doubtful authenticity itself dating from the late Middle Ages.

"Simon" was also Levenda's creation. He cultivated an elusive, secretive persona, giving him a fantastic and blatantly implausible line of [BS] to cover the book's origins. He had no telephone. He always wore business suits, in stark contrast to the flamboyant Renaissance fair, proto-goth costuming that dominated the scene. (Alan Cabal, "The Doom That Came to Chelsea," *Chelsea News* [June 10, 2003]. http://www.nypress.com/the-doom-that-came-to-chelsea/, retrieved 8/7/17).

In *The Dark Lord*, Levenda not only analyzed Kenneth Grant's magickal system and documented the synchronicities between Crowley and Lovecraft, he validated the supernatural authenticity of the fake *Necronomicon* that he created!

But this doesn't mean the *Necronomicon* is fake in the supernatural sense.

We can conclude that the hoax Necronomicons—at least the Hay-Wilson-Langford-Turner and Simon versions—falsely claim to be the work of the mad Arab Abdul Alhazred, but in so falsely attributing themselves, they signal their genuine inclusion in the grimoire genre. The misattribution is the mark of their genre, and their very falsity is the condition of their genuineness. The hoax Necronomicons are every bit as "authentic" as the Lesser Key of Solomon or the Sixth and Seventh Books of Moses. (Dan Clore, "The Lurker on the Threshold of Interpretation: Hoax Necronomicons and Paratextual Noise," *Lovecraft Studies* No. 42–43 [Autumn 2001]. http://www.geocities.ws/clorebeast/lurker.htm, retrieved 8/7/17).

So, while the published edition of the *Necronomicon* was obviously invented long after the deaths of H. P. Lovecraft and Aleister Crowley, it's still a genuine tool for the practice of sorcery. And, as Grant and Levenda contend, the evidence points to Lovecraft and Crowley, the atheist and the occultist, hearing from the same demonic sources.

Now, you're probably wondering what this detour into fairly recent Western culture has to do with ancient cults of the dead. Hang on, because it's going to get even weirder. Lovecraft's fiction has been laundered and recycled into mainstream Western culture as a "scientific" alternative to God.

22

The Dead in Space

f Lovecraft used horror to introduce the idea of contact with an alien "other" to the masses, the growing popularity of science fiction in the twentieth century established ET as a common trope in popular entertainment. It's hard to imagine, but our great-grandparents would have had no idea what the phrase "little green men" was supposed to mean.

Nineteenth-century forerunners like Jules Verne and H. G. Wells demonstrated that fiction based on speculative science would sell. Verne's 1865 *From the Earth to the Moon* was the first major work to feature space travel; in 1898, Wells produced the first ET invasion story with his classic *The War of the Worlds*. Another Welles—Orson—transformed *The War of the Worlds* into a compelling radio drama on Halloween Eve in 1938, although the story that the program caused a national panic is, sadly, a myth. (Newspapers lost a lot of advertising revenue to the new medium during the Great Depression and took advantage of a golden opportunity to slam radio—an early example of "fake news.")[295]

The popularity of the genre took off in the 1920s with the arrival of the first pulp magazines that featured science fiction, such as *Amazing Stories*, *Weird Tales*, *Astounding Stories*, and *Wonder Stories*. The Golden

Age of science fiction arrived in 1937 when John W. Campbell took over as editor of *Astounding Science Fiction*. Campbell is widely considered the most influential editor of the early years of the genre, publishing first or early stories by Isaac Asimov, Lester del Rey, Robert Heinlein, A. E. Van Vogt, and Theodore Sturgeon, thus helping to launch the careers of many of the biggest names in twentieth-century science fiction.

In spite of his insistence that his writers research the science behind their stories, Campbell had an interest in parapsychology that grew over the years. Writers learned that topics like telepathy helped them sell stories to *Astounding*.[296] In 1949, Campbell discovered L. Ron Hubbard and published his first article on Dianetics, which Campbell described as "one of the most important articles ever published."[297] He suggested to some that Hubbard would win the Nobel Peace Prize for his creation.

Three years before selling Campbell on Dianetics, Hubbard participated in an event that falls smack into the "you can't make this stuff up" category: From January to March, 1946, Hubbard and Jack Parsons, rocket engineer and one of the founders of the Jet Propulsion Laboratory, performed a series of sex-magick rituals called the Babalon (sic) Working. It was intended to manifest an incarnation of the divine feminine, an ancient concept that reaches back to Inanna of ancient Sumer. Hubbard and Parsons based their ritual on the writings of Aleister Crowley described in his 1917 novel *Moonchild*.

So, through L. Ron Hubbard and Joseph Campbell, science fiction fans were connected to the Two Degrees of Aleister Crowley at the same time readers of gothic horror were plugged into the same spiritual source through the works of H. P. Lovecraft and his friends.

Campbell managed to capture the paranoia and dread that marked Lovecraft's work in his classic 1938 novella *Who Goes There?* The story has been adapted for the big screen three times—1951's *The Thing from Another World*, 1982's *The Thing*, starring Kurt Russell, and a 2011 prequel, also titled *The Thing*.

The Kurt Russell film, set in Antarctica, draws on key Lovecraftian themes—an ancient extraterrestrial horror that poses an existential threat to all life on earth, the loss of self as one is assimilated by the monster, and a claustrophobic setting. *The Thing* was set at an Antarctic research station, where the bitter cold confines most of the action to the interior of the base. The paranoia-inducing monster imitates its victims perfectly (similar to the ETs in the 1956 classic, *Invasion of the Body Snatchers*), which causes the base scientist, played by Wilford Brimley, to snap when he realizes just how quickly the creature could destroy the earth if it escapes the Antarctic—which makes Brimley's character an awful lot like the protagonists in many of Lovecraft's stories.

Even the setting near the South Pole recalls Lovecraft, whose classic novella *At the Mountains of Madness* introduced a theme that's been revisited over the years in films like *The X-Files* and *Alien vs. Predator*—there's something beneath the ice down there that shouldn't be disturbed.

> It is absolutely necessary, for the peace and safety of mankind, that some of earth's dark, dead corners and unplumbed depths be let alone; lest sleeping abnormalities wake to resurgent life, and blasphemously surviving nightmares squirm and splash out of their black lairs to newer and wider conquests.[298]

Not coincidentally, UFO enthusiasts are claiming to find alien craft half-buried in the Antarctic on a fairly regular basis these days.

By the time Campbell began to elevate science fiction out of the swamp of pulp fiction in the late 1930s, the concept of unfriendly (or, at best, uncaring) ETs intervening in earth's affairs was already several decades old. By the late 1940s, it was fodder for kiddie cartoons; Marvin the Martian and his Uranium PU-36 Explosive Space Modulator debuted in 1948, one year after Kenneth Arnold's UFO sighting at Mount Rainier and the famous crash near Roswell, New Mexico.

In the decades since, science fiction has become, in the words of Dr.

Michael S. Heiser, "televangelism for the ET religion."[299] People looking in from outside the genre may assume sci-fi is all rockets, ray guns, and lasers, but a great deal of it theological. Films like *Prometheus, Mission to Mars, Knowing,* and *2001: A Space Odyssey,* for example, conflate space travel, extraterrestrial intelligence, and religion. The 1994 film *Stargate* kicked off a long-running science-fiction franchise that centered on the return of the old gods to earth. Surprise—they're aliens!

The television series *Stargate SG-1* and its spinoffs continued that theme. The Norse pantheon was introduced in the series as the Asgard, whose appearance, according to the storyline, inspired stories of the alien greys (not a good look for Thor). In other words, the *Stargate* franchise built an entire alternate history for the world's largest religions that can be boiled down to one short sentence: They were all aliens. *SG-1* ran from 1997 through 2007, surpassing *The X-Files* as the longest-running science-fiction television series in North America at the time.

Comic heroes have also mined human theology for story arcs. It's hard to overstate the influence on three generations of American kids reading, and now watching through blockbuster Hollywood films, the thrilling adventures of gods in spandex:

> This culture is far more influential (and insidious) than most realize. Most contemporary action movies take their visual language from comic books. The rhythm of constant hyper-violence of today's action movies comes straight from Jack Kirby. Elvis Presley idolized Captain Marvel Jr., to the point of adopting his hairstyle....
>
> Although most of us don't realize it, there's simply nothing new about devotion to superheroes. Their powers, their costumes, and sometimes even their names are plucked straight from the pre-Christian religions of antiquity. When you go back and look at these heroes in their original incarnations, you can't help but be struck by how blatant their symbolism is and how

strongly they reflect they belief systems of the pagan age. What even fewer people realize is that this didn't occur by chance, but came directly out of the spiritual and mystical secret societies and cults of the late 19th century—groups like the Theosophists, the Rosicrucians, and the Golden Dawn. These groups turned their backs on the state cult of Christianity and reached back in time to the elemental deities of the ancient traditions.[300]

How has eighty years of pop culture promoting the ETI meme shaped our ideas about contact? Seth Shostak, lead astronomer for the SETI (Search for Extraterrestrial Intelligence) Institute, hits the nail on the head:

I think we are ready for ET contact in some sense, because the public has been conditioned to the idea of life in space by movies and TV. And if you go into a classroom with a bunch of 11 year olds and ask them, "How many of you kids think there are aliens out there?" they all raise their hands! Why? Is it because their parents have been educating them about astrobiology? No. It's because they've seen them on TV!...

I think that Hollywood is by far the biggest term in the equation of the public's reaction to confirmation of alien life.[301]

Exactly. But the public hasn't just been conditioned to accept the idea of extraterrestrial intelligence; we've been programmed to identify these ETIs as the old gods of earth, thus rebranding the fallen angels and demons who've been with us since the beginning and taking them out of a biblical context. Without that framework, they're no longer rebellious, destructive spirit beings; they're simply misunderstood space travelers demonized, as it were, by the small-minded leader of a group of nomadic Semites named Moses.

We showed in an earlier chapter that those demons are the spirits of the Nephilim, the mighty men of old venerated as Rephaim by the ancient Amorites and, all too often, the people of Israel.

It's the greatest marketing campaign in history. And we can lay a large share of the blame on a former hotel-manager-turned-"ancient aliens"-apologist, Erich von Däniken.

Interest in the occult enjoyed a renaissance in the Western world in the 1960s and '70s. Oddly enough, it was a French journal of science fiction that helped spark the revival, and it did so by translating and republishing the works of H. P. Lovecraft for a new audience. *Planète* was launched in the early '60s by Louis Pauwles and Jacques Bergier, and their magazine drew a new legion of admirers to Lovecraft. More significantly, however, was the book Pauwles and Bergier coauthored in 1960, *Les Matins des Magiciens* (*Morning of the Magicians*), which was translated into English in 1963 as *Dawn of Magic.*[302]

The book covered everything from pyramidology (the belief that the Egyptian pyramids held ancient secrets) to supposed advanced technology in the ancient world. Likewise, the authors praised Arthur Machen, the Irish author of horror fiction, about surviving Celtic mythological creatures, and they discussed the genius of H. P. Lovecraft in the same breath as the scientist Albert Einstein and psychoanalyst Carl Jung. From Lovecraft, Bergier and Pauwles borrowed the one thought that would be of more importance than any other in their book. As we have seen, *Morning of the Magicians* speculates that **extraterrestrial beings may be responsible for the rise of the human race and the development of its culture, a theme Lovecraft invented** (Emphasis added).[303]

The success of Pauwles and Bergier inspired others to run with the concepts they'd developed from the writings of Lovecraft. The most successful of these, without question, was Erich von Däniken's *Chariots of the Gods*, the best-selling English language archaeology book of all time.[304]

You can say one thing for von Däniken—he's not shy about challenging accepted history:

I claim that our forefathers received visits from the universe in the remote past, even though I do not yet know who these extraterrestrial intelligences were or from which planet they came. I nevertheless proclaim that these "strangers" annihilated part of mankind existing at the time and produced a new, perhaps the first, *homo sapiens*.[305]

The book was published in 1968, the same year Stanley Kubrick's epic adaptation of Arthur C. Clarke's *2001: A Space Odyssey* hit theaters. The film, based on the idea that advanced alien technology had guided human evolution, was the top-grossing film of the year, and was named the "greatest sci-fi film of all time" in 2002 by the Online Film Critics Society.[306] By 1971, when *Chariots of the Gods* finally appeared in American bookstores, NASA had put men on the moon three times, and the public was fully primed for what von Däniken was selling.

Chariots of the Gods has transformed the UFO research community and the worldviews of millions of people around the world. In 1973, *Twilight Zone* creator Rod Serling produced a documentary around *Chariots* titled *In Search of Ancient Astronauts*, which featured astronomer Carl Sagan and Wernher von Braun, architect of the Saturn V rocket.[307] The following year, a feature film with the same title as the book was released to theaters. By the turn of the twenty-first century, von Däniken had sold more than sixty million copies of his twenty-six books, all promoting the idea that our creators came from the stars.[308]

This, despite the fact that von Däniken told *National Enquirer* in a

1974 interview that his information came not through archaeological fieldwork, but through out-of-body travel to a place called Point Aleph, "a sort of fourth dimension" outside of space and time.[309]

The claims of von Däniken, to be kind, don't hold water. His theories have been debunked in great detail[310] and he's even admitted to just making stuff up,[311] but lack of evidence has never stopped crazy ideas for long. Remember how true believers refused to believe the Fox sisters when they debunked their own spiritualist movement.

Likewise, the work of the late Zecharia Sitchin continues to attract a faithful following, even though it's based translations from ancient Sumerian tablets that are either just badly wrong or invented from scratch to sell his theory. In a nutshell, Sitchin, who passed away in 2010, claimed that Mesopotamian iconography showed the existence of a forgotten planet called Nibiru beyond Neptune. This planet, Sitchin claimed, follows a highly elliptical orbit into the inner solar system about every 3,600 years with catastrophic consequences. Sitchin also equated the Anunnaki, the gods of Sumer, with the biblical Nephilim, and claimed that they arrived on earth some 450,000 years ago to mine gold in Africa.

Sitchin's theories are behind much of the Planet X angst that clogs the Internet. Bible scholar Dr. Michael S. Heiser, who can read Sumerian, has thoroughly debunked Sitchin's theories, even going so far as to post his personal tax returns to show that he wasn't trying to profit by publicly challenging Sitchin.[312] That hasn't stopped Sitchinites from continuing to spread the idea that the gods of the ancient world were astronauts from outside the solar system.

And now, thanks to a new generation of people who, like *The X-Files'* Fox Mulder, want to believe, *Ancient Aliens* and its imitators are still mining von Däniken gold five decades after his first book hit the shelves.

This deception is deliberate, and it's been very well executed. The old gods and their demon spawn, disguised as extraterrestrials, have been reaching out to some very important people.

23

Starships of the Dead

Without a doubt, *Star Trek* has been one of the most influential entertainment franchises in history. Captains Kirk and Picard, Mr. Spock, McCoy, Scotty, Data, Worf, and others are iconic characters, recognized all over the world. Oddly, though, series creator Gene Roddenberry is linked to CIA mind-control experiments, a group of "aliens" who claim to be the creators of humanity, and (why not?) the assassination of John F. Kennedy.

Let's back up to World War II. During the war, Andrija Puharich, the son of immigrants from the Balkans, attended Northwestern University outside Chicago where he earned a bachelor's degree in philosophy in 1942 and his MD in 1947. Through an invitation from a well-off family friend who'd married into the Borden dairy family, Puharich found himself in Maine in early 1948, where he established a research institute to pursue his interest in parapsychology, the Round Table Foundation of Electrobiology, usually shortened to the Round Table.[313]

An early member of the Puharich Round Table was Aldous Huxley, author of *Brave New World* and *The Doors of Perception*, a book about his experiences with mescaline. Puharich financed his research with gifts from donors, one of whom was Henry Wallace, who'd been vice president under Franklin D. Roosevelt. Wallace, a 32nd-degree Freemason, persuaded Roosevelt to add the reverse of the Great Seal of the United States, the pyramid and the all-seeing eye, to the one-dollar bill.[314]

This book isn't big enough to hold a full account of what Puharich was up to for the United States Army in the 1950s,[315] but the upshot is that he was apparently researching parapsychology and chemical substances that might stimulate the human mind to reach into realities beyond those we can normally perceive with our natural senses. At one of his gatherings in Maine, on New Year's Eve in 1952, Puharich and his Round Table, working with a Hindu channeler named Dr. D. G. Vinod, conducted a seance that apparently made contact with a group calling itself The Nine.[316] Thus began a truly breathtaking chapter in America's mostly hidden programs that searched for ways to weaponize the occult.

> Some months later, on June 27, 1953, the night of the full moon, Puharich gathered around him what was to be a core group of the Round Table Foundation for another session with Vinod. The membership of this group of nine members—á la The Nine—is illuminating. Henry Jackson, Georgia Jackson, Alice Bouverie, Marcella Du Pont, Carl Betz, Vonnie Beck, Arthur Young, Ruth Young, and Andrija Puharich. Dr. Vinod acted as the medium.
>
> Imagine the Fellowship of the Ring, with government funding and a security classification that was, well, "cosmic."[317]

This group included old money. *Very* old money. The Du Pont name is obvious, but some of the others were no less prominent. Alice Bouverie was an Astor—a descendent of John Jacob Astor and the daughter of Col. John Jacob Astor IV, who built the Astoria Hotel and went down with the Titanic. Arthur Young was the designer of the Bell helicopter; his wife had been born Ruth Forbes. Yes, *that* Forbes.

Ruth Young's previous marriage had been to George Lyman Paine, who was from another old-money family with roots in the early days of the American colonies. Their son, Michael Paine, married a woman named Ruth Hyde, and in 1963, Michael and Ruth Paine became friends with a young couple newly arrived from Russia, Lee and Marina Oswald.

Yes, *that* Lee Oswald. Lee Harvey.

So. A Du Pont, an Astor, and a Forbes/Paine, in a psychic research group funded by the US government, communicating telepathically with…who? Or what?

And what was the monkey-god doing there?

Dr. Vinod sat on the floor, the nine members of the group in a circle around him, with a copper plate on his lap, prayer beads in his hands, and a small statue of "Hanoum," a Hindu god that the author believes to be Hanuman, the Monkey King. If this is so, it is interesting in that Hanuman was a human being, a minister, before becoming divine due to his devotion and courage. The half-human, half-divine image is one that becomes more important and more obvious as this study progresses. Another important aspect of Hanuman is his depiction in much Indian art as holding an entire mountain in one hand (and a club in the other). When—in the Ramayana and during the battle of Rama and Ravana—Lakshmana was mortally wounded, Hanuman raced to a mountain covered with different healing herbs. Not knowing which one Lakshmana required, Hanuman simply brought the entire mountain. Hanuman—as well as his fellow monkey-men, the Vanaras of southern India—is often shown with his hand in front of his mouth, signifying "silence" as well as obedience, in much the same way western occultists depict Harpocrates. In this sense, replete with silence, obedience, a club, and a mountain of herbs, Hanuman might easily have been the patron saint of MK-ULTRA.[318]

What an interesting, um, coincidence. Occultist Aleister Crowley believed *The Book of the Law* was dictated to him by Aiwass, the messenger of Hoor-Paar-Kraat—Harpocrates, the god of silence.

Anyway, The Nine disclosed that they wanted the Round Table to lead a spiritual renewal on earth, and eventually revealed that they were extraterrestrials orbiting the planet in a giant, invisible spacecraft.

Remember, members of some of the wealthiest families in America bought this story. These were highly intelligent, very successful people. And Puharich later wrote, "We took every known precaution against fraud, and the staff and I became thoroughly convinced that we were dealing with some kind of an extraordinary extraterrestrial intelligence."[319] In other words, if this was a hoax, it was pulled off by entities intelligent enough to fool some very smart people.

Who might have a motive for such a deception? The clue is in the Nine's declared identity: "God is nobody else than we together, the Nine Principles of God."[320]

Ah. So, The Nine were extraterrestrial *and* divine. That's the point of this chapter. Coincidentally (or not), while the Round Table was hearing from The Nine, Aleister Crowley's acolyte Kenneth Grant was developing his occult system based on an extraterrestrial chaos-god from Sirius, Set/Typhon.

Dr. Vinod returned to India in the mid-1950s after the early Round Table sessions, and contact with The Nine was interrupted for more than fifteen years. Then, in 1971, Puharich discovered Israeli psychic Uri Geller.

Geller, best known for his alleged power to bend silverware with his mind, became for a time the new link to The Nine. Through Geller, The Nine informed Puharich that his life's mission was "to alert the world to an imminent mass landing of spaceships that would bring representatives of The Nine."[321]

Obviously, that didn't happen. Geller moved on in 1973, so Puharich had to find someone else to bridge the gap between earth and the giant, invisible craft allegedly orbiting the earth. He eventually connected with former race car driver Sir John Whitmore and Florida psychic Phyllis Schlemmer, who became the authorized spokesperson for their contact within The Nine, who identified himself as "Tom."[322]

> Puharich, Whitmore and Schlemmer then set up Lab Nine at Puharich's estate in Ossining, New York. The Nine's disciples included multi-millionaire businessmen (many hiding behind pseudonyms and including members of Canada's richest family, the Bronfmans), European nobility, scientists from the Stamford Research Institute and at least one prominent political figure who was a personal friend of President Gerald Ford.[323]

Another member of the Bronfman clan has been in the news recently. Clare Bronfman, daughter of Seagrams chairman, Edgar Bronfman, pleaded guilty in April 2019 to charges stemming from her involvement in the NXVIUM sex cult.[324] Apparently, alternate forms of spirituality are popular with the Bronfmans.

So, if connecting members of some of the wealthiest families in North America, a personal friend of an American president, and parties linked to the Kennedy assassination to a group of entities who claimed to be extraterrestrial gods isn't weird enough, another member of the rebranded "Lab Nine" in 1974 and '75 was *Star Trek* creator Gene Roddenberry, who reportedly wrote a screenplay based on The Nine. Some believe that concepts from the channeling sessions Roddenberry attended surfaced in the early *Star Trek* movies and in the series *Star Trek: The Next Generation* and *Star Trek: Deep Space Nine*.

If DS9 wasn't inspired by The Nine, it would be one heck of a coincidence, wouldn't it?

Before Lab Nine folded in 1978, the identities of Tom and the Other Eight were finally revealed: Tom was actually Atum,[325] he said, the creator of the Great Ennead, the Egyptian gods worshiped at Heliopolis, near modern-day Cairo. Besides Atum, the Ennead included his children Shu and Tefnut; their children Geb and Nut; and their children Osiris, Isis, Set, Nephthys, and sometimes the son of Osiris and Isis, Horus.[326]

Connecting dots between Andrija Puharich, who was almost certainly a CIA asset during much of the time he conducted parapsychological research,[327] and the volunteers of his Round Table and Lab Nine, we can tie the United States government (and specifically the US Army and CIA during the period of mind-control research projects like ARTI-CHOKE, BLUEBIRD, and MKULTRA),[328] members of upper-class society from the East Coast and Canada, the creator of the most successful science-fiction entertainment franchise in history, extraterrestrials, and gods. And not just any gods—it was the pantheon that included the chaos-god, Set, who Crowleyite Kenneth Grant believed was the spirit of the age.

Oh, yes—and the Kennedy assassination.

How do we wrap our heads around this? Considering that Puharich was, in all likelihood, doing this research for the American government, and that he led the witnesses, suggesting to Geller and at least one of his successors while they were under hypnosis that they were being contacted by The Nine,[329] this may have been a long PSYOP to stir up belief in the existence of extraterrestrial intelligences, who were the old gods worshiped by our distant ancestors.

To what end? For Puharich and his superiors, maybe it was an experiment on group dynamics, or maybe a research into how people would react to the imminent arrival of extraterrestrial visitors. Or maybe, as with the Paul Bennewitz affair,[330] it was an intelligence op to misdirect the wealthy members of Lab Nine and their influential social circles toward an ETI explanation for anomalous aerial phenomena and away from secret government projects.

Ancient alien evangelists have effectively proselytized the American public in recent years. Recent research shows that more adults in the US believe in ETs than in the God of the Bible.[331] The irony is that long-time UFO researchers—the serious ones, anyway—are disturbed by the impact the ancient alien meme has had on their work.

MUFON, the Mutual UFO Network, which bills itself "the world's oldest and largest UFO phenomenon investigative body,"[332] is all in lately, endorsing pseudoscientific and often New Age and openly occultic interpretations of the UFO phenomenon instead of sticking to what can be supported by evidence—by which we mean something more solid that uncorroborated accounts by "insiders." For example, the theme of MUFON's 2017 national convention was "The Case for a Secret Space Program," which was described by one critic as "blatantly unscientific and irrational."[333]

The conference featured among its speakers a man who claims he was recruited for "a '20 & Back' assignment which involved age regression (via Pharmaceutical means) as well as time regressed to the point of beginning service." In plain English, he allegedly served twenty years with an off-planet research project. Then he was sent back in time to a few minutes after he left and "age-regressed" so that no one would notice that he's twenty years older than the rest of us.[334]

We'll pause until you stop laughing.

Another speaker claimed he was preidentified as a future president of the United States in a CIA/DARPA (Defense Advanced Research Projects Agency) program called Project Pegasus, which purportedly gathered intel on past and future events, such as the identities of future presidents. The speaker also claimed he was a roommate of Barack Obama in 1980 as part of an alleged CIA project called Mars Jump Room,[335] a teleportation program to send trainees to a secret base on the Red Planet.[336]

The content was so over the top that Richard Dolan, a respected ufologist and longtime advocate for ETI disclosure, found it necessary to publicly explain why he appeared on a MUFON-sanctioned discussion panel with men who claimed, with no corroboration whatsoever, they'd been part of a "secret space program."

When I learned I would be on a panel with Corey [Goode], Andy [Basiago], Bill [Tompkins], and Michael [Salla], I phoned Jan [Harzan, MUFON's executive director] and politely asked him what was he thinking. I mentioned my concern about MUFON's decision to bring in individuals with claims that are inherently impossible to verify. MUFON, after all, is supposed to have evidence-based standards.[337]

Maybe it shouldn't surprise us that MUFON has morphed from an "evidence-based" organization to one that actively promotes unverifiable claims at its national convention. As controversy grew over the theme of MUFON's 2017 symposium, it was revealed that MUFON's "Inner Circle," a group that provides "advisory guidance" to MUFON because its members—thirteen in all, a curiously coincidental number—have "shown unparalleled generosity towards MUFON by donating in excess of $5,000 in a single donation," included New Age teacher J. Z. Knight.[338]

Knight, who, strangely enough, was born in Roswell, New Mexico (in March, 1946, just about the time Jack Parsons and L. Ron Hubbard were wrapping up their Babalon Working), claims to channel the spirit of Ramtha the Enlightened One, a warrior who lived thirty-five thousand years ago in the mythical land of Lemuria. Knight says Ramtha fought against the tyrannical Atlanteans before eventually bidding his troops farewell and ascending to heaven in a flash of light.[339]

Ten years after Ramtha's first appearance, Knight founded Ramtha's School of Enlightenment, through which she has become a very wealthy woman by selling counseling sessions based on the wisdom of the ancient Lemurian warrior. (While Ramtha has no need for creature comforts, Ms. Knight apparently likes nice things.) As of 2017, the school employed eighty full-time staff,[340] and annual profits from book and audio sales ran into the millions.[341] According to Knight, Ramtha's teachings can be boiled down to mind over matter: "Ramtha tells people that if they learn what to do, the art of creating your own reality is really a divine act. There's no guru here. You are creating your day. You do it yourself."[342]

There we go: "Ye shall be as gods." Call us skeptical, but your authors assume that Ms. Knight still looks both ways before crossing the street. Creating your own reality has its limits.

As Christians, we must look past the human actors in movements like this. In the case of The Nine, how did the spirits benefit from their charade? Spreading spiritual confusion is our guess. Seeding these ideas through influential members of high society and the military-industrial complex would be a good way to do it. It's one thing to mock a blue-collar worker from rural America when he claims he's in contact with aliens, but it's a different story when those spreading the ET gospel are from the wealthiest, most politically influential families in the world.

Spreading confusion about the Big Questions—where did we come from, why are we here, where do we go when we die—may be enough for the principalities, powers, thrones, and dominions. On the other hand, it may just be a PSYOP to prepare for the final conflict—the war of Gog and Magog, which culminates at Armageddon, the battle for the holy mountain of God.

Ask yourself this question: If contactees in the UFO community are hearing from beings so advanced that they've solved the monumental technological challenges of traveling across the vast black gulfs of inter-stellar space, why are their messages telepathic? On a physical level, that's no different from communicating with spirits through a medium. Some true believers contend that it's not spiritual, it's simply advanced technology that we don't yet understand.

Fine. If these super-advanced entities really want to communicate with us earthlings, why narrowcast a message to one person at a time in a way that can't be corroborated? (And why are their messages so contra-dictory? They can't seem to decide where they're from—but we digress.) They've crossed the galaxy but they can't broadcast a radio signal? Use a webcam? Flash their headlights? Send up a flare? Land on the White House lawn and say, "Klaatu barada nikto"?

Skeptics are free to believe what they like, but the Hebrew prophets and apostles had other witnesses to the messages and miracles of God. According to Paul, the risen Christ appeared to "more than five hundred brothers at one time,"[343] a resurrection, remember, that Jesus prophesied and then fulfilled to confirm his claim of godhood. As of this writing, we're still waiting for independent confirmation that Blavatsky's ascended masters, Crowley's Aiwass, Atum of The Nine, or J. Z. Knight's Ramtha are who they claim to be.

We assume they're real. Why do their followers assume they're not lying?

This is an important question. Drawing the wrong conclusion could leave you on the wrong side of eternity. The principalities and powers are preparing their ground game for the final assault on the holy mountain of God. Deceiving the world into misidentifying them when they finally appear is just one more lie in a long string of mistruths that lead all the way back to Eden.

Part Eight

RETURN OF THE DEAD

24

Warriors of the Dead

The Bible records a military excursion in the days of Abraham that must have been a huge geopolitical incident at the time. Chapter 14 of Genesis tells us that kings from as far away as modern Iran marched their armies across Mesopotamia to go to war against a coalition in the southern Levant who apparently challenged the authority of their sovereigns in the east. Chedorlaomer of Elam led the invading group, aided by his allies, Amraphel of Shinar (Sumer), Arioch of Ellasar, and Tidal of Goiim.

Historians haven't been able to identify these men; Chedorlaomer may be a transliteration of Kudur-Lagamar ("Servant of Lagamar," a goddess in the Elamite pantheon),[344] although that name isn't among the forty or so kings of Elam that we know about. Once upon a time, it was believed that Amraphel was the famous Hammurabi of Babylon, but the War of the Nine Kings took place about a hundred years before Hammurabi's time, and it's unlikely the great king would have been depicted as a junior member of the coalition. Arioch is a name found in extrabiblical sources from that period, as well as in the Book of Daniel, but Ellasar in unidentified—likewise, the kingdom of Goiim, which means "nations" or "Gentiles." That could be anywhere. The king's name may be a transliteration of a name known among the Hittite royal house, Tudhaliya,[345] but the earliest of the kings with that name, like Hammurabi, arrived on the scene long after this war.

Our own timeline of the age of the patriarchs puts this conflict around 1850 BC.[346] The lands of the Bible were emerging from a century of chaos after the collapse of the Third Dynasty of Ur, the last Sumerian rulers to reign over Mesopotamia. The events of Genesis 14 are plausible in that environment even if we can't nail down the participants.

The same goes for the kings of the Dead Sea coalition. There haven't been any archaeological discoveries that can positively identify Sodom, much less the cities of the plain—although, as we noted earlier, the site of Tall el-Hammam in Jordan, about eight miles northeast of the Dead Sea and six miles northwest of Mount Nebo, is the most likely candidate for Sodom.[347]

The point of this chapter, however, is not the battle in the Valley of Siddim. It's what happened *before*.

> In the fourteenth year Chedorlaomer and the kings who were with him came and defeated the Rephaim in Ashteroth-karnaim, the Zuzim in Ham, the Emim in Shaveh-kiriathaim, and the Horites in their hill country of Seir as far as El-paran on the border of the wilderness. Then they turned back and came to En-mishpat (that is, Kadesh) and defeated all the country of the Amalekites, and also the Amorites who were dwelling in Hazazon-tamar. (Genesis 14:5–7)

On their way to fight the kings of Sodom, Gomorrah, and their allies, probably for control of the King's Highway, a vital trade route connecting Egypt to Mesopotamia, the kings of the east had to defeat Rephaim tribes along the road, which ran east of the Jordan River, parallel to the Jordan Rift Valley. The first few battles were fought against tribes whose lands later fell to the people of Ammon, Moab, and Edom. Kadesh was at the southern boundary of the land allotted to Judah,[348] and it was the campsite for Israel for most of their time in the wilderness before crossing the Jordan—and possibly located at Petra.[349] Seir refers to the Shara mountains, which run along the east side of the Aravah, the valley that connects the Dead Sea to the Red Sea at Eilat and Aqaba. Hazazon-tamar is equated with Ein Gedi,[350] an oasis near Qumran and Masada, about halfway up the west side of the Dead Sea.

This mission was apparently directed against troublemaking city-states, Rephaim tribes, and their allies from Mount Hermon to the Gulf of Aqaba. This was no quick police action. Marching from western Persia to the area around the Dead Sea was a three- or four-month journey. Then, based on the location of the battle sites and our best guess about the tar pits, which today are clustered around the west side of the Dead Sea (today they manifest as sinkholes, and the danger areas are mostly north of Ein Gedi),[351] the kings of the east apparently traveled south along the King's Highway, doubled back to Kadesh (Petra), and then marched north along the west side of the Dead Sea, defeating the Amorites at Ein Gedi, and then fought the Sodom alliance somewhere *north* of the sea, not south, as is traditionally believed. That route makes sense, and it fits the theory that Tall el-Hammam was Sodom. It would also explain how Abraham, who was pasturing his flocks west of the Jordan, was able to get out after the eastern alliance so quickly.

All of this, however, is prelude to the point of this chapter: The tribes called Rephaim along the King's Highway were a big enough security problem in the days of Abraham that an army *marched all the way from Persia to put them down.* By the time Moses began directing the conquest of Canaan in 1406 BC, only Og of Bashan was hanging on, the last of the remnant of the Rephaim. Yet, ritual texts from Ugarit a couple hundred years later treated the Rephaim as a special group among the spirits in the underworld—the way Ezekiel described the "mighty Nephilim of ancient times" in Sheol more than six hundred years later.

As we noted earlier, the *Rpum* (Rephaim) in the Ugaritic texts were connected to a "semi-mythical warrior tribe," the Tidanu, known from Sumerian texts a couple hundred years before the time of Abraham. The violent tendencies of this group, then, were part of their image. They were summoned in rituals described in several texts that have only been translated since World War II, and some only since the 1980s, so the context they give us to understand some of the weirder parts of the Bible, like the Rephaim/Nephilim references in Ezekiel 32, Isaiah 14, and a few other scattered references in the Old Testament, weren't available to Bible scholars until now.

Probably the most striking of the Ugarit texts is for a ritual that was apparently performed at the coronation of Ammurapi III, the last king of Ugarit, around 1200 BC. It was clearly a necromancy rite, summoning the Rephaim to bless the new king.

> "Sacrifice of the Shades" liturgy:
> You are summoned, O Rephaim of the earth,
> You are invoked, O council of the Didanu!
> Ulkn, the Raphi', is summoned,
> Trmn, the Raphi', is summoned,
> Sdn-w-rdn is summoned,
> Tr 'llmn is summoned,
> The Rephaim of old are summoned!
> You are summoned, O Rephaim of the earth,
> You are invoked, O council of the Didanu![352]

The "council of the Didanu" is another reference to that warlike tribe of venerated ancestors, the Tidanu, which, you remember, is the origin of the name of the old Greek gods, the Titans. That assembly shows up in other Ugaritic texts, such as *The Legend of Keret*, a tale of a king lamenting his misfortunes, including the lack of an heir. In the story, the high god El blesses Keret:

Be greatly exalted, Keret,
among the *rpum* of the underworld,
in the convocation of the assembly of Ditan.[353]

This further links the Rephaim to the council/assembly of the Didanu/Ditanu/Tidanu. And a fragmentary ritual text, RS 24.248 (KTU 1.104), mentions "the temple of Ditanu," making it clear that this council or assembly was more than just the honored dead; they were counted among the gods.[354]

Interestingly, and probably not coincidentally, one of the veiled references to the Rephaim in the Old Testament mocks those who hoped to join that assembly after death:

One who wanders from the way of good sense
will rest in the assembly of the dead [*rephaim*]. (Proverbs 21:16)

The best known of the Ugaritic texts are designated KTU 1.20–1.22, the so-called Rephaim Texts. Scholars argue over their precise meaning because they're hard to translate, but it seems clear that the spirits of the mighty warriors of long ago were summoned to a ritual meal, similar to the *kispum*, at the tabernacle of the Canaanite creator-god, El.

The saviours [*rpum*] will feast:
seven times the divinities
    [*ilnym* (Ugaritic form of Hebrew *elohim*)],
eight times the dead....
The saviours hurried to his sanctuary,
to his sanctuary hurried the divinities.[355]

The sanctuary belonged to the Canaanite creator-god, El. All three of the Rephaim texts refer to El's sanctuary, palace, house, plantations, or threshing floor, where a banquet awaits the Rephaim. (Note: The concept of meeting a god on a threshing floor is an idea we explore else-where in this book.) Several lines toward the end of KTU 1.22 describe El's abode as a "lofty banqueting-house on the peak in the heart of the Lebanon,"[356] it's probable that the location of El's sanctuary was located on Mount Hermon, which is significant.[357] It's also important to note that some scholars translate KTU 1.22, column i, lines 8 and 9, to read, "There rose up Baal Rapiu, the warriors of Baal and the warriors of Anat [the Canaanite war-goddess]."[358]

But what's even more significant is how these "warriors of Baal" trav-eled to El's threshing floor:

The [Rephaim] hurried to his sanctuary,[359]
to his sanctuary hurried the [elohim].
The chariots they harnessed;
the horses they hitched,…
They mounted their chariots,
they came on their mounts.
They journeyed a day
and a second.
After sunrise on the third
the [Rephaim] arrived at the threshing-floors,
the [elohim] at the plantations.
Then Danel the man of healing [literally, "man of Rapiu"]
answered,
the hero, the devotee of *Hrnm*
[possibly a reference to Mount Hermon],[360] replied
The [Rephaim] arrived at the threshing-floors,
the [elohim] at the plantations.[361] (Emphasis added)

The reference to the travel time of the Rephaim and their arrival at the sanctuary of El "after sunrise on the third" day is found in all three of the Rephaim texts. If you're a Christian, the significance is impossible to miss. Especially when you add this bit:

> There, shoulder to shoulder were the brothers,
> whom El made to stand up in haste.
> There the name of El revivified the dead,
> the blessings of the name of El revivified the heroes.
> There rose up Baal Rapiu,
> the warriors of Baal and the warriors of Anat.[362]

Did you catch that? The purpose of the ritual, essentially a *kispum* rite for the spirits of the "mighty men who were of old," was to *resurrect them from the dead*.

And they arrived at dawn of the third day.

Yeah. "Wow," is right.

So, who is Baal Rapiu? "Lord Rapiu" may refer to Rapi'u, the underworld god who ruled from Ashtaroth and Edrei in Bashan, or it may be an epithet ("Lord of the Rephaim") of the storm-god Baal, king of the Canaanite pantheon. Other scholars translate that sentence, "There rose up the Rephaim of Baal,"[363] which fits with the following description of the Rephaim as the warriors of Baal and the war-goddess Anat.

Now, not all scholars of the Ugaritic texts agree that these rituals were intended to resurrect the Rephaim. That said, it's clear that the Amorites believed the dead weren't gone; they still had the power to affect the living, and the Rephaim were an exalted group in the afterlife who served the great gods Baal and El.

Why? We can only speculate, but from the clues in the Bible and the pagan texts with which the prophets would have been familiar (they were writing under the influence of the Holy Spirit, after all), it appears that the Infernal Council created their monstrous offspring to destroy humanity. When God derailed that plan through the Flood, the dark gods fell back to Plan B: turning the Rephaim spirits into the warriors of Baal—an end-times army that will march on the holy mountain of God.

25

Valley of the Travelers

One of the most well-known characters of end-times prophecy is Gog of Magog. In fact, it's safe to say he is *the* most well-known, since he is simply the Old Testament conception of the Antichrist. The war described by Ezekiel culminates in Armageddon, the battle for Zion, and the foot soldiers in the army of Gog/Antichrist will be the demonic spirits of the Rephaim.

Let's establish at the beginning of this chapter that Magog is not Russia, so we can forget about Vladimir Putin being Gog. As we go through this chapter, we'll explain why we should look for Gog to come from someplace closer to Jerusalem than Moscow.

The word of the LORD came to me: "Son of man, set your face toward Gog, of the land of Magog, the chief prince of Meshech and Tubal, and prophesy against him and say, Thus says the Lord GOD: Behold, I am against you, O Gog, chief prince of Meshech and Tubal. And I will turn you about and put hooks into your jaws, and I will bring you out, and all your army, horses and horsemen, all of them clothed in full armor, a great host, all of them with buckler and shield, wielding swords. Persia, Cush, and Put are with them, all of them with shield and helmet; Gomer and all his hordes; Beth-togarmah from the uttermost parts of the north with all his hordes—many peoples are with you." (Ezekiel 38:1–6)

In recent years, Magog has often been interpreted as southern Russia, hence the idea that a coalition led by Russia will attack Israel. This is assumed as settled in some prophecy circles these days, where Magog is almost a synonym for Russia. This is an error.

The prophets wrote for us twenty-first-century readers, yes, and many aspects of Bible prophecy are only coming into focus now as archaeologists dig more evidence out of the ground. However, the prophets wrote for the people alive in their time, too. And the simple fact is that no one alive in the days of Ezekiel would have had a clue about the identity of a nation called Russia, or anything similar.

The idea that Ezekiel was inspired to prophesy a starring role for Russia in the end times emerged in the nineteenth century when scholars Wilhelm Gesenius and C. F. Keil translated the Hebrew word *rosh* in Ezekiel 38:3 as a proper noun,[364] which changes the verse from "Gog, chief prince of Meshech and Tubal" to "Gog, prince of Rosh, Meshech, and Tubal." But it was the Scofield Reference Bible, published in 1909 and revised in 1917, that popularized the belief that Russia would lead a world coalition in a war against Israel in the last days:

That the primary reference is to the northern (European) powers, headed up by Russia, all agree. The whole passage should be read in connection with Zechariah 12:1–4; 14:1–9; Matthew 24:14–30; Revelation 14:14–20; 19:17–21. "Gog" is the prince, "Magog," his land. The reference to Meshech and Tubal (Moscow and Tobolsk) is a clear mark of identification. Russia and the northern powers have been the latest persecutors of dispersed Israel, and it is congruous both with divine justice and with the covenants... that destruction should fall at the climax of the last mad attempt to exterminate the remnant of Israel in Jerusalem.[365]

Just as during the years following the Bolshevik Revolution, America—after the Cold War and again since the election of President Donald Trump—has been primed to identify Russia as the great end-times enemy of God and Israel. But it just doesn't fit the text. More importantly, it completely misses the supernatural significance of this prophecy.

Ezekiel's primary audience was Jews of the sixth century BC. So, here's the question to ask: What would his readers have taken away from the text?

First, they wouldn't have read *rosh* as a name. That's certain. It means "chief" or "head," as in Rosh Hashanah ("head of the year"), the Jewish New Year. In the Bible, when *rosh* doesn't refer to somebody's head, it's used the way English speakers use the word "head"—head of a company, head of the nation, etc. Thus, "*rō'š* is therefore best understood as a common noun, appositional to and offering a closer definition of *nāśî'*,"[366] thus yielding the ESV translation above, "Gog, of the land of Magog, the chief prince of Meshech and Tubal."

But, some argue, the hordes of Magog come from the "uttermost parts of the north." And it's true: When you draw a straight line north from Jerusalem on a map, there is nothing farther north than Russia. But this obscures the supernatural fulfillment of the prophecy by looking for villains in the natural realm. To put it bluntly, it's a coincidence that *rosh* sounds like "Russia." Identifying Moscow with "Meshech" or Tobolsk with "Tubal" because they sound alike is bad hermeneutics. The *Expositor's Bible Commentary* puts it this way: "There is no etymological, grammatical, historical, or literary data in support of such a position."[367]

Contrary to what you may have been taught, the nations of the northern coalition are relatively easy to identify. Magog, Meshech, Tubal, Gomer, and Beth-Togarmah were all known in Ezekiel's day, and they were all located in Anatolia—modern-day Turkey.[368] This is significant for reasons we'll roll out in just a moment.

First, let's look at the other members of this end-times alliance against Israel. As with the nations from the north, Ezekiel's readers were familiar with Persia (Iran), Cush (Ethiopia), and Put (Libya). Likewise, it's a simple matter for us, 2,500 years later, to pinpoint those nations on a map. However, aside from Iran, it's hard to see any reality in which Ethiopia and Libya (which isn't a nation in the true sense of the word as we write this) pose any threat to Israel.

Yes, if God says it, we believe it, too. But let us suggest another interpretation that makes more sense.

Go back to a map. Locate Turkey, Iran, Ethiopia, and Libya. If you draw lines from Jerusalem to those nations, you basically have the four cardinal directions on a compass—north, east, south, and west. In Ezekiel's day, the nations the prophet listed as the army of the apocalypse were probably the farthest known places to his readers in each of those directions. Ezekiel's point was not that these specific nations would someday emerge as a clear and present danger to God's chosen people; he was prophesying a day when *the whole world*—armies from the four corners of the earth—would make war on Israel.

This is consistent with other apocalyptic prophecies in the Old Testament, such as this from Zechariah:

Behold, I am about to make Jerusalem a cup of staggering to all the surrounding peoples. The siege of Jerusalem will also be against Judah. On that day I will make Jerusalem a heavy stone for all the peoples. All who lift it will surely hurt themselves. And all the nations of the earth will gather against it. (Zechariah 12:2–3)

The phrase "on that day" is commonly used by the Hebrew prophets for the Day of the Lord, the time of His wrath against the unrepentant nations of the earth. You can find other prophecies of a climactic battle pitting the world against Jerusalem in chapters 3 and 4 of Joel and Zechariah 14. That's what's in view in Ezekiel 38 and 39—Armageddon, the war for God's mount of assembly.

Now, you may also have been taught that Armageddon will be fought at Megiddo. There is some logic behind that; ancient Megiddo commanded a key pass through the Carmel range to the Valley of Jezreel. Several important battles have been fought there in history, including one in 609 BC at which King Josiah of Judah was mortally wounded while fighting the Egyptian army. Identifying Megiddo as the site of the final battle of our age has become, if anything, even more of a given than pegging Russia as the land of Magog.

But there are two problems with putting Armageddon at Megiddo. First, the assumption that Armageddon is derived from *Har Magedōn* ("mountain of Megiddo") is incorrect. To put it simply, there is no mountain at Megiddo. There is a tell, yes, but a tell is an artificial hill created by the debris of human civilization. At Megiddo, archaeologists say they've found about twenty-six layers' worth going back nine thousand years.

The other problem is that it doesn't square with the prophecies of Joel, Zechariah, or Ezekiel that clearly point to the final battle at Jerusalem. This is for all the marbles, and it's why Armageddon is there. It makes no sense for God to "gather all the nations against Jerusalem to battle," descend Himself on the Mount of Olives,[369] splitting it in two—and then move the battle to Megiddo, nearly seventy miles away.

Remember that the goal of the rebel from Eden is to "sit on the mount of assembly in the far reaches of the north."[370] Scholar Charles C. Torrey pointed out in 1938 that the Hebrew for the phrase "mount of assembly" is *har-mō'ēd*, and that it is there we should look to solve the riddle of the meaning of "Armageddon."[371]

In transliterating from Hebrew to Greek, the apostle John was forced to make a choice. The Hebrew character *ayin* (ע), which is represented in our alphabet by a sort-of reverse apostrophe (ʿ), has no corresponding sound in Greek or English. The closest Greek letter available to John was *gamma*. When it was time for English speakers to reverse engineer the Hebrew underlying the Greek, it was assumed that the *gamma* represented the English *G* sound, and *har-mō ʿēd* was transformed into *Har Magedōn.*[372]

Not only does *har-mō ʿēd*, "mount of assembly," make more sense in light of this battle being fought for Zion, God's mount of assembly; Ezekiel identified the mount of assembly of the enemy forces at Armageddon. Remember in our chapter about Lucifer (i.e., Baal), the "abominable branch" of Isaiah 14? We noted that his mount of assembly was *yarkete tsaphon*, or Mount Zaphon, the mountain in southern Turkey today called Jebel al-Aqra. The Hebrew phrase *yarkete tsaphon* only appears in two places in the Bible other than Isaiah 14:13, and one of them is in the prophecy of the war of Gog and Magog.

Yarkete tsaphon, a mountain known to be sacred to Baal (Satan) nearly four thousand years ago, will be the rally point for the army of Antichrist before it marches on Israel to assault the holy mountain of God.

We've explained in detail elsewhere why the Gog-Magog war and the conflict that ends at Armageddon are one and the same.[373] To summarize, God Himself appears on the field at the end of the fighting in Ezekiel 39:7 as "the Holy One in Israel," the only time in the Bible that title uses the phrase "*in* Israel" rather than "*of* Israel." Further, the gruesome sacrificial meal that follows the battle in Ezekiel 39:17–20 is the same one prophesied by John in Revelation 19:17–21. The purpose of this chapter is to establish just who will be fighting for the Infernal Council at Armageddon.

Think of Gog, the Antichrist, as the enemy's commander-in-chief. Ezekiel identifies his home base—Mount Zaphon, the mountain of

Baal. So, how did we reach the conclusion that he'll lead an army of Rephaim—in other words, demons or demonically possessed humans?

We refer back to the Rephaim texts of ancient Ugarit, where the feast served up by the creator-god El for the Rephaim is described:

> He slaughtered oxen and sheep,
> he felled bulls
> and the fattest of rams,
> year-old calves,
> skipping lambs,
> kids.
> Like silver to vagabonds were the olives,
> (like) gold to vagabonds were the dates.[374]

The word rendered "vagabonds" is translated by other scholars as "onlookers," "invitees," "those who came over," and "travelers." The Ugaritic word is 'brm, an equivalent to the Hebrew word behind the place name "Abarim," which we find along the route of the Exodus.

One of the stations where the Israelites made camp was Iye-Abarim, or "Ruins of the Travelers." As we noted in another chapter, that was the next station of the Exodus after Oboth ("spirits of the dead"). Mount Nebo, where Moses was granted his only look at the Promised Land, was called "this mountain of Abarim."[375]

That begs the question: Who or what were the Travelers?

We find an important clue in Job 33:18, where the Hebrew verb 'abar, from the root 'br, describes the process of death, like the Greek concept of crossing the river between life and death.[376] We've already noted that while the Israelites camped on the plains of Moab, northeast of the Dead Sea, they worshiped Baal-Peor, the "lord of the entrance to the underworld," and ate sacrifices offered to the dead. Oboth ("Spirits of the Dead") was nearby. Apparently, this was a place believed to be haunted, for lack of a better word. And if the Ugaritic term for the

Rephaim, *brm*, is "travelers" in the sense of "those who cross over," well, then, we have a winner, Johnny—because that's exactly where Ezekiel puts the final battle of the Gog-Magog war, which is Armageddon.

> On that day I will give to Gog a place for burial in Israel, the Valley of the Travelers, east of the sea. It will block the travelers, for there Gog and all his multitude will be buried. It will be called the Valley of Hamon-gog. (Ezekiel 39:11)

"East of the sea" refers to the Moab (present-day Jordan) side of the Dead Sea, right where the Israelites camped in sight of the ruins of Sodom. The Travelers are the spirits of the Rephaim—the "warriors of Baal" who'd been worshiped for at least two thousand years by the time of Ezekiel.

And they're coming back as an army at Armageddon.

26

Lord of the Dead

A s mentioned earlier, the fourteenth chapter of Isaiah is one of the most remarkable in the entire Bible. The first portion, verses 1 through 23, give us more information about the history of the supernatural war going on around us than just about any other section of Holy Scripture.

On the surface, it's a condemnation of the king of Babylon. However, Babylon wasn't the dominant power in Mesopotamia during Isaiah's lifetime. Assyria emerged as the neighborhood bully in the Near East about two hundred years before the prophet's birth, and it would be another century after Isaiah's death before the Chaldean rulers of Babylon threw off the Assyrian yoke and dragged the elite of Judah from Jerusalem into captivity.

So, why did God direct the prophet to "take up this taunt against the king of Babylon"? Obviously, Isaiah was given a glimpse of the future. He prophesied the rise of the Persian King Cyrus, who would end the Chaldean empire less than twenty-five years after the peak of its glory under Nebuchadnezzar.

But Isaiah 14 is more than that; it's a condemnation of the king of

Babylon by comparing him with the divine rebel from Eden. In that sense, the chapter is a parallel to Ezekiel 28. Like Isaiah, the prophet Ezekiel, writing about a hundred years later while in exile with the Jews in Babylonia, compared the king of Tyre to the "anointed guardian cherub" who was kicked out of Eden. But when we look under the hood of Isaiah's prophecy, we see that while he used the rebel from Eden as a symbol to prophesy the fall of the king of Babylon, he also foretold the ultimate doom of Satan and his colleagues in the last days.

> How the oppressor has ceased,
> the insolent fury ceased!
> The LORD has broken the staff of the wicked,
> the scepter of rulers,
> that struck the peoples in wrath
> with unceasing blows,
> that ruled the nations in anger
> with unrelenting persecution.
> The whole earth is at rest and quiet;
> they break forth into singing.
> The cypresses rejoice at you,
> the cedars of Lebanon, saying,
> "Since you were laid low,
> no woodcutter comes up against us." (Isaiah 14:4b–8)

Verses 4 through 8 are prelude. They set up the rest of this prophecy. You can see how the description of the unnamed Babylonian king would just as easily apply to Satan. The charge of "unrelenting persecution" echoes God's condemnation of the rebellious sons of God in the Divine Council for judging unfairly and playing favorites with the wicked.[377]

> Sheol beneath is stirred up
> to meet you when you come;

it rouses the shades to greet you,
all who were leaders of the earth;
it raises from their thrones
all who were kings of the nations.
All of them will answer
and say to you:
"You too have become as weak as we!
You have become like us!'
Your pomp is brought down to Sheol,
the sound of your harps;
maggots are laid as a bed beneath you,
and worms are your covers." (Isaiah 14:9–11)

This is where we bring in the dead. The "shades" of verse 9 are Rephaim. Nearly all English translators have opted against using the Hebrew *rephaim*, maybe because it was thought that rendering the verse "it rouses the Rephaim to greet you" was too weird and confusing for readers who'd remember the living Rephaim tribes of Abraham's day and Moses' showdown with Og on the Golan Heights. In other words, the idea of Isaiah referring to the spirits of mighty men who walked the earth before the Flood might have made them a bit uncomfortable.

To be fair, most Bible translators, English and otherwise, didn't have access to the texts from the ancient Amorite kingdom of Ugarit, which were only discovered in 1928. Many of the tablets, most of which were written during the period of the judges in Israel, have only been translated within the last fifty years, and scholars don't always agree on the translations. Bible scholars tasked with translating Hebrew and Greek manuscripts may not be aware of the latest work on Ugaritic language and religion, or the relevance of those fields to some of the weirder parts of the Bible—like the Rephaim.

Their description by Isaiah matches their depiction in the Ugaritic texts: Chariot warriors of the underworld, warriors of their chief god

Baal, closely linked to the council of the Ditanu, the ancient Amorite tribe which several Amorite royal houses, including the founders of Babylon, claimed as ancestors. Remember, that's the tribe whose name found its way into Greek as the name of their old gods, the Titans, whom we identify with the Hebrew Watchers—the angels who sinned[378] and were banished to Tartarus, the abyss.

We need to pause for a moment to distinguish between Sheol and the abyss. Sheol was essentially the same as Hades to the later Greeks, the destination for run-of-the-mill dead. Tartarus was another level of the underworld reserved for threats to the divine order. In Greek cosmology, those were the Titans and a few other supernatural monsters, like Typhon, the god of chaos.

However, we need to remember that the Greek demigods, heroes of old who were the semi-divine children of gods and humans, were simply Rephaim by different names. Scholar Amar Annus made the connection clear in an important paper published in 1999, in which he also traced the etymology of "Titan" to the Amorite tribe Ditanu/Tidanu.[379] These heroes, according to the Greek poet Hesiod, "lived in the time of Cronos when he was reigning in heaven." Upon death, they became *daimones*, spirits who wandered the earth dispensing wealth and delivering humans from harm.[380] While the story is similar to the origin story of demons in 1 Enoch, the nature of Greek *daimones* is the opposite of the demons in Hebrew cosmology.

> But now the giants who were begotten by the spirits and flesh— they will call them evil spirits on the earth, for their dwelling will be on the earth. The spirits that have gone forth from the body of their flesh are evil spirits, for from humans they came into being, and from the holy watchers was the origin of their creation. Evil spirits they will be on the earth, and evil spirits they will be called. The spirits of heaven, in heaven is their dwelling; but the spirits begotten on the earth, on the earth is their dwelling. And the

spirits of the giants < lead astray >, do violence, make desolate, and attack and wrestle and hurl upon the earth and < cause illnesses >. They eat nothing, but abstain from food and are thirsty and smite. These spirits (will) rise up against the sons of men and against the women, for they have come forth from them.[381]

While some might dismiss this theory on the origin of demons because it comes from outside the Bible, it was the default belief of the early church. Respected early theologians like Philo, Justin Martyr, and Origen understood that demons were the spirits of the Nephilim.[382]

These spirits were the ones who greeted Satan (i.e., Baal, the storm-god) upon his arrival in Sheol—the guardian cherub who'd been demoted from the King's Guard in Eden to become the accursed lord of the dead.

> How you are fallen from heaven,
> O Day Star, son of Dawn!
> How you are cut down to the ground,
> you who laid the nations low!
> You said in your heart,
> "I will ascend to heaven;
> above the stars of God
> I will set my throne on high;
> I will sit on the mount of assembly
> in the far reaches of the north;
> I will ascend above the heights of the clouds;
> I will make myself like the Most High." (Isaiah 14:12–14)

These are the five famous "I wills" that summarize the goals of Satan and his colleagues, who were driven by pride, envy, or rage at being made mere supervisors of God's ultimate creation, humanity, to dare to dream of overthrowing their Creator.

The phrase rendered "far reaches of the north," *yarkete tsaphon*, deserves special attention. It's only used three places in the Bible: Here; Psalm 48, a comparison between God's mount of assembly and another mountain in the north; and Ezekiel 38 and 39, which is the prophecy of the war of Gog of Magog.

Tsaphon is the Hebrew word for "north." It was not always so. In most other Semitic languages, north is *sim'al*. But everyone in the ancient world knew that *Tsaphon* was the mountain where Baal built his palace, and the importance of Baal on the lives of the pagans who lived around ancient Israel was such that the name of his sacred mountain, located north of Israel near the city of Antioch, became the word for the compass point north.[383]

So, when we read Ezekiel's prophecy of Gog, the great end-times enemy of Israel, we learn that "the uttermost north," *yarkete tsaphon*, is Mount Zaphon, the mountain sacred to Baal, whom Jesus identified as Satan. And here in Isaiah, we should understand that this long supernatural war, from Eden to today, is about establishing a rival "mount of assembly" to challenge Zion.

But you are brought down to Sheol,
to the far reaches of the pit.
Those who see you will stare at you
and ponder over you:
"Is this the man who made the earth tremble,
who shook kingdoms,
who made the world like a desert
and overthrew its cities,
who did not let his prisoners go home?" (Isaiah 14:15–17)

Satan's descent to "the far reaches of the pit" suggests that he no longer held a place of honor, a real blow to the arrogant *elohim*. Remember, in Ezekiel 32 the prophet allotted "the midst of Sheol" to "the mighty chiefs," the chiefs of the *gibborim*. And his fall brings him down to where even the semi-divine spirits of the Rephaim exclaim, "You too have become as weak as we! You have become like us!"

Greek myth records a story that is startlingly similar. The demigod Bellerophon, who tamed the flying horse Pegasus and is called by some "the greatest hero and slayer of monsters, alongside Cadmus and Perseus, before the days of Herakles,"[384] may be "a transparent transcription of West Semitic Ba 'al Rapi'u"[385]—that is, "lord of the Rephaim."

As the story goes, Bellerophon, son of the sea-god Poseidon and a mortal woman named Eurynome, decided after a series of heroic adventures that he'd earned the right to live in Olympus with the gods. As he flew Pegasus toward the mountain, a gadfly sent by Zeus startled the horse, throwing Bellerophon back to earth. Blinded, Bellerophon wandered the earth the rest of his life miserable and alone, hated by gods and men.

This is so similar to the fall of Satan, the *original* "lord of the Rephaim," that it's a good bet the ancient Greeks had heard the same story.

> All the kings of the nations lie in glory,
> each in his own tomb;
> but you are cast out, away from your grave,
> ike a loathed branch,
> clothed with the slain, those pierced by the sword,
> who go down to the stones of the pit,
> like a dead body trampled underfoot.
> You will not be joined with them in burial,
> because you have destroyed your land,
> you have slain your people. (Isaiah 14:18–20)

It is logical to interpret this section of the chapter as a jab at the pride of the future king of Babylon: "You will not be remembered or buried with honor among the great kings of the nations." And that prophecy was probably fulfilled in 539 BC, when Babylon fell to the Medes and Persians. Nabonidus, the last king of Babylon, was captured in battle. We don't know for sure what happened to him, but it's a safe bet that Cyrus didn't allow his defeated enemy to build any great monument for posterity.

However, there is more here than meets the English-reading eye. The phrase "loathed branch," *nétzer nit'av*, has been a difficult one for translators. On one level, it is undoubtedly a comparison to the branch Isaiah referred to earlier in his book:

> There shall come forth a shoot [*nétzer*] from the stump of Jesse,
> and a branch from his roots shall bear fruit.
> And the Spirit of the LORD shall rest upon him,
> the Spirit of wisdom and understanding,
> the Spirit of counsel and might,
> the Spirit of knowledge and the fear of the LORD. (Isaiah 11:1–2)

This is a prophecy of the coming Messiah. Contrasting the fallen lord of the Rephaim as a "loathed branch" to the One on whom the seven spirits of God will rest is the type of wordplay for which Isaiah is famous. But it goes deeper than that.

Scholar Christopher B. Hays has suggested an explanation that is mind-blowing, but extremely relevant to our study of the spirits of the dead. Isaiah, who lived at a time when his king, Hezekiah, was currying favor with Judah's southern neighbor, used an Egyptian word to communicate an even more specific insult to the lord of the Rephaim:

> [The] term ["loathed branch"] is best explained as a loanword from the common Egyptian noun *ntr*. *Ntr* is generally translated "god," but is commonly used of the divinized dead and their physical remains. It originally came into Hebrew as a noun refer-

ring to the putatively divinized corpse of a dead king, which is closely related to the Egyptian usage.[386]

Not to put too fine a point on it, but the divinized dead—the Rephaim—and a loathed "god"—Satan—is exactly what Isaiah was writing about! Yes, the rebel from Eden, who aspired to replace the Creator, was no Branch—no Messiah, the basic meaning of the verse. But on a deeper level, Satan was cast from heaven like a "loathed dead god," a description of the Rephaim—venerated spirits of the divinized dead kings of old.

Ironically, as we've noted elsewhere in this book, the kings who succeeded Hezekiah, his son Manasseh and grandson Amon, apparently aspired to join the assembly of the Rephaim, which may explain why they were buried in the Garden of Uzza rather than the royal tombs.

But Isaiah wasn't finished. He turned his gift of wordplay to a prophecy of the ultimate destruction of Satan and his demonic minions.

May the offspring of evildoers
nevermore be named!
Prepare slaughter for his sons
because of the guilt of their fathers,
lest they rise and possess the earth,
and fill the face of the world with cities.

The key here is in the word translated "cities." Now, while Sharon is a country girl, raised in a town so small you can walk from one end to the other in about ten minutes, Derek was raised in Chicago, and spent more than half his life in places with populations numbered in the hundreds of thousands or millions. What's wrong with cities? Didn't God place His name in a city—Jerusalem?

Once again, we have to look at the language of a neighboring people to get the actual sense of this verse. The Hebrew word for "ciy," *'iyr*, is identical to the Aramaic word for "Watcher"—the class of angelic beings who sinned against God by vowing to corrupt humanity through blood and magic.

The plural forms of the word are *'iyrim* in Hebrew and *'iyrin* in Aramaic. Thanks to Dr. Michael Heiser, we have a good example of how an Aramaic loanword can be imported into the Bible and then "corrected" with the Hebrew *-im* plural suffix, which transformed the Aramaic *naphil(a)* ("giant") into the Bible's *nephilim*.[387]

You can see how swapping in "Watchers" for "cities" can change the meaning of the verse, but the important thing is that here, in Isaiah 14, it fits the context. There are plenty of places in the Old Testament where *'iyrim* means "cities." We're not trying to shoehorn a pet definition into a verse here to find Watchers and giants where none exist. The entire chapter up to this point has been about the Rephaim, who were the spirits of the Nephilim giants of old, and their master, the rebel from Eden, the entity we know as Satan.

Their doom has been foretold—just like the destruction of Babylon:

"I will rise up against them," declares the LORD of hosts, "and will cut off from Babylon name and remnant, descendants and posterity," declares the LORD. "And I will make it a possession of the hedgehog, and pools of water, and I will sweep it with the broom of destruction," declares the LORD of hosts. (Isaiah 14:22–23)

Isaiah's prophecy is devastating for the Fallen. For us, dear reader, death is just the transition between our physical existence and our eternal home. We're even promised an upgrade on these organic shells that house our spirits—sometimes not very well.

For the divine rebels, though, a day is coming when death really means the end.

Part Nine

DEATH OF THE DEAD

27

Gog of the Dead

All this begs the question: Who or what is Gog?

Modern prophecy students look to political leaders such as Vladimir Putin, whose long tenure has made him an attractive candidate here in the West. But since we've placed the "uttermost parts of the north" inside the borders of present-day Turkey, should we consider its president as of this writing, Recep Tayyip Erdogan?

He's another attractive candidate for Gog of Magog because of his neo-Ottoman ambitions. Erdogan has made it clear that the days of secular rule in Turkey are over. As Derek wrote in *I Predict! What 12 Global Experts Believe You Will See by 2025*:

> The rise of Erdogan's Justice and Development Party (AKP) has given Erdogan the clout to roll back some of the secular reforms of Mustafa Kemal Ataturk, who modernized Turkey and aligned it with the West after the collapse of the empire in 1923. Ottoman Turkish and Arabic script will again be taught in government schools, and the number of students enrolled in state-run Islamic seminaries has grown from 62,000 in 2002, when Erdogan first

came to power, to over 1 million. Considering Erdogan's public call for Muslims to work toward wresting control of Jerusalem away from Israel, it is no surprise that some Middle East observers are asking in so many words: Is Turkey attempting to resurrect the Ottoman Empire on the back of the Islamic State?[388]

In December of 2017, Erdogan called on the fifty-seven member nations of the Organization of Islamic Cooperation to form a united military front against Israel.[389] If the political and religious rivalries within Islam could be overcome—which, to be clear, is not a sure bet to say the least—the OIC could theoretically field a five-million-man army backed by Pakistan's nuclear arsenal.

Not a pleasant thought. It makes you wonder how Israeli political and military leaders sleep at night. But the hatred that divides the factions within Islam is at least as strong as that between Islam and the *kafir*, which is anyone and everyone who rejects the teachings of Muhammad. It's not likely we'll see Sunnis and Shias on the same side of any battlefield, so the odds of an alliance between Turkey and Iran, or the Saudis and Iran, are pretty slim.

Similarly, the Sunnis of Turkey and their Sunnis of Saudi Arabia don't particularly like one another, either. With Erdogan flexing the muscle of Turkey's army, which is the second largest in NATO after the US,[390] the Saudis have grown increasingly suspicious of his intentions. Saudi Arabia has controlled Islam's holiest sites for nearly a century, after the collapse of the Ottoman Empire in the early 1920s, but the Turks haven't forgotten their glory years. The Ottomans controlled Mecca and Medina, the Levant, most of the Mediterranean, and southeastern Europe for more than six hundred years. It's hard for us Americans to grasp the impact of Islam in general, and the Ottomans in particular, on world history, but think about this: Sixty years after the Pilgrims landed at Plymouth Rock, the Ottoman Turks laid siege to Vienna. Check a map—Austria is a long way from Turkey.

The point is that Turkey, or at least the ruling AKP party of President Erdogan, wants to restore Turkey to great power status, at least in the Middle East. The Saudis aren't keen to give up that status. Their priority is containing the growing power of Iran, even if that means cooperating with Israel, which they've been doing through back channels. Just days before this book went to the editor, Saudi Crown Prince Mohammad bin Salman told Jewish leaders at a gathering in New York that the Palestinian Authority should accept the peace proposals put forward by the Trump administration "or shut up and stop complaining."[391]

Obviously, this isn't what Fatah or Hamas wanted to hear, and it's certainly a different tone from President Erdogan's call for a united Muslim army to march on Jerusalem. But it makes the point clear: Even the world's leading Sunni powers don't get along. So, the notion that they'll work together against Israel, especially with Israel useful to the Saudis as an ally against Iran, seems far-fetched. Without supernatural intervention, of course. And that's where we're going with this:

> The battle of Gog and Magog would be something expected after the initiation of Yahweh's plan to reclaim the nations and, therefore, draw his children, Jew or Gentile, from those nations. *The Gog invasion would be the response of supernatural evil against the messiah and his kingdom.* This is in fact precisely how it is portrayed in Revelation 20:7–10.
>
> Gog would have been perceived as either a figure empowered by supernatural evil or an evil quasi-divine figure from the supernatural world bent on the destruction of God's people. For this reason, Gog is regarded by many biblical scholars as a template for the New Testament antichrist figure.[392]

While human actors will be involved, the true identity of Gog, leader of the Magog coalition, is found in the spirit realm. Ezekiel spelled it out for us by pointing to Isaiah 14. He may even have added a subtle clue in this verse:

> You will advance, **coming on like a storm.** You will be like a cloud covering the land, you and all your hordes, and many peoples with you. (Ezekiel 38:9, emphasis added)

By naming *yarkete tsaphon* as the point of origin for the armies of Gog, Ezekiel identified the mountain of the storm-god, Baal, which was the mount of assembly of the divine rebel from Eden, Satan.

Does this mean Gog is Satan? No, Gog is the Old Testament Antichrist figure. John the Revelator clearly distinguishes between the Antichrist (the Beast) and Satan (the dragon).

Identifying Gog as the Antichrist is not a new idea. Our Jewish brothers and sisters have been aware of Gog's starring role in the end times for a long, long time:

> An important part in the eschatological drama is assigned to Israel's final combat with the combined forces of the heathen nations under the leadership of Gog and Magog, barbarian tribes of the North. Assembled for a fierce attack upon Israel in the mountains near Jerusalem, they will suffer a terrible and crushing defeat, and Israel's land will thenceforth forever remain the seat of God's kingdom.[393]

In Jewish eschatology, Gog is the great end-times enemy who attacks YHWH and His people, Israel, in a climactic battle that coincides with the arrival of Messiah.[394] While there are as many differences of opinion about end-times prophecy among Jews as there are among Christians, it's clear that Gog is the Antichrist character described by Paul and John in their prophecies of the end times.

This view of Gog by Jews of the Second Temple period is hinted at by some of the choices made by translators of the Septuagint. For example, they made an interesting choice in rending the first two verse of Amos chapter 7. First, the ESV:

This is what the LORD God showed me: behold, he was forming locusts when the latter growth was just beginning to sprout, and behold, it was the latter growth after the king's mowings. (Amos 7:1)

Contrast that with the Septuagint translation:

Thus the LORD showed me, and behold, a swarm of locusts coming early, and behold, one locust, Gog, the king. (Amos 7:1, Septuagint translation by Lancelot C. L. Brenton, 1851)

Explaining how the Jewish translators of the Septuagint rendered that passage the way they did is a task for experts in ancient Hebrew and Greek, which we are not. The point is that the Jewish scholars who translated the Septuagint saw an army of invading locusts, similar or even identical to the supernatural army of Joel 2, and in trying to make sense of a difficult phrase, they chose to connect it to a well-known supernatural villain—Gog, the great enemy of Israel in the last days.

Regardless of which human face is worn by the commander of this great end-times army, the real leader, Gog, is unquestionably a creature from the abyss who leads an army from cosmic (supernatural) north in a final assault on the holy mountain of God.

28

War of the Dead

So, the picture begins to come into focus. The hordes of Magog will be led by a supernatural entity called Gog by the prophets Ezekiel and John. Let's be clear: This does *not* mean humans will play no part in the great war led by Gog of Magog. Far from it. That said, we believe texts from the ancient Amorite kingdom of Ugarit confirm our hypothesis that the giants of the ancient world, the Nephilim/Rephaim, will be on the battlefield in the last great war of the age. The clue is the location of Magog's defeat.

> On that day I will give to Gog a place for burial in Israel, the Valley of the Travelers, east of the sea. (Ezekiel 39:11a)

As we noted earlier, the Hebrew word translated into English as "traveler" is *ōběrîm*, a plural form of the verb *'br*, which means "to pass from one side to the other."[395] And this brings us to the point: We've identified the area that Ezekiel called the Valley of the Travelers as the east side of the Jordan Rift Valley, specifically ancient Moab east and just northeast of the Dead Sea. Here's why that's important: The Rephaim texts from Ugarit specifically refer to the spirits of the Rephaim as "travelers."

> [El is speaking:]
> "I shall summon the [elohim] into the midst of my palace."
> To his sanctuary the [Rephaim] hurried indeed,
> to his sanctuary hurried indeed the [elohim].
> They harnessed the chariots;
> the horses they hitched.
> They mounted their chariots,
> they came on their mounts.
> They journeyed a day
> and a second.
> After sunrise on the third
> the [Rephaim] arrived at the threshing-floors,
> the [elohim] at the plantations....
> **Like silver to vagabonds [travelers] were the olives,**
> **(like) gold to vagabonds were the dates.**[396] (Emphasis added)

In the preceding text, (Ugaritic text KTU 1.22), the word chosen by the translator for the Ugaritic *'brm*, "vagabonds," is simply another word for "travelers." Scholar Klaas Spronk translates *l 'brm*, the equivalent of the Hebrew *'br* mentioned above, as "those who came over."[397] This has the same meaning. In short, the Rephaim traveled, came over, or crossed over from the realm of the dead to the land of the living; thus, the Rephaim are the Travelers.

Remember, this area east of the Jordan River is exactly where Chedorlaomer and his coalition of kings from the east defeated the Rephaim in the time of Abraham. It is exactly where the cousins of Israel, the Edomites, Moabites, and Ammonites, drove out the Rephaim between the time of Abraham and the Exodus. The last of the remnant of the

Rephaim, Og of Bashan, was sent to the underworld to join his *ăbōṯ*, his fathers, by Moses and the host of Israel.

But the spirits of the Rephaim were believed to travel to the land of the living in that valley where Israel camped before launching its attack on Jericho. Two hundred years after the conquest of Canaan by Israel, the Amorites of Ugarit still performed rituals to summon those Travelers to banquets at the threshing floor of El on the summit of Mount Hermon.

This is key to understanding Ezekiel's prophecy: He was shown that the hordes of Magog would be slaughtered and buried in the wilderness near Moab, east of the Dead Sea. This area is connected to the dead—and not just the dead, but dead spirits who "traveled," or "crossed over," to the land of the living. Why? Because that's where the Travelers—i.e., the spirits of the Rephaim/Nephilim—and those who venerated them in the days of Abraham and Moses lived when they walked the earth.

So, let's look at the significance of Gog. Remember, his home base is *yarkete tsaphon*, Mount Zaphon. This is the place Isaiah identified as the mount of assembly of the divine rebel in Eden, Ezekiel's anointed guardian cherub, the throne guardian who schemed to overthrow his sovereign Lord. And it was known to the world as the place where the storm-god, Baal, lived in his palace of gold and silver.

Not coincidentally, it was also where the Greeks believed their storm-god, Zeus, defeated the chaos serpent Typhon, who dove under the mountain to escape the thunderbolts of Zeus and in so doing carved out the channel of the Orontes River. This is another telling of the *chaoskampf*, the name scholars give to the common ancient Near Eastern myth of a warrior god defeating chaos to create or preserve order. The Bible has the original story, of course, in which Yahweh crushed the heads of Leviathan (Psalm 74:14), but, as we've already mentioned, the story was repeated by Amorites from Babylon (Marduk vs. Tiamat) to Ugarit (Baal vs. Yamm). The story traveled north to the Hurrians and Hittites (Teshub or Tarhunz, the storm-god, vs.

the chaos-dragon Illuyankas), and finally west to Greece, where it was transformed into the epic battle between Zeus and the hundred-headed serpentine monster, Typhon.

To make this point clear, in the Gospel of Matthew, Jesus specifically connected the storm-god, Baal, to Satan:

> Then a demon-oppressed man who was blind and mute was brought to him, and he healed him, so that the man spoke and saw. And all the people were amazed, and said, "Can this be the Son of David?" But when the Pharisees heard it, they said, "It is only by Beelzebul, the prince of demons, that this man casts out demons." Knowing their thoughts, he said to them, "Every kingdom divided against itself is laid waste, and no city or house divided against itself will stand. And if Satan casts out Satan, he is divided against himself. How then will his kingdom stand? (Matthew 12:22–26)

Beelzebul means "Baal the Prince." Because you're observant, you saw how Jesus specifically identified the storm-god as Satan there. And then, in the Revelation of John, He linked Satan to the storm-god, Zeus:

> And to the angel of the church in Pergamum write: "The words of him who has the sharp two-edged sword. I know where you dwell, where Satan's throne is. Yet you hold fast my name, and you did not deny my faith even in the days of Antipas my faithful witness, who was killed among you, where Satan dwells." (Revelation 2:12–13)

Pergamum was in western Asia Minor, near the Aegean Sea. It was home to a famous and elaborate altar to Zeus, where he was hailed as a savior. Most scholars lean toward the view that Jesus had that altar in mind when He called out Satan's throne. So, Zeus = Baal = Satan.

284

Because Isaiah identified Mount Zaphon as the mount of assembly of the rebel from Eden, we can build a good case that the divine rebel was Satan. As a servant of Satan, that's where Gog, the Antichrist, will assemble his army. The uttermost parts of the north, *yarkete tsaphon*, refers to Mount Zaphon, today called Jebel al-Aqra in Turkey.

Many of us, fascinated by the prophecy of Ezekiel, have tried for years to pin down the identity of Gog by interpreting the headlines. That's pulled us in the wrong direction as we looked for a human ruler to fit the role. While a human will undoubtedly be connected to this figure, we've lost sight of the fact that we should be looking for a supernatural character.

Here's where we'll get even *more* supernatural.

Remember that we've cited several texts from the Amorite kingdom of Ugarit calling the spirits of the Rephaim "warriors of Baal." Also remember that, in the previous section, we showed you where the Rephaim spirits—demons—were called Travelers, because they traveled from one plane of existence to another.

Consider this question: When Baal's servant, Gog, leads his army to the mountains of Israel, how many "warriors of Baal" will be marching with the troops?

By that time, the Church of believers in Jesus Christ will be off the earth. This war ends with Armageddon. To ask the question another way, with the Church gone and the "restrainer" Paul mentioned in 2 Thessalonians 2:6 removed to give the Antichrist free rein, how many soldiers in the army of the Antichrist will be demonically possessed? Some of them? All of them?

If, as we believe, demons are the spirits of the Rephaim, the demigod sons of the Watchers/Titans who died in Noah's Flood, then the horde of Gog will be an army of the living dead. It will be, in a very real sense, the ultimate zombie apocalypse.

This is consistent with Second Temple Jewish beliefs about the prophesied fate of the Nephilim. The Book of Enoch tells us that God's judgment on the Nephilim will take place on "the day of the consummation of the great judgment, when the great age will be consummated."[398] That's the Day of the Lord, when Armageddon will be fought—and we repeat, the Gog-Magog war ends at Armageddon.

Ezekiel specifically identified the battlefield where Gog's warriors are slain as the Valley of the Travelers—the valley of the spirits of the Rephaim. Now, catch this, as we include the second part of a verse we cited earlier:

> On that day I will give to Gog a place for burial in Israel, the Valley of the Travelers, east of the sea. **It will block the travelers, for there Gog and all his multitude will be buried.** (Ezekiel 39:11, emphasis added)

Block the travelers? What does *that* mean?

It could suggest that so many bodies will fall in the valley that people literally won't be able to travel along the King's Highway in Jordan. Okay, in a war of this size, especially because God intervenes and rains fire from heaven on Magog (notice how Yahweh uses what's supposed to be Baal's weapon, the thunderbolt), that seems plausible. But this is an army of demonically possessed soldiers—yes, it sounds weird when you say it out loud, but go with it—so maybe there's something more to this than a physical obstacle created by a multitude of dead bodies.

The Hebrew word translated "block," *wəhōsemet*, is based on the root *chasam*,[399] which is only used twice in the Old Testament. The other verse is Deuteronomy 25:4: "You shall not muzzle an ox when it is treading out the grain." So, "block" means "muzzle." To muzzle an animal is to restrain it so it can't eat or bite, which is much more specific than creating an impassable obstacle. How demons are muzzled, we don't know, but we trust God has a plan for that.

Some scholars, following the KJV, take this to mean it will "stop the noses" of travelers along the King's Highway, apparently because of the stench of the decaying dead. But let's view this in the context of the necromancy rituals from Ugarit.

Their rites summoned the spirits of the Travelers, the Rephaim, to ritual meals at the house or sanctuary of El. Since Ezekiel wrote under God's direction, we can assume that he was aware of this. Then the prophecy of the destruction of the army of Gog is a reversal of those rituals. On the day of the Lord, instead of arriving at a ritual meal to be revivified by "the blessings of the name of El," they will be *muzzled*—prevented from doing whatever they did when they traveled, came over, or crossed over from the land of the dead to the realm of the living. Why? Because they'll be muzzled with extreme prejudice.

Let's go back to Isaiah. By this time, you may not be surprised to learn that we've found another prophecy hidden in the prophet's writings.

O LORD our God,
other lords besides you have ruled over us,
but your name alone we bring to remembrance.
They are dead, they will not live;
they are shades [Rephaim], they will not arise;
to that end you have visited them with destruction
and wiped out all remembrance of them.
(Isaiah 26:13–14, emphasis added)

The word translated "shades" is *rephaim*, which gives this Scripture a very different meaning. The Rephaim were once the "other lords" who ruled over God's people, or over the earth. That's why God "visited them with destruction."

This can be taken a couple of ways. By the time Moses and the Israelites arrived in the Transjordan, only Og of Bashan was left of the Rephaim. The other tribes had been wiped out by the people of Ammon, Moab, and Edom.[400] But it could also be a reference to the Nephilim who walked the earth in the days of Noah, the "mighty men who were of old" whose earth-shaking deeds inspired worship down to the days of David and beyond.[401]

Isaiah then continues with a prophecy of the latter days:

Your dead shall live; their bodies shall rise.
You who dwell in the dust, awake and sing for joy!
For your dew is a dew of light,
and the earth will give birth to the dead [Rephaim]....
For behold, the LORD is coming out from his place
to punish the inhabitants of the earth for their iniquity,
and the earth will disclose the blood shed on it,
and will no more cover its slain. (Isaiah 26:19, 21)

This requires a little unpacking. Verse 21, the second half of the passage cited above, clearly prophesies a day when Yahweh dispenses justice on the earth.

Verse 19, on the other hand, is difficult to grasp. It seems to foretell the resurrection, but the earth giving birth to the Rephaim appears to contradict verse 14. We just read that they're dead and "will not rise." So, which is it?

Let's bring in the Septuagint translation for comparison. This can be helpful when trying to get a sense of a difficult passage in the Old Testament because it's a window into the minds of Jewish religious scholars who lived a couple of centuries before Jesus.

The dead will rise, and those in the tombs will be raised, and those in the earth will rejoice; for the dew from you is a remedy for them, but the land of the impious will fall. (Isaiah 26:19, LXX)[402]

That's a lot different from "the earth will give birth to the Rephaim." What or where is "the land of the impious"?

Scholar Brook W. R. Pearson reads it this way:

It is probable that the reference...is meant to indicate the pit of
Tartarus, and that the inhabitants of this place are to be differ-
entiated from the rest of the dead. Given the prominence of the
Titans in other Hellenistic period Jewish literature, it is hard to
believe that the initial audience of this passage could have seen
them as anything but the Titans, and their "land" as anything
but Tartarus.[403]

In other words, Isaiah and the Jewish scholars who translated his
work into Greek understood the connection between the Rephaim (the
giants of old), the Watchers, and the old gods of the Greeks, the Titans.
Bear in mind that our English translations come from the Masoretic
Text, a Hebrew translation that wasn't finalized until the seventh and
tenth centuries AD, or between 900 and 1,200 years after the Hebrew
text used by the translators of the Septuagint, which has since been lost.
We suggest that the scholars who worked on the Septuagint had a better
handle on the sense of the verse.

It's our belief that Isaiah was prophesying the ultimate demise of
these demon kings of old, the Rephaim, who'd plagued Israel throughout its history and still afflict the world to this day. And this, we believe,
was confirmed by Ezekiel in his prophecy of the end of the war of Gog
and Magog.

Remember the curious phrase, "it will block the Travelers, for there
Gog and all his multitude will be buried"? Here's how we process that verse:

- Ezekiel's Travelers are the Rephaim; in other words, the demonic
  spirits of the Nephilim destroyed in the Flood.
- The Travelers/Rephaim will be part of the army of Gog,
  probably as spirits possessing the human soldiers fighting for the
  Antichrist.

- Isaiah prophesied a future resurrection for the faithful, an event that we believe is the same one prophesied by Paul in 1 Corinthians 15:35–55.
- The Travelers/Rephaim, however, will be "blocked." In other words, they will *not* be resurrected—as Isaiah put it, "They are dead, they will not live; they are [Rephaim], they will not arise."
- Further, "the land of the impious (ungodly, profane) ones will fall," the domain of the Titans—the Watchers of Genesis 6:1–4.

A day is coming when the abyss opens, and the gatekeeper of the underworld—Resheph/Apollo, called Apollyon by John—leads a hellish assault on the people still on earth, no doubt assisted by their demonic progeny. But their revenge is short-lived—just five months.[404]

That's exactly how long it took the waters of Noah's Flood to recede from the earth. The Watchers will have five months to wreak vengeance on humanity for the five months they watched from the abyss, helpless, while their monstrous children, the Nephilim, perished in the Flood.

Then comes the end—with none to help them.

Conclusion

This has been a whirlwind tour through human history that's taken us from the original garden, Eden, to a sci-fi future prophesied by apostles of the modern ancient-aliens UFO cult. You've seen the long game played by the Infernal Council as they deceived our ancestors into worshiping the demonic spirits of the Nephilim in the belief that they were honoring their dead ancestors and the kings of old. This practice is documented as far back as the third millennium BC, and it was so deeply ingrained in Mediterranean cultures that archaeologists have solid evidence that the Christians of Rome as late as the fourth century AD, after the faith was legalized by Constantine, still practiced ritual communal meals in cemeteries for, and with, the dead.

It was a very old custom. As we saw, Abraham, more than two thousand years earlier, was distressed that he had no living heir, other than his servant Eleazar, to serve as his "son of the cup" and perform the monthly rituals he thought were necessary to be properly cared for in the afterlife.

To us, providing food and drink to the dead seems silly, but there are still places in the world today where that would fit right in to local religious customs. Such offerings are not very different from the gifts of food, tobacco, and alcohol left at shrines for Mexican folk saints like Jesús Malverde and Santa Muerte ("Saint Death"). Ancestor veneration continues in much of the Far East, where the Roman Catholic was compelled to lift a ban on ancestral rites in Korea in 1939.[405] Even we Americans can get close to the ancient rites with some of our burial customs and the care and maintenance of gravesites.

The Bible only gives us one example of a human spirit returning to the land of the living, that of Samuel, who was tasked with delivering a message to King Saul. Demons, however, are scattered throughout the Bible, although they're mentioned far more often in the New Testament. For that matter, we never see the prophets of the Old Testament engaged in deliverance or exorcism.

We do, however, see attacks by the prophets on pagan veneration of those spirits. It was a practice that drew in the Israelites from the time they arrived on the plains of Moab practically down to the Babylonian captivity. It brought disaster in the form of a plague that killed twenty-four thousand Israelites before they crossed the Jordan, and God condemned those who offered sacrifices to the dead in gardens, tombs, and among the smooth stones of the valley—sometimes human children.

Ezekiel prophesied that the last act of these demon spirits will be to fall in the Valley of the Travelers, soldiers in the army of Gog of Magog, the Antichrist. This will be the Battle of Armageddon, fought for control of the Lord's *har-mō'ēd*, His mount of assembly, Zion. And when we are raised from the dead and transformed into imperishable beings when the last trumpet sounds (theology we don't hear much about in church), the Travelers—the Rephaim, spirits of the dead Nephilim—will be *blocked*. We believe this is the ultimate end for the hybrid spawn of the Watchers.

Armageddon will be, in a real sense, the ultimate zombie apocalypse. But victory has been decreed, as has the ultimate destruction of the Watchers, the rebellious host of heaven, Satan, and their demonic henchmen. Our mission, dear reader, is to make disciples of all nations while there is still time. The Enemy will try to stop you from fulfilling your commission, and will stop at nothing to discourage, distract, and demoralize you.

Take heart. We have the tools we need. It's up to us, through the power of the Holy Spirit, to stand our ground and rescue the wounded on the battlefield. Many of them have been so thoroughly deluded by the Enemy's lies and deception that they don't even realize they're standing in the middle of a battlefield.

So be it. Our Savior took the nails for us. We can withstand what the Enemy throws at us. God's got your back.

Think about this: For literally millennia, the rulers of the fallen realm have convinced their pagan followers to provide them food and drink—sometimes in the form of bread, water, or wine offered to teraphim or temple idols, and often—far too often—as human blood.

Now, remember:

...that the Lord Jesus on the night when he was betrayed took bread, and when he had given thanks, he broke it, and said, "This is my body, which is for you. Do this in remembrance of me."

In the same way also he took the cup, after supper, saying, "This cup is the new covenant in my blood. Do this, as often as you drink it, in remembrance of me." For as often as you eat this bread and drink the cup, you proclaim the Lord's death until he comes. (1 Corinthians 11:23–26)

You see, the rebellious sons of God demand sacrifice from us—even the sacrifice of our children—as food and drink so that they and their demon spawn might live.

Our Lord and Savior sacrificed Himself, becoming the Bread and Water of Life so that *we* might live.

That's the fundamental difference between our Lord and the other "lords" we've foolishly served since we were expelled from Eden. Until our Savior returns, leading the cavalry of heaven to rescue the faithful, the battle rages on.

And finally, let us remember the greatest weapon of all given to the children of Adam: prayer. Since Sharon first wrote the following passage for *The Redwing Saga's* fifth book, *Realms of Fire*, she's been asked again and again to print it, email it, and recite it for eager readers. It is a prayer that often brings tears, for it comes from a humble servant, representing all of us. We'd like to end with this. As you read it, remember that we stand upon a battlefield, and that our great General, the LORD of Hosts, still commands that field, and the enemy's plans are doomed to failure. May each of you put on the full armor and be ready to stand as we enter the final phases of this ongoing war.

From *Realms of Fire*, Book 5, The Redwing Saga

"Before we begin, I would ask Mr. Cornelius Baxter to offer a prayer both for the meal and for our discussion," Charles Sinclair told the members.

Baxter stepped forward, completely surprised. "Sir, are you sure?"

"I can think of no one more qualified," the marquess answered.

The formidable butler with the humble heart bowed his head. "Then, let us pray," he said, his sonorous voice low. "Our Gracious and wonderful Saviour and King, we humbly come to your throne this morning, many of us weighed down with the troubles of the day already, some with health issues, some with financial woes, others with concerns about family and friends, some carrying fear and doubt that darkens the soul and devours the mind—but no matter what our worries, no matter what our concerns or our anxieties, no matter the dross or decay of the world that rises to the top and surrounds, they all vanish and are vanquished in the light of Your face!

"It is unusual for me to speak before such an honourable gathering of fellow soldiers. I say this not because most of these men bear noble titles, but because they bear noble scars. Physical as well as spiritual. I have watched the members of this circle rush into battle wearing naught but your promises upon their mortal frames, wielding nary an ax, but flashing the sword of the spirit in the eyes of the enemy. A double-edged blade likened unto the Word of God that proceeds out of them with a fiery vengeance! But as brave as these deeds are—as valiant as their exploits in armour might be—this circle's greatest achievements are accomplished not on the battlefield but within the quietness of the prayer closet. Before these warriors take to their feet, they spend time on their knees; each and every one of them, and it is my honour to be called their fellow. I know not what plans the enemy now devises, my Lord, but you do. Help us to unmask their faces and uncover their secrets. Let us rise to the fight until our arms grow numb, and our breath be gone. Let us crawl when our legs will no longer run, whisper when our voices fail, feel our way forward when our eyes become blind.

"Bind upon our hearts a love for one another that knows no language other than love and knows no title other than brother or sister. Help us to serve you with all our strength, soul, and mind until the end of our days. And when those days are done, my Lord, let us continue to cheer our beloved fellows whilst we kneel before your throne. As St. Paul wrote, '*Wherefore seeing we also are compassed about with so great a cloud of witnesses, let us lay aside every weight, and the sin which doth so easily beset us, and let us run with patience the race that is set before us, Looking unto*

Jesus the author and finisher of our faith; who for the joy that was set before him endured the cross, despising the shame, and is set down at the right hand of the throne of God.'

"Saviour and King, I shall consider it a privilege to be counted amongst that cloud of witnesses one day, standing alongside men like Paul and Peter and James, cheering on this group of servant-soldiers who continue to battle upon the field. May that day come for us all when our Saviour returns. In the meantime, we consider it all the greatest joy to partake of only a small share of that which you endured on our behalf. Thank you for each man and woman here today. In the name of our King, I ask it. Even Christ Jesus. Amen."[406]

They are dead, they shall not live; they are deceased, they shall not rise: therefore hast thou visited and destroyed them, and made all their memory to perish. (Isaiah 26:14)

And the Spirit and the bride say, Come.

And let him that heareth say, Come.
And let him that is athirst come.
And whosoever will, let him take the water of life freely.
(Revelation 22:17)

Notes

1. The Hebrew word *iyrim* is translated "cities" in English Bibles. However, as we'll see later in this book, the context of Isaiah 14 argues for using the Aramaic *iyr* ("Watcher") as the root behind the word.

2. Genesis 6:4 (ESV).

3. Robert Matthews, "Believe It or Not, They're All the Same Species." *The Telegraph*, December 26, 2004. https://www.telegraph.co.uk/news/worldnews/northamerica/usa/1479800/Believe-it-or-not-theyre-all-the-same-species.html, retrieved 5/7/19.

4. 1 Enoch 6:1–2, 7:1–3. George W. E. Nickelsburg, *1 Enoch: The Hermeneia Translation* (Minneapolis, MN: Fortress Press, 2012), Kindle Edition, pgs. 22–24.

5. 1 Enoch 9:7.

6. Epic of Erra, Tablet 1, line 47. Helge Kvanvig, Primeval History: Babylonian, Biblical, and Enochic: An Intertextual Reading (Leiden: Brill, 2011), pp. 161–2.

7. 1 Peter 3:18–19, ESV.

8. For example, 1 Enoch 10:2 and 1 Enoch chapters 83 and 84.

9. See Genesis 14.

10. Deuteronomy 3:11.

11. Conrad l'Heureux, "The *yelide harapa*—A Cultic Association of Warriors." *Bulletin of the American Schools of Oriental Research* No. 221, (Feb., 1976), pp. 83-85. L'Heureux argues that the biblical definition "descendants" is too narrow and literal. The Hebrew word *yelide* referred to "one who is born into the group by adoption, initiation or consecration," and that "the second element in the phrase might then be the name of the group, or its emblem, or the name of the group's patron, whether human or divine." In other words, "Sons of the Rephaim" was probably an exclusive warrior cult who worshiped the spirits of the Nephilim.

12. E. C. B. MacLaurin, "Anak/ʾανξ." *Vetus Testamentum*, Vol. 15, Fasc. 4 (Oct., 1965), pp. 468-474.

13. Matthew Suriano, "Dynasty Building at Ugarit: The Ritual and Political Context of KTU 1.161," *Aula Orientalis* 27 (2009), p. 107.

14. Andrea Polcaro, "The Bone Talisman and the Ideology of Ancestors in Old Syrian Ebla: Tradition and Innovation in the Royal Funerary Ritual Iconography." In P. Matthiae (ed.), *Studia Eblaitica* (Wiesbaden: Harrassowitz Verlag, 2015), pp. 179–204.

15. Brian B. Schmidt, "Israel's Beneficent Dead: The Character and Origin of Israelite Ancestor Cults and Necromancy." (Oxford: University of Oxford doctoral thesis, 1991), pp. 158–159.

16. Amar Annus, "Are There Greek Rephaim? On the Etymology of Greek *Meropes* and *Titanes*." *Ugarit-Forschungen* 31 (1999), pp. 13–30.

17. Isaiah 14:12. Interestingly, Shachar was a deity attested in texts from the Amorite kingdom of Ugarit.

18. Isaiah 36 and 37.

19. W. G. E. Watson, "Helel." In K. van der Toorn, B. Becking, & P. W. van der Horst (Eds.), *Dictionary of Deities and Demons in the Bible* (Leiden; Boston; Köln; Grand Rapids, MI; Cambridge: Brill; Eerdmans, 1999), p. 392.

20. KTU 1.4, v, 49–55. In Nicolas Wyatt, *Religious Texts from Ugarit,* 2nd ed. (London; New York: Sheffield Academic Press, 2002), pp. 103–104.

21. Matthew 12:26 and Luke 11:18.

22. Revelation 2:13.

23. See Derek's book, *Last Clash of the Titans*, which digs into Ezekiel's prophecy of the Gog-Magog war, and explains in depth why all of the nations mentioned by Ezekiel aside from Persia, Cush (Ethiopia), and Put (Libya), were located in Anatolia, modern-day Turkey.

24. Christopher B. Hays, "An Egyptian Loanword in the Book of Isaiah and the Deir 'Alla Inscription: Heb. *nṣr*, Aram. *nqr*, and Eg. *nṯr* as "[Divinized] Corpse." *Journal of Ancient Egyptian Interconnections* Vol. 4:2 (2012), p. 18.

25. Ibid., p. 17.

26. Isaiah 36:6.

27. Robin Ngo, "King Hezekiah in the Bible: Royal Seal of Hezekiah Comes to Light," *Bible History Daily* (May 18, 2019). https://www.biblicalarchaeology. org/daily/news/king-hezekiah-in-the-bible-royal-seal-of-hezekiah-comes-to-light/, retrieved 6/9/19.

28. Meir Lubetsky, "King Hezekiah's Seal Revisited," *Biblical Archaeology Review* 27:4 (2001), pp. 44–50.

29. George C. Heider, *The Cult of Molek: A Reassessment* (Sheffield: JSOT Press, 1985), pp. 90-91.

30. Jan N. Bremmer, "Remember the Titans!" In C. Auffarth and L. Stuckenbruck (eds.), *The Fall of the Angels* (Leiden; Boston: Brill, 2004), pp. 43–44.

31. Ibid., p. 44.

32. John F. Miller, "Roman Festivals," in *The Oxford Encyclopedia of Ancient Greece and Rome* (Oxford University Press, 2010), p. 172.

33. Porphyry, *On Abstinence from Animal Food,* 2.54 (http://www.tertullian.org/ fathers/porphyry_abstinence_02_book2.htm, retrieved 6/15/19).

34. Porphyry, *Abst.* 2.56.

35. Diodorus Siculus, *Library of World History* 13.86.3; 20.14.6 (http://penelope. uchicago.edu/Thayer/E/Roman/Texts/Diodorus_Siculus/home.html, retrieved 6/15/19); also Tertullian, *Apologeticus* 9.22 (http://www.tertullian.org/articles/ mayor_apologeticum/mayor_apologeticum_07translation.htm, retrieved 6/15/19).

36. Plutarch, *On Superstition* 13.4 (http://penelope.uchicago.edu/Thayer/E/Roman/ Texts/Plutarch/Moralia/De_superstitione*.html, retrieved 6/15/19).

37. Diodorus Siculus, op. cit., 20.14.7.

38. Tertullian, op. cit.

39. Bremmer, op. cit., p. 46.

40. Nicolas Wyatt, "À la Recherche des Rephaïm Perdus." *The Archaeology of Myth: Papers on Old Testament Tradition* (Sheffield: Taylor and Francis, 2010), p. 56.

41. Michael Heltzer, *The Suteans* (Naples: Instituto Universitario Orientale, 1981), p. 99.

42. Thorkild Jacobsen, Cuneiform Texts in the National Museum, Copenhagen, Chiefly of Economical Contents (Leiden: Brill, 1939), p. 7.

43. Walther Sallaberger,"From Urban Culture to Nomadism: A History of Upper Mesopotamia in the Late Third Millennium." In: C. Kuzucuoğlu and C. Marro (eds.), *Sociétés humaines et changement climatique à la fin du troisième millé-naire: une crise a-t-elle eu lieu en Haute Mésopotamie?* (Istanbul: Institut Fran-çais d'Études Anatoliennes-Georges Dumézil, 2007), pp. 444–445.

44. Annus (1999), op. cit., p. 19.

45. Ugaritic text KTU 1.15. III, 13–15, cited by Annus, op. cit.

46. KTU 1.161, in Nicolas Wyatt, *Religious Texts from Ugarit (2nd ed.).* (London; New York: Sheffield Academic Press, 2005), p. 210.

47. Jordi Vidal, "The Origins of the Last Ugaritic Dynasty." *Altorientalishce Forsc-hungen* 33 (2006), p. 168.

48. Og of Bashan, defeated by the Israelites around 1406 BC, was described in the Bible as the last of the remnant of the Rephaim (Deuteronomy 3:11).

49. Annus, op. cit., p. 20.

50. Derek P. Gilbert, *Last Clash of the Titans* (Crane, Mo.: Defender, 2018), pp. 86–87.

51. Hesiod, *Works and Days*, l. 121.

52. Genesis 10:16.

53. Daniel Bodi, "Is There a Connection Between the Amorites and the Arameans?" *Aram* 26:1 & 2 (Oxford: Aram Publishing, 2014), p. 385.

54. Renata MacDougal, *Remembrance and the Dead in Second Millennium BC Mesopotamia* (University of Leicester: Doctoral dissertation, 2014) pp. 58–59.

55. Ibid., p. 22.

56. Ibid.

57. Ibid., p. 26.

58. Nicolas Wyatt, "After Death Has Us Parted," in *The Perfumes of Seven Tamarisks* (Munster: Ugarit-Verlag, 2014) p. 261.

59. Ibid.

60. Karel van der Toorn, "The Nature of the Biblical Teraphim in the Light of the Cuneiform Evidence," *The Catholic Biblical Quarterly, Vol. 52, No. 2* (April, 1990), pp. 215–216.

61. LKA 83, Lines 1–10, cited by MacDougal, op. cit., p. 53.

62. Jo Ann Scurlock, "Death and the Afterlife in Ancient Mesopotamian Thought," in *Civilizations of the Ancient Near East,* ed. Jack M. Sasson (New York: Scribner, 1995) p. 1889.

63. Wyatt, op. cit., p. 276.

64. Scurlock, op. cit., p. 1884.

65. Wyatt, op. cit., p. 264.

66. Ibid., p. 265.

67. MacDougal, op. cit., p. 25.

68. BM 17495, CT 43 106, cited by MacDougal, op. cit., p. 58.

69. Ibid., p. 24.

70. Wyatt, op. cit., p. 261.

71. Scurlock, op. cit, p. 1889.

72. Wyatt, op. cit., p. 261.

73. Gog of Magog, in Ezekiel 39:11—the Valley of the Travelers.

74. Genesis 19:30-38.

75. And the name of the aforementioned Amorite king Ammi-ditana essentially means "my people are the Ditanu," the ancient Amorite tribe whose name is the origin of the name of the old Greek gods, the Titans. See Annus (1999), op. cit.

76. MacDougal, op. cit., p. 55.

77. 1 Samuel 25:1.

78. Wyatt, op. cit., p. 282.

79. See Genesis 24.

80. 1 Enoch 6:6.

81. Edward Lipiński, "El's Abode: Mythological Traditions Related to Mount Hermon and to the Mountains of Armenia." *Orientalia Lovaniensa Periodica* II (Leuvan, 1971), p. 29.

82 Ibid.

83. 1 Enoch 15:11. George W. E. Nickelsburg, *1 Enoch: The Hermeneia Translation* (Minneapolis: Fortress Press, Kindle Edition, 2012), p. 37.

84. Barry, J. D., Mangum, D., Brown, D. R., Heiser, M. S., Custis, M., Ritzema, E., … Bomar, D., *Faithlife Study Bible* [*Nu 25:8*] (Bellingham, WA: Lexham Press, 2016).

85. Dr. Phillip J. Silvia, "The 3.7kaBP Middle Ghor Event: Catastrophic Termination of a Bronze Age Civilization." American Schools of Oriental Research annual meeting (Denver, November 17, 2018), p. 1.

86. Ibid., p. 3.

87. Ibid., p. 1.

88. Based on Strong's Hebrew #58, meaning a "grassy meadow or plain."

89. Steven Collins and Latayne C. Scott, *Discovering the City of Sodom* (New York: Howard Books, 2013).

90. Joseph Tropper, "Spirit of the Dead." In K. van der Toorn, B. Becking, & P. W. van der Horst (Eds.), *Dictionary of Deities and Demons in the Bible (2nd extensively rev. ed.)* (Leiden; Boston; Köln; Grand Rapids, MI; Cambridge: Brill; Eerdmans, 1999), p. 806.

91. 1 Samuel 28:3–25.

92. l'Heureux, op. cit.

93. For a highly entertaining, biblically based account of the influence of the giants on human history, Brian Godawa's *Chronicles of the Nephilim* series is highly recommended.

94. Spronk (1986), op. cit., p. 229.

95. Klaas Spronk, "Travellers." In K. van der Toorn, B. Becking, & P. W. van der Horst (Eds.), *Dictionary of Deities and Demons in the Bible* (2nd extensively rev. ed.) (Leiden; Boston; Köln; Grand Rapids, MI; Cambridge: Brill; Eerdmans, 1999), p. 876.

96. Klaas Spronk, "Baal of Peor." In K. van der Toorn, B. Becking, & P.W. van der Horst (Eds.), *Dictionary of Deities and Demons in the Bible* (2nd extensively rev. ed.) (Leiden; Boston; Köln; Grand Rapids, MI; Cambridge: Brill; Eerdmans, 1999), p. 147.

97. KTU 1.5, ii, 1. In Nicolas Wyatt, *Religious Texts from Ugarit* (2nd ed.) (London; New York: Sheffield Academic Press, 2002), p. 120.

98. Theodore J. Lewis, "Death Cult Imagery in Isaiah 57." *Hebrew Annual Review* 11 (1987), p. 271.

99. Susan Ackerman, "Sacred Sex, Sacrifice, and Death." *Bible Review 6:1* (February 1990). https://www.baslibrary.org/bible-review/6/1/9, retrieved 7/23/19. Fertility rites in sacred groves are mentioned in Isaiah 1:29-30, Hosea 4:12–13, and Ezekiel 20:28.

100. 2 Kings 23:10, Jeremiah 7:31 and 19:6.

101. Faithlife Study Bible. See also Lewis, op.cit., pp. 272–273.

102. Spronk, K. (1999). "Travellers." op. cit., p. 876.

103. Tropper, J. (1999). "Spirit of the Dead." In K. van der Toorn, B. Becking, & P. W. van der Horst (Eds.), *Dictionary of Deities and Demons in the Bible* (2nd extensively rev. ed.) (Leiden; Boston; Köln; Grand Rapids, MI; Cambridge: Brill; Eerdmans), p. 806.

104. Spronk (1986), op. cit., p. 229.

105. Major Contributors and Editors. (2016). "Iye-Abarim." In J. D. Barry, D. Bomar, D. R. Brown, R. Klippenstein, D. Mangum, C. Sinclair Wolcott, … W. Widder (Eds.), *The Lexham Bible Dictionary* (Bellingham, WA: Lexham Press).

106. Schuster, R. (2017). "Monumental Carved Dolmen More Than 4,000 Years Old Found in Golan Rewrites History of Civilization." *Haaretz* (March 6, 2017), https://www.haaretz.com/archaeology/huge-dolmen-found-in-golan-rewrites-history-of-civilization-1.5444970, retrieved 3/26/18.

107. Yassine, K. (1985). "The Dolmens: Construction and Dating Reconsidered." *Bulletin of the American Schools of Oriental Research*, No. 259 (Summer, 1985), pp. 63–69.

108. Sharon G, Barash A, Eisenberg-Degen D, Grosman L, Oron M, et al. (2017)

"Monumental Megalithic Burial and Rock Art Tell a New Story about the Levant Intermediate Bronze 'Dark Ages.'" *PLOS ONE* 12(3): e0172969. https://doi.org/10.1371/journal.pone.0172969, retrieved 3/28/18.

109. Savage, S. (2010). "Jordan's Stonehenge: The Endangered Chalcolithic/ Early Bronze Age Site at al-Murayghât–Hajr al-Mansûb," *Near Eastern Archaeology* 73:1, p. 32.

110. Spronk, K. (1986), op. cit., p. 228.

111. Yassine, K. (1985), op. cit.

112. Ibid., p. 66.

113. Sharon G., et al (2017). op. cit., p. 1.

114. Ibid., p. 10.

115. Ibid., p. 17.

116. See Jude 1:9.

117. Strong's Concordance #H6465, http://lexiconcordance.com/hebrew/6465.html, retrieved 3/27/18.

118. Spronk, K. (1999). "Baal of Peor." In K. van der Toorn, B. Becking, & P. W. van der Horst (Eds.), *Dictionary of Deities and Demons in the Bible* (2nd extensively rev. ed.) (Leiden; Boston; Köln; Grand Rapids, MI; Cambridge: Brill; Eerdmans), p. 147.

119. KTU 1.5, ii, 1. In Wyatt, N. (2002). *Religious Texts from Ugarit* (2nd ed.) (London; New York: Sheffield Academic Press), p. 120.

120. Barry, J. D., Mangum, D., Brown, D. R., Heiser, M. S., Custis, M., Ritzema, E., … Bomar, D. (2012, 2016). *Faithlife Study Bible* (Nu 25:8), (Bellingham, WA: Lexham Press).

121. Torres, H. (2016). "57% Percent of Pastors, 64% of Youth Pastors in U.S. Struggle with Porn Addiction, Survey Shows." *Christian Today*, January 30, 2016. https://www.christiantoday.com/article/57-percent-of-pastors-and-64-of-youth-pastors-in-u-s-struggle-with-porn-addiction-survey-shows/78178.htm, retrieved 3/27/18.

122. Diane Wolkstein and Samuel N. Kramer, *Inanna, Queen of Heaven and Earth: Her Stories and Hymns from Sumer* (New York: Harper & Row, 1983), p. 60.

123. Ezekiel 8:14.

124. 1 Samuel 28:12.

125. KTU 1.108:1–3. Translation by Nicolas Wyatt, *Religious Texts from Ugarit* (2nd ed.). (London; New York: Sheffield Academic Press, 2002), p. 395.

126. RS 24:244:40–41. Translation by Dennis Pardee & Theodore J. Lewis, *Ritual and Cult at Ugarit* (Vol. 10). (Atlanta, GA: Society of Biblical Literature, 2002), p. 177. Ugaritic text RS 24:251:42 also places the god Milku in Ashtaroth.

127. 1 Kings 11:5 calls Milcom "the abomination of the Ammonites," but 1 Kings 11:7 uses the same description for Molech.

128. George Heider, *The Cult of Molek: A Reassessment* (Sheffield: University of Sheffield, 1985), p. 96.

129. Ibid., p. 129.

130. Rebecca Doyle, Faces of the Gods: Baal, Asherah and Molek and Studies of the Hebrew Scriptures. Doctoral thesis (University of Sheffield, 1996), p. 129.

131. MacDougal, op. cit., pp. 85–86.

132. Ibid., p. 89.

133. Ibid, p. 92.

134. M. L. Barré, "dLAMMA and Rešep at Ugarit: The Hittite Connection." *Journal of the American Oriental Society*, 98:4 (January 1, 1978), pp. 465–467.

135. Paola Xella, "Resheph." In K. van der Toorn, B. Becking, & P. W. van der Horst (Eds.), *Dictionary of Deities and Demons in the Bible* (2nd extensively rev. ed.). (Leiden; Boston; Köln; Grand Rapids, MI; Cambridge: Brill; Eerdmans, 1999), p. 701.

136. Giovanni Pettinato, *The Archives of Ebla: An Empire Inscribed in Clay.* (Garden City, NY: Doubleday & Company, Inc., 1981), p. 248.

137. Genesis 12:6–7.

138. Genesis 34.

139. Genesis 34:30.

140. Genesis 48:22.

141. Maciej M. Münnich, *The God Resheph in the Ancient Near East* (Tübingen: Mohr Siebeck, 2013), p. 114.

142. Maciej M. Münnich, "Two Faces of Resheph in Egyptian Sources of the New

Kingdom." In Iconography and Biblical Studies: Proceedings of the Iconography Sessions at the Joint EABS / SBL Conference, 22–26 July 2007, Vienna, Austria (AOAT, 361; Münster: Ugarit, 2009), p. 54.

143. Douglas N. Petrovich, "Amenhotep II and the Historicity of the Exodus-Pharaoh." https://www.academia.edu/1049040/_2006_Amenhotep_II_

144. Xella, op. cit., p. 702.

145. Manfred Hutter. "Abaddon." In K. van der Toorn, B. Becking, & P. W. van der Horst (Eds.), *Dictionary of Deities and Demons in the Bible* (2nd extensively rev. ed.). (Leiden; Boston; Köln; Grand Rapids, MI; Cambridge: Brill; Eerdmans, 1999), p. 1.

146. "Apollo: Greek God of the Sun and Light." *Greek Mythology*, www.greekmythology.com, retrieved 7/27/19.

147. 2 Kings 21:18, 26.

148. 2 Kings 21:11.

149. 2 Kings 21:3–7.

150. MacDougal, op. cit., p. 26.

151. Nicola Laneri, "Embodying the Memory of the Royal Ancestors in Western Syria During the 3rd and 2nd Millennia BC: The Case of Ebla and Qatna." In D. Nadali (ed.), *Envisioning the Past Through Memories* (New York: Bloomsbury Academic, 2016), pp. 58–59.

152. Ibid., p. 62.

153. Polcaro, op. cit., p. 190.

154. Ibid., p. 191.

155. Paolo Matthiae, "The Royal Ancestors' Cult in Northern Levant Between Early and Late Bronze Age: Continuity and Problems from Ebla to Ugarit." *BAAL (Bulletin d'Archeologie et d'Architecture Libanaises)*, Hors-Serie X (2015), p. 22.

156. Ibid., p. 6.

157. Vidal, op. cit.

158. Francesca Stavrakapolou, "Exploring the Garden of Uzza: Death, Burial and Ideologies of Kingship." *Biblica* Vol. 87 (2006), p. 13.

159. M. Dahood and G. Pettinato, "Ugaritic *ršp gn* and Eblaite *rasap gunu(m)ki*." *Orientalia*, NOVA SERIES, Vol. 46, No. 2 (1977), p. 230.

160. Ibid.

161. Stavrakapolou, op. cit., p. 9.

162. Nicolas Wyatt, "After Death Has Us Parted." In *The Perfumes of Seven Tamarisks* (Munster: Ugarit-Verlaine, 2014), p. 285.

163. Ismar Schorsch, "The Story of Pig as Taboo," *Jewish Theological Seminary* (April 17, 2004). http://www.jtsa.edu/the-story-of-pig-as-taboo, retrieved 7/13/19.

164. Wyatt, op. cit.

165. 2 Kings 21:18. 2 Chronicles 33:20 notes simply that "Manasseh slept with his fathers, and they buried him in his house."

166. 2 Kings 21:26. 2 Chronicles 33 does not note the location of Amon's burial.

167. 2 Kings 18:3.

168. Although, to be fair, 2 Chronicles 33:10–16 records that Manasseh repented and humbled himself before God.

169. 2 Kings 21:11.

170. Wyatt, op.cit, p. 286.

171. Carl Gallups, *Gods of Ground Zero* (Crane, Mo.: Defender, 2018). See especially pages 241–243.

172. Ezekiel 28:13–14.

173. Wyatt, "A Royal Garden: The Ideology of Eden," p. 11.

174. John 19:41–42.

175. Ezekiel 28:14.

176. See Matthew 21:33–45, Mark 12:1–12, and Luke 20:9–19.

177. Matthew 21:41.

178. H. M. Barstad, "Sheol." In K. van der Toorn, B. Becking, & P. W. van der Horst (Eds.), *Dictionary of Deities and Demons in the Bible* (2nd extensively rev. ed.). (Leiden; Boston; Köln; Grand Rapids, MI; Cambridge: Brill; Eerdmans, 1999), pg. 768.

179. Proverbs 27:20.

180. Isaiah 5:14.

181. Leviticus 7:30–34.

182. Louise M. Pryke, *Ishtar* (New York and London: Routledge, 2017), p. 205.

183. Wolkstein and Kramer, op. cit., p. 56.

184. Rita Lucarelli, "The Guardian-demons of the Book of the Dead." *British Museum Studies in Ancient Egypt and Sudan* 15 (2010), p. 87.

185. Ibid., p. 86.

186. Amar Annus, "On the Origin of Watchers: A Comparative Study of the Antediluvian Wisdom in Mesopotamian and Jewish Traditions," *Journal for the Study of the Pseudepigrapha* vol. 19:4 (2010), pp. 277–320.

187. Genesis 37:35; Numbers 16:30–33; 1 Samuel 2:6; Job 7:9 and 17:16, etc.

188. Ugaritic texts KTU 1.20–1.22, the Rephaim Texts.

189. Brian R. Doak, "Ezekiel's Topography of the (Un-)Heroic Dead in Ezekiel 32:17–32." *Journal of Biblical Literature*, Vol. 132, No. 3 (2013), p. 611.

190. Ezekiel 32:18.

191. Ezekiel 32:23.

192. Ezekiel 32:24–30.

193. Ezekiel 32:23–26, 30.

194. Doak, op. cit, p. 616.

195. Ibid., p. 612.

196. Ronald S. Handel, "Of Demigods and the Deluge: Toward an Interpretation of Genesis 6:1–4." *Journal of Biblical Literature* 106 (1987), p. 22.

197. Karl Kerenyi, *The Heroes of the Greeks* (London: Thames and Hudson, 1959), p. 75.

198. Wyatt (2005), op. cit., p. 52. Wyatt cited the earlier work of Michael C. Astour, *Hellenosemitica: An Ethnic and Cultural Study in West Semitic Impact on Mycenaean Greece* (Leiden: Brill, 1967), p. 230.

199. Pindar, *Olympian Odes*, xiii.87–90, and *Isthmian Odes*, vii.44; *Bibliotheke* ii.3.2; Homer, *Iliad* vi.155–203 and xvi.328; Ovid, *Metamorphoses* ix.646.

200. Michael Freikman and Naomi Porat, "Rujm el-Hiri: The Monument in the Landscape." *Tel Aviv*, 44:1 (2017), p. 31.

201. Ibid., p. 22.

202. Jaimie Waters, in his 2013 Johns Hopkins doctoral dissertation, *Threshing Floors as Sacred Spaces in the Hebrew Bible,* adds this footnote: Anderson and Freedman read *dāgān* with verse 2 to create a more balanced poetic line in

verse 1b. Cf. Anderson and Freedman, Hosea, 5:19. The word for grain, *dāgān*, could be a play on the Canaanite deity Dagan who is associated with grain. If this was the case, it would suggest that these threshing floors were dedicated to Dagan worship. This is an interesting possibility, especially since the oracle focuses on punishment for worship of non-Yahwistic gods. However, throughout Hosea, Baal is repeatedly mentioned in connection to non-Yahwistic cultic activities, so I think it is better to translate *dāgān* simply as grain, leaving open the possibility that he may have been one of several gods worshiped on threshing floors."

203. Schmidt, op. cit., p. 66.

204. Ibid.

205. Scholar Nicolas Wyatt translates the Ugaritic *rp'um* ("Rephaim") as "saviours," an interesting choice to say the least. Others choose to leave the word untranslated, rendering it *rp'um* or *rapiuma*.

206. KTU 1.20:ii:5–9, in Nicolas Wyatt, *Religious Texts from Ugarit 2nd ed.* (London; New York: Sheffield Academic Press, 2002), pp. 316–317.

207. KTU 1.22:ii:21–25. Ibid., p. 320.

208. Edward Lipiński, "El's Abode: Mythological Traditions Related to Mount Hermon and to the Mountains of Armenia." *Orientalia Lovaniensa Periodica II* (1971), pp 13–69.

209. KTU 1.20:ii:5–9, in Spronk, op. cit., p.165.

210. Spronk, op. cit., pp. 168–169.

211. Prosic, Tamara, "The 'Threshing Floor' As Sacred Space in the Hebrew Bible: A Spatial and Anthropological Perspective", in J Okland, J Comelis de Vos & K Wenell (eds), *Constuctions of Space III: Biblical Spatiality and the Sacred*. 1st edn, Library of Hebrew Bible/Old Testament Studies, vol. 540, (London: Bloomsbury Academic, 2016), pp. 58–74.

212. Hoskins, Michael, "Orientations of Dolmens in Western Europe," published in *The Role of Astronomy in Society and Culture Proceedings*, No. 260, 2009, pages 116–126. Accessed online via adsbit.harvard.edu on April 30, 2019.

213. Derek P. Gilbert, *Last Clash of the Titans* (Crane, MO: Defender, 2018), p. 123.

214. Guillermo del Olmo Lete, "Bashan." In K. van der Toorn, B. Becking, & P. W.

van der Horst (Eds.), *Dictionary of Deities and Demons in the Bible* (2nd extensively rev. ed.). (Leiden; Boston; Köln; Grand Rapids, MI; Cambridge: Brill; Eerdmans, 1999), p. 161.

215. Collins and Scott, *op. cit.*, p. 31.

216   Charles Warren, "The Summit of Hermon, With An Illustration," *Palestine Exploration Fund Quarterly Statement,* 2.5 (Jan. 1 to March 31, 1870), p. 212.

217. The opening quote is taken from "Word of Tree and Whisper of Stone: El's Oracle to King Keret (Kirta), and the Problem of the Mechanics of its Utterance" by Nicholas Wyatt, published in the *Vetas Testamentaum* 57, 2007, pp. 1–28.

218. Robert D. Miller III, "Baals of Bashan." *Revue Biblique* 121 (2014) pp. 506–515.

219. Nicolas Wyatt, "A la recherche des Rephaïm perdus," in J. M. Michaud (ed.) *Le royaume d'Ougarit de la Crète à l'Euphrate: Nouveaux axes de recherche* (Proche-Orient et Littérature Ougaritique II, Sherbrooke, QC: Éditions GGC, 2007), pp. 597–598.

220. W. Rollig, "Lebanon." In Van der Toorn, Becking, Van der Horst, editors; *Dictionary of Demons and Deities in the Bible*, 2nd edition (Grand Rapids, Mich.: William B. Eerdmans Publishing, 1999), p. 506.

221. Black, Cunningham, Robson, Zólyomi, *The Literature of Ancient Sumer,* p. 96, Oxford University Press, New York, pub. 2004. Accessed via Google Books online.

222. Ibid, p. 93.

223. Ibid. p. 93.

224. Ibid. p. 94.

225. Ibid. p. 198.

226. Wolkstein and Kramer, *The Descent of Inanna: From the Great Above to the Great Below*, accessed online via http://www.boblyman.net/engwr302/myth/inanna.htm (Aug. 6, 2019).

227. Kramer, Samuel Noah, *Sumerian Mythology*, p. 65, University of Pennsylvania Press, 1972.

228. Ibid. p. 66.

229. Ibid, p. 67

230. Black and Cunningham editors, *The Literature of Ancient Sumer*, p. 94, Oxford University Press, 2006.

231. Ibid, p. 95.

232. Ibid. p. 95.

233. Ibid, p. 96.

234. Joan, Eahr Amelia, *Re-Genesis Encyclopedia: Synthesis of the Spiritual Dark*, Section 167.800, Motherline Integral Research, Labyrinth Learning, and Eco–Thealogy. Part I. Revised Edition II, 2018.

235. Ibid.

236. Tablet IV, Epic of Gilgamesh, lines 5–8, accessed via pdf at http://uruk-warka.dk/Gilgamish/The%20Epic%20of%20Gilgamesh.pdf (August 7, 2019).

237. Ibid.

238. Ibid.

239. Ibid.

240. Ibid.

241. Wolkstein and Kramer, *Inanna Queen of Heaven and Earth,* p. 63, Harper & Row Publishers, pub. 1983, content made available in html format through archive.org (https://archive.org/stream/input-compressed-2015mar28a29/done-compressed-2015mar28a29_djvu.txt - accessed Aug. 7, 2019)

242. Corbi, Maria, Principles of an Epistemology of Values: The permutation of collective cohesion and motivation, p. 119, Springer Publications, 2016.

243. Glassner and Herron, *The Invention of Cuneiform Writing*, p. 202, JHU Press, 2003.

244. Matthews, V. H., Chavalas, M. W., & Walton, J. H. *Bible Background Commentary: Old Testament* (electronic ed.), InterVarsity Press: Downers Grove, IL, published 2000.

245. Black, J.A., Cunningham, G., Fluckiger-Hawker, E, Robson, E., and Zólyomi, G. "The Sumerian King List: Translation," *The Electronic Text Corpus of Sumerian Literature* (http://etcsl.orinst.ox.ac.uk/section2/tr211.htm), retrieved 12/24/16.

246. C. S. Coon, "The Eridu Crania: A Preliminary Report," *Sumer* 5 (1949), p 103.

247. Solecki, Rose; Akkermans, Peter M. M. G.; Agelarakis. Anagnostis; Meikle-john, Christopher; Smith, Philip E.L. "Artificial cranial deformation in the Proto-neolithic and Neolithic Near East and its possible origin: Evidence from four sites," *Paléorient* vol. 18, no. 2 (1992), pp. 83–97.

248. Black, J.A., Cunningham, G., Fluckiger-Hawker, E, Robson, E., and Zólyomi, G. "Enmerkar and the Lord of Aratta," *The Electronic Text Corpus of Sumerian Literature* (http://etcsl.orinst.ox.ac.uk/cgi-bin/etcsl.cgi?text=t.1.8.2.3#), retrieved 12/17/16.

249. Black, J.A., Cunningham, G., Fluckiger-Hawker, E, Robson, E., and Zólyomi, G. "A *cir-namcub* to Inana (Inana I)," *The Electronic Text Corpus of Sumerian Literature* (http://etcsl.orinst.ox.ac.uk/cgi-bin/etcsl.cgi?text=t.4.07.9&charenc=j#), retrieved 12/17/16.

250. A. W. Sjoberg, "In-nin Sa-gur-ra: A Hymn to the Goddess Inanna," *Zeitschrift für Assyriologie* 65, no. 2 (1976), p. 225.

251. Black et al, "Enmerkar and the Lord of Aratta," op. cit.

252. Fu'ād Safar, Seton Lloyd, Muhammad 'Alī Muṣṭafá & Mu'assasah al-'Āmmah lil-Āthār wa-al-Turāth, *Eridu* (Baghdad: Republic of Iraq, Ministry of Culture and Information, State Organization of Antiquites and Heritage, 1981).

253. Becker, Helmut and Fassbinder, Jörg W.E. (2003), "Magnetometry at Uruk (Iraq): The City of King Gilgamesh," *Archaeologia Polona, 41*, pp. 122–124.

254. 1 Enoch 6:6.

255. Nickelsburg, George W. E. *1 Enoch: The Hermeneia Translation*. Fortress Press. Kindle Edition, p. 26.

256. Amar Annus, "On the Origin of Watchers: A Comparative Study of the Antediluvian Wisdom in Mesopotamian and Jewish Traditions." *Journal for the Study of the Pseudepigrapha*, Vol 19, Issue 4 (2010), pp. 277–320.

257. Greenfield, J.C. (1999). "Apkallu," *Dictionary of Deities and Demons in the Bible*. Van der Toorn, K., Becking, B., & Van der Horst, P. W. (Eds.). Brill, p. 73.

258. George, Andrew (1999). *The Epic of Gilgamesh* (London: Penguin Books), 111–112.

259. Lipiński, op. cit., p. 19.

260. Ibid.

261. Livingston, David (2003). "Who Was Nimrod?" http://davelivingston.com/ nimrod.htm, retrieved 12/27/17.

262. "Anunna." *Ancient Mesopotamian Gods and Goddesses*. http://oracc.museum. upenn.edu/amgg/listofdeities/anunna/index.html, retrieved 12/27/17.

263. Pritchard, James B., ed. (2010). *The Ancient Near East: An Anthology of Texts and Pictures* (Princeton University Press), p. 34.

264. Lieck, Gwendolyn (1998). *A Dictionary of Ancient Near Eastern Mythology* (New York City, New York: Routledge), p. 141.

265. Gilbert, *Last Clash of the Titans*, pp. 29–35.

266. 2 Peter 2:4.

267. Wyatt (2002), op. cit., p. 131.

268. Probably the proper name of a peak in the Hermon range. See Lipinski, op. cit., p. 40.

269. Ibid., p. 41.

270. George, *op. cit.*, p. 199.

271. This is well established, but see, for example: Klaas Spronk, *Beatific Afterlife in Ancient Israel and in the Ancient Near East* (Kevelaer: Butzon & Bercker, Neukirchen-Vluyn, 1986).

272. Frölich, Ida (2014). "Mesopotamian Elements and the Watchers Traditions", in *The Watchers in Jewish and Christian Traditions* (ed. Angela Kim Hawkins, Kelley Coblentz Bautch, and John Endres; Minneapolis: Fortress), p. 23.

273. Annus (2000), op. cit., pp. 13–30.

274. Jude 6.

275. "The Death of Gilgamesh: translation." *The Electronic Text Corpus of Sumerian Literature*, http://etcsl.orinst.ox.ac.uk/section1/tr1813.htm, retrieved 12/31/17.

276. Marchesi, Gianni (2004). "Who Was Buried in the Royal Tombs of Ur? The Epigraphic and Textual Data," *Orientalia*, NOVA SERIES, Vol. 73, No. 2, p. 154.

277. Aubrey Baadsgaard, Janet Monge, Samantha Cox, and Richard L. Zettler, "Human Sacrifice and Intentional Corpse Preservation in the Royal Cemetery

of Ur." *Antiquity* Vol. 85, No. 327 (March 2011), pp. 36–37.

278. Jeremy Black and Anthony Green, *Gods, Demons, and Symbols of Ancient Mesopotamia* (London: British Museum Press, 1992), p. 89.

279. For example, in Psalm 82.

280. Leviticus 17:7, Deuteronomy 32:17, 1 Corinthians 10:20.

281. Rev. Simeon Stefanidakis, "Forerunners to Modern Spiritualism: Emanuel Swedenborg (1688-1772), http://www.fst.org/spirit2.htm, retrieved 7/25/17.

282. http://www.swedenborg.com/product/life-planets/, retrieved 7/25/17.

283. *Doctrine and Covenants*, 130:22. https://www.lds.org/scriptures/dc-testament/dc/130.22?lang=eng#21, retrieved 7/30/17.

284. *The Pearl of Great Price*, Moses 1:29–34. https://www.lds.org/scriptures/pgp/moses/1.29-34?lang=eng#28, retrieved 7/30/17.

285. Margaret Fox Kane, quoted in Reuben Briggs Davenport, *The Deathblow to Spiritualism* (New York: G.W. Dillingham, 1888), pp. 75–76.

286. Ibid., p. 77.

287. Leonard Zusne and Warren Jones, *Anomalistic Psychology: A Study of Magical Thinking* (New York; London: Psychology Press, 2014), p. 212.

288. David J. Hess, Science in the New Age: The Paranormal, Its Defenders and Debunkers, and American Culture (Madison, WI: University of Wisconsin Press, 1993), p. 20.

289. Helena P. Blavatsky, *The Key to Theosophy* (London: Theosophical Publishing Society, 1889), p. 43.

290. Alvin Boyd Kuhn, *Theosophy: A Modern Revival of Ancient Wisdom*. (PhD thesis). *American Religion Series: Studies in Religion and Culture* (Whitefish, MT: Kessinger Publishing, 1992 [originally published 1930]), pp. 63–64.

291. Jason Colavito, The Cult of Alien Gods: H. P. Lovecraft and Extraterrestrial Pop Culture (New York: Prometheus Books, 2005), p. 44.

292. Howard Phillips Lovecraft (David E. Schultz & S. T. Joshi, eds.), *Lord of a Visible World: An Autobiography in Letters* (Athens: Ohio University Press, 2000), p. 187.

293. Aleister Crowley, *The Equinox of the Gods*. Hermetic.com (https://hermetic.com/crowley/equinox-of-the-gods/remarks-on-the-method-of-receiving-liber-

legis?redirect=1#the-actual-writing), retrieved 8/8/19.

294   Peter Goodgame, "The First Pharaoh." *RedMoonRising.com* (http://www.red-moonrising.com/Giza/AfricOrig8.htm, retrieved 8/15/19).

295. Chilton, Martin. "The War of the Worlds Panic Was a Myth." *The Telegraph*, May 6, 2016. http://www.telegraph.co.uk/radio/what-to-listen-to/the-war-of-the-worlds-panic-was-a-myth/, retrieved 8/6/17.

296. McCaffery, Larry. "An Interview with Jack Williamson." July 1991. http://www.depauw.edu/sfs/interviews/williamson54interview.htm, retrieved 8/6/17.

297. Astounding Science Fiction, April 1950, p. 132.

298. Lovecraft, H. P. "At the Mountains of Madness." *Astounding Stories*, 16, No. 6 (February 1936), 8–32; 17, No. 1 (March 1936), 125–55; 17, No. 2 (April 1936), 132–50. http://www.hplovecraft.com/writings/texts/fiction/mm.aspx, retrieved 8/8/17.

299. The title of one of Dr. Heiser's presentations at the Modern Challenges to the ET Hypothesis Conference at the 2017 UFO Festival in Roswell.

300. Knowles, Christopher, and Joseph Michael Linsner. *Our Gods Wear Spandex: The Secret History of Comic Book Heroes* (San Francisco: Weiser Books, 2007), p. 18.

301. Graham, Robbie. "SETI Astronomer says We're Ready for Alien Contact… Thanks to Hollywood." *Mysterious Universe*, July 19, 2017. http://mysteriousuniverse.org/2017/07/seti-atronomer-says-were-ready-for-alien-contact-thanks-to-hollywood/, retrieved 8/6/17.

302. Colavito, Jason (2005). *The Cult of Alien Gods: H.P. Lovecraft And Extraterrestial Pop Culture.* Amherst, NY: Prometheus Books. Kindle Edition (Kindle location 1227).

303. Ibid (Kindle locations 1296–1300).

304. Ibid (Kindle location 1338).

305. Von Däniken, Erich (1968). *Chariots of the Gods: Unsolved Mysteries of the Past.* New York: Berkley Books, p. viii.

306. "2001: A Space Odyssey Named the Greatest Sci-Fi Film of All Time by the Online Film Critics Society" (June 12, 2002). https://web.archive.org/web/20061126071451/http://ofcs.rottentomatoes.com/pages/pr/top100scifi,

retrieved 8/27/17.

307. Von Braun was one of the 1,600 or so Nazi scientists, engineers, and technicians secretly brought to the US after the war during Operation Paperclip.

308. Colavito, op. cit. (Kindle location 1346).

309. Sheaffer, Robert (1974). "Erich von Däniken's 'Chariots of the Gods': Science or Charlatanism?" Originally published in *NICAP UFO Investigator*. https://www.debunker.com/texts/vondanik.html, retrieved 8/27/17.

310. See, for example, Chris White's excellent three-hour film *Ancient Aliens Debunked*, available for free at AncientAliensDebunked.com.

311. "Erich von Daniken: Fraud, Lies and Bananas." *Forgetomori* (April 8, 2012). http://forgetomori.com/2012/aliens/erich-von-daniken-fraud-lies-and-bananas/, retrieved 8/27/17.

312. https://www.sitchiniswrong.com/taxreturns.htm, retrieved 8/10/19.

313. Levenda, Peter (2005). *Sinister Forces—The Nine: A Grimoire of American Political Witchcraft.* Walterville, Oregon: TrineDay. Kindle Edition, Kindle Locations 7603–7604.

314. Melanson, Terry (2001). "The All-Seeing Eye, The President, The Secretary and The Guru." http://www.conspiracyarchive.com/NWO/All_Seeing_Eye.htm, retrieved 8/14/17.

315. For that we recommend Peter Levenda's excellent book, *Sinister Forces: The Nine.*

316. Levenda, op. cit., Kindle Locations 7734–7737.

317. Levenda, op. cit., Kindle Locations 7765–7769.

318. Levenda, op. cit., Kindle Locations 7809–7815.

319. Puharich, A. (1974). *Uri; a Journal of the Mystery of Uri Geller.* (Garden City, NY: Anchor Press), p. 18.

320. Penre, Wes (1999). "The Council of Nine." *Fortean Times*. Republished at UriGeller.com: http://www.urigeller.com/plan-nine-outer-space/. Retrieved 8/22/17.

321. Ibid.

322. Ibid.

323. Ibid.

324   Joseph Spector, "NXIVM: Clare Bronfman, Heiress to Seagram's, Pleads Guilty in Sex Cult Case." *Democrat and Chronicle,* April 19, 2019 (https://www.democratandchronicle.com/story/news/politics/albany/2019/04/19/nxivm-clare-bronfman-heiress-seagrams-plead-guilty-deal/3520356002/, retrieved 8/15/19).

325. Ibid.

326. Christiane., Zivie-Coche, (2004). *Gods and Men in Egypt: 3000 BCE to 395 CE.* Cornell University Press.

327. Penre, op. cit.

328. Ibid.

329. Ibid.

330. Josh Peck and Derek P. Gilbert, *The Day the Earth Stands Still* (Crane, MO: Defender, 2017), pp. 74–77.

331. Ibid., pp. 1–2.

332. http://www.mufon.com, retrieved 8/23/17.

333. Sheaffer, Robert (August 1, 2017). "MUFON Unravels." *Bad UFOs.* http://badufos.blogspot.com/2017/08/mufon-unravels.html, retrieved 8/26/17.

334. https://www.mufonsymposium.com/corey-goode, retrieved 8/26/17.

335. https://www.mufonsymposium.com/andrew-bassagio, retrieved 8/26/17.

336. Salla, Dr. Michael E. (December 26, 2015). "Jump Room to Mars: Did CIA Groom Obama & Basiago as Future Presidents?" *Exopolitics.org.* http://exopolitics.org/jump-room-to-mars-did-cia-groom-obama-basiago-as-future-presidents/, retrieved 8/26/17.

337. Dolan, Richard (July 18, 2017). "On Corey, Andrew, and the Whistleblowers". https://www.facebook.com/notes/richard-dolan/on-corey-andrew-and-the-whistleblowers/1394366947350897/, retrieved 8/26/17.

338. http://www.mufon.com/the-inner-circle.html, retrieved 8/26/17.

339. Knight, Judy Zebra (2005). *Ramtha, the White Book.* Yelm, WA: JZK Publishing.

340. Iwasaki, John (February 10, 1997). "JZ Knight Not Faking It, Say Scholars— But They Bristle at the Idea She's Buying Them." *Seattle Post-Intelligencer.* p. B1.

341. Brenner, Keri (January 27, 2008). "Disillusioned Former Students Target

Ramtha." *The Olympian*. Via the Cult Education Institute. https://www.cult-education.com/group/1113-ramtha-school-of-enlightenment/17846-disillusio-ned-former-students-target-ramtha-.html, retrieved 8/26/17.

342. Ibid.

343. 1 Corinthians 15:6.

344. Kenneth Kitchen, *Ancient Orient and Old Testament* (London: Inter-Varsity Press, 1966), p. 44.

345. Barry, J. D., Mangum, D., Brown, D. R., Heiser, M. S., Custis, M., Ritzema, E., … Bomar, D. "Genesis 14:1." *Faithlife Study Bible* (Bellingham, WA: Lexham Press, 2012).

346. Exodus 12:40-41 says the people of Israel lived in Egypt 430 years. Working backward from a pretty solid Exodus date of 1446 BC, that would put Jacob and his sons in Egypt around 1876 BC. That's too early for the number of generations between Jacob and Moses. The solution is in Galatians 3:16–17, where Paul writes that the Exodus was 430 years after God's covenant with Abraham. That means Abraham arrived in Canaan around 1876 BC, which was under Egyptian control at that time, so technically the 430-year timeline is correct. Jacob migrated to Egypt in 1661 BC, when Amorite Hyksos dynasties ruled the Nile delta, people with a culture similar to that of the nomadic Hebrews. That could explain how a Hebrew rose to be the second most powerful person in the kingdom, and how later, after native Egyptian kings in the south forced out the Hyksos around 1550 BC, a new king arose over Egypt "who did not know Joseph."

347. Collins and Scott, op. cit.

348. Joshua 15:1–3.

349. Scholars and historians as far back as Josephus in the 1st century, including the esteemed twelfth-century rabbi Maimonides, place Kadesh at Petra.

350. 2 Chronicles 20:2.

351. Nir Hasson, "The Dead Sea: A dramatic look at Israel's endangered natural wonder." *Haaretz* > (https://www.haaretz.com/st/c/prod/global/deadsea/eng/5/, retrieved 8/15/19).

352. Matthew Suriano. "Dynasty Building at Ugarit: The Ritual and Political Context of KTU 1.161," *Aula Orientalis* 27 (2009), p. 107.

353. Nicolas Wyatt, *Religious Texts from Ugarit* (2nd ed.) (London; New York: Sheffield Academic Press, 2002), p. 210.

354. Vidal, op. cit., p. 169.

355. KTU 1.20 i 1–3, ii 2–3. Wyatt, op. cit, pp. 315–316.

356. Ibid.

357. Edward Lipiński, "El's Abode: Mythological Traditions Related to Mount Hermon and to the Mountains of Armenia," *Orientalia Lovaniensa Periodica* II (1971), pp. 13–69.

358. Klaas Spronk, Beatific Afterlife in Ancient Israel and in the Ancient Near East (Kevelaer: Butzon & Bercker, 1986), p. 171.

359. In these translations by Ugaritic scholar Nicolas Wyatt, I have substituted "Rephaim" (Ugaritic *rpum*) for Wyatt's choice, "saviours," and "elohim" (Ugaritic *ilnym*) for Wyatt's preferred word, "divinities."

360. Spronk (1986), op. cit., pp. 168–169. Note that the *Book of 1 Enoch* identifies one of the Watchers who descended on Mount Hermon as Daniel, which is the same name as the one in this text.

361. KTU 1.20:ii:2–7. Wyatt (2002), op. cit., pp. 316–317.

362. KTU 1.22:ii:21-25. Ibid., p. 320.

363. Theodore Lewis, "Toward a Literary Translation of the Rapiuma Texts," in Ugarit, Religion, and Culture: Proceedings of the International Colloquium on Ugarit, Religion, and Culture, Edinburgh, July 1994. Essays presented in honour of John C. L. Gibson. Ugaritisch-Biblische Literatur 12 (ed. N. Wyatt, W.G.E. Watson, and J.B. Lloyd); (Münster: Ugarit-Verlag, 1996), p. 130.

364. Joel Richardson, "Rosh: Russia or Chief?" https://joelstrumpet.com/rosh- russia-or-chief/, retrieved 3/10/18.

365. C. I. Scofield, "Ezekiel 38:2." *Scofield Reference Notes* (1917 Edition). https://www.biblestudytools.com/commentaries/scofield-reference-notes/ezekiel/ezekiel-38.html, retrieved 3/10/18.

366. Daniel I. Block, *The Book of Ezekiel, Chapters 25–48* (Grand Rapids, MI: Wm. B. Eerdmans Publishing Co., 1997), p. 435.

367. Ralph H. Alexander, *Ezekiel*. In: *Expositor's Bible Commentary: Jeremiah-Ezekiel* (Grand Rapids: Zondervan, 1986), p. 854.

368. Gilbert (2018), op. cit., pp. 152–155.

369. Zechariah 14:2–4.

370. Isaiah 14:13.

371. Charles C. Torrey, "Armageddon." *The Harvard Theological Review*, Vol. 31, No. 3 (Jul., 1938), pp. 237–248.

372. Ibid., pp. 247–248.

373. See chapter 8 of Derek's book, *Last Clash of the Titans*. That's the reason for the book's title—Armageddon will literally *be* the last clash of the Titans.

374. KTU 1.22 i 13-15. Wyatt, op. cit, pp. 321–322.

375. Numbers 27:12, Deuteronomy 32:49.

376. Spronk (1999), op. cit, p. 876.

377. Psalm 82:2.

378. Genesis 6:1–4, an incident further explained in 1 Enoch chapters 6–11.

379. Annus (1999), op.cit., p. 22.

380. Hesiod, *Works and Days*, lines 110–130.

381. 1 Enoch 15:8–12. George W. E. Nickelsburg and James C. VanderKam, *1 Enoch: The Hermeneia Translation* (Minneapolis: Fortress Press, 2012), Kindle edition.

382. Gilbert (2017), op. cit., p. 38.

383. David Talshir, "The Relativity of Geographic Terms: A Re-investigation of the Problem of Upper and Lower Aram." *Journal of Semitic Studies* XLVIII/2 (2003), pp. 264–265.

384. Karl Kerenyi, *The Heroes of the Greeks* (London: Thames and Hudson, 1958), p. 75.

385. Wyatt (2010), op. cit., p. 52.

386. Christopher B. Hays, "An Egyptian Loanword in the Book of Isaiah and the Deir 'Alla Inscription: Heb. *nṣr*, Aram. *nqr*, and Eg. *nṯr* as "[Divinized] Corpse." *Journal of Ancient Egyptian Interconnections*, Vol. 4:2 (2012), p. 17.

387. Dr. Michael S. Heiser, "The Nephilim." *SitchinIsWrong.com,* https://www.sitchiniswrong.com/nephilim/nephilim.htm, retrieved 8/5/19.

388. Gilbert, D. (2016). I Predict! What 12 Global Experts Believe You Will See Before 2025. (Crane, MO: Defender).

389. Furnish, T. (2018). "Talking Turkey about the Mahdi," *Occidental Jihadist,* https://occidentaljihadist.com/2018/03/12/talking-turkey-about-the-mahdi/, retrieved 3/17/18.

390. Dillinger, J. (2018). "29 Largest Armies in the World." *World Atlas,* https://www.worldatlas.com/articles/29-largest-armies-in-the-world.html, retrieved 3/18/17.

391. "MBS: Palestinians Should 'Accept Trump Proposals or Shut Up,'" *Al Jazeera,* April 30, 2018. https://www.aljazeera.com/news/2018/04/mbs-palestinians-accept-trump-proposals-shut-180430065228281.html, retrieved 5/2/18.

392. Michael S. Heiser, *The Unseen Realm: Recovering the Supernatural Worldview of the Bible* (Bellingham, WA: Lexham Press, 2015), pp. 364–365.

393. Kohler, K. (1906). "Eschatology." *The Jewish Encyclopedia*, http://www.jewishencyclopedia.com/articles/5849-eschatology, retrieved 3/30/19.

394. Kohler, K., and Ginzburg, L. (1906). "Armilus." *The Jewish Encyclopedia*, http://www.jewishencyclopedia.com/articles/1789-armilus, retrieved 3/30/18.

395. Spronk, K. (1999). "Travellers." op. cit., p. 876.

396. KTU 1.22 ii, 20-27; I, 15. In Wyatt, N. (2002). *Religious Texts from Ugarit* (2nd ed.), (London; New York: Sheffield Academic Press), p. 322.

397. Spronk (1986), op. cit., p. 172.

398. Nickelsburg, George W. E. *1 Enoch: The Hermeneia Translation* (Fortress Press. Kindle Edition), p. 37.

399. Strong's H2629.

400. Deuteronomy 2:9–23.

401. Evidence points to the worship of the Rephaim/Nephilim as the origin of the Greek hero cults. See Annus, "Are There Greek Rephaim?" previously cited.

402. Brannan, R., Penner, K. M., Loken, I., Aubrey, M., & Hoogendyk, I. (Eds.). *The Lexham English Septuagint* (Is 26:19). (Bellingham, WA: Lexham Press, 2012).

403. Brook W. R. Pearson, "Resurrection and the Judgment of the Titans." *Journal for the Study of the New Testament Supplement Series 186* (London: Roehampton Institute, 1999), p. 50.

404. Revelation 9:10.

405. Chang-Won Park, *Cultural Blending in Korean Death Rites* (New York: Continuum International Publishing Group, 2010), pp. 12–13.

406. Gilbert, Sharon, *Realms of Fire: Book 5 of The Redwing Saga* (Crane, MO: Rose Avenue Fiction, 2019).